# How to Beat a
# BROKEN
# GAME

# How to Beat a
# BROKEN GAME

*The Rise of the Dodgers in
a League on the Brink*

# PEDRO MOURA

**PUBLIC**AFFAIRS
*New York*

PublicAffairs
Hachette Book Group
1290 Avenue of the Americas, New York, NY 10104
www.publicaffairsbooks.com
@Public_Affairs

Printed in the United States of America

First Edition: March 2022

Published by PublicAffairs, an imprint of Perseus Books, LLC, a subsidiary of Hachette Book Group, Inc. The PublicAffairs name and logo is a trademark of the Hachette Book Group.

The Hachette Speakers Bureau provides a wide range of authors for speaking events. To find out more, go to www.hachettespeakersbureau.com or call (866) 376-6591.

The publisher is not responsible for websites (or their content) that are not owned by the publisher.

Print book interior design by Jeff Williams.

Library of Congress Control Number: 2021950931

ISBNs: 9781541701427 (hardcover), 9781541701434 (ebook)

LSC-C

Printing 1, 2022

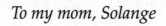

*To my mom, Solange*

# Contents

# Chapter 1

THE NIGHT THE LOS ANGELES DODGERS FINALLY won the World Series, nothing happened until Mookie Betts, the smallest, lightest man on the field, wrested control. In the sixth game's sixth inning, the Tampa Bay Rays removed their thriving ace, Blake Snell, fearful of Betts taking a third look at him. Betts thumped a double on the first strike he saw from a skilled Rays reliever. On the game-tying wild pitch, he scampered to third base. On a routine grounder with Tampa Bay's infield in, he maximized his secondary lead, accelerated at contact, slid headfirst, and touched home a few tenths of a second before he could be tagged. "If it was anybody but Mookie on third," said Tampa Bay third baseman Joey Wendle, "we would've got him at home." Betts rose, howled, and pumped his right fist five times. The Dodgers would be winners. All series, Betts proved the most comprehensive contributor, and the most entertaining. He homered. He executed double steals. He secured screaming line drives. He demonstrated modern baseball at its best, superlatively skilled and impossibly instinctual.

Baseball at its worst surrounded him. The decisive game featured almost as many strikeouts as balls in play. After Betts's sixth-inning romp, no one but him reached second base again in 2020. And no one was watching. The last time fewer Americans watched a World Series, the World Series was not on television. The Dodgers' thirty-two-year championship drought was over, but their sport's struggle continued.

The evidence attests that baseball is broken. The games become more of a bore every year, and the league's early efforts to speed pace of play changed little. It is simpler to explain the problem than it is to suggest a solution. More than our pitiful attention spans, the prime culprit is the advent and spread of data into the consciousness of the executives running the sport and, more recently, the athletes playing it. Once they grasped what earned them money in the modern game, hitters adjusted their swings to pursue it. They started hitting balls harder and launching them into the air more often, accepting a corresponding increase in strikeouts. Pitchers were already throwing harder than ever, so hard they made it halfway through a game just over half the time. They changed their games to negate hitters' gains, throwing fewer fastballs and throwing them high, where uppercut swings can't reach. Strangely sticky concoctions enabled them to generate gratuitous spin.

The battle of extremes yields an imbalanced product devoid of action and drained of surprises. Even no-hitters became the norm for a time in 2021. Sacrifice bunting, calculated to be inefficient, is a rare relic. Base stealing is often considered foolhardy. On average, balls in play are now spaced more than four minutes apart, more than twice as slow as a century ago. A typical 2020 game featured 33 percent fewer balls in play than the average 2005 game.

"I'm worried," said longtime manager Buck Showalter. "Young or old, if you're not worried, you don't love the game." Even on that, there is disagreement. "I definitely don't worry about it," said Giants manager Gabe Kapler. "Baseball has always gone through ebbs and flows. The game survives through it all." But more stakeholders side with Showalter, one of fifteen men on commissioner Rob Manfred's competition committee, a group of baseball lifers reestablished in 2017 to dissect the sport's struggle attracting new fans. Showalter reports that the league understands the extent of the problem. "We've just made the game too predictable," he said. "And it's not the players' fault, because they're gonna chase what pays the most."

Showalter indicts the financial incentives and the defensive shift. Most insiders assign blame differently. Fellow former manager Jim Leyland faults hitters for lingering too long outside the batter's box waiting for their walk-up songs, refocusing their eyes. Marlins manager Don Mattingly sources it to swing changes. "It's been building," he said. "Now, we're at a point where it's getting so much more attention because it's a game that, sometimes, is unwatchable." Speaking to ESPN, Cubs manager David Ross likened the modern game to a nightly derby. "We are not trying to play baseball," he said. "We are trying to hit home runs."

Others omit blame in favor of frustration. "It's disgusting to watch, really," said recently retired reliever J. P. Howell. "What is this, a barroom brawl? This isn't our art." Tigers manager A. J. Hinch said he harbored "great concern" that a game dominated by strikeouts, walks, and home runs would not entertain the masses. "We're trending in the wrong direction," he said. "It doesn't mean we can just snap our fingers and make a rule change or do one simple thing and all of a sudden we're going to turn into a more balanced sport."

As it did to many fields, the COVID-19 pandemic amplified the inequity. It is far easier for a marooned pitcher to simulate game action than it is for a hitter. Most minor leaguers did not play any actual games in 2020, and the 2021 return laid bare their weaknesses. Strikeouts shot up further.

As a business, baseball is also broken, or, like the game, at least imbalanced. The start of this century brought unprecedented sustained labor peace, but players and owners have grown more and more at odds in recent seasons. Soon after the sport's COVID shutdown in March 2020, players agreed to be paid on a prorated basis for any games played. Team owners later tried to alter the terms of the deal. When players balked, the disagreement went public, and it stayed that way until Manfred, acting on behalf of the owners, imposed a sixty-game season to begin in July. When coronavirus outbreaks inevitably occurred, the league blamed players for their lack of vigilance, not its insufficient protocols. When a COVID-positive Justin Turner emerged from a Globe Life Field spare room minutes after the Dodgers won, it was he who was condemned, not league officials, who failed to follow protocols that called for him to be sent away from the premises when he tested positive.

Looming over the turmoil was the league's collective bargaining agreement, expired as of December 1, 2021. The sport's state cannot be traced to one document, but it was painfully obvious that the players lost the last negotiations. Billionaire owners obtained millions more in annual profits; players secured more buses to travel to spring-training games and earlier start times on travel days. Twenty years ago, the middle class could count on employment into their midthirties, often at the best salaries of their careers. Now, only the game's stars are paid that way past thirty. Players used to be underpaid before they reached free agency and overpaid thereafter. Now they are underpaid, then unemployed. Predictably, players coalesced around the necessity of negotiating a more equitable deal.

Again, the pandemic rendered that goal more difficult, financially and logistically. Major leaguers are among the few rich people in America who suffered financially from 2020. If owners are to be believed, they, too, lost millions, though their prize assets continued to appreciate. In 2021, it was in both sides' interest to delay the annual rite of spring training, so as to allow desiring players to be vaccinated before they began crisscrossing the country in April. But the owners did not formally offer such a suspension until hundreds of players had already secured housing, and, in many cases, traveled to their temporary homes. They deemed it too late. Spring training began in mid-February.

On February 21, the final few players were trickling into camps across Arizona and Florida, undergoing physicals and COVID-19 tests. It should have been a time of hope, of the season's requisite renewal. Instead it was a painful period.

Earlier that month, Kevin Mather, the president and CEO of the Seattle Mariners, had addressed the Bellevue Breakfast Rotary Club over Zoom. Mather, a former accountant who rose through the ranks over thirty years in baseball, began by saying he planned to ramble. Ramble he did. Among other soon-sore subjects, he brazenly revealed the team's plans to manipulate the service time of two prospects, including prized outfielder Jarred Kelenic. He derided two foreign players' English fluency. He called franchise cornerstone Kyle Seager overpaid and predicted the season would be his last in Seattle, prompting Seager's wife to ask if they should sell their house. After the rotary club posted the video to YouTube, a Mariners superfan stumbled on it and tweeted it. Thirty-nine hours later, after players league-wide lambasted him, Mather lost his job.

Cubs first baseman Anthony Rizzo said he was glad the sentiment had been made public, so "people can see how it is." Twins third baseman Josh Donaldson offered what he described as his appreciation. "You just said what everyone already knew, but now we have official evidence that is going to help a lot of players," he wrote. "Again, thank you!! Bravo." Yankees ace Gerrit Cole said it was evidence that teams operate in "bad faith." Kelenic himself referenced a desire to put 2020 behind him. "This should be an exciting time for baseball," he told *USA Today*. "Now, the day before spring training, this is what I have to deal with."

The union called it a "highly disturbing yet critically important window into how players are genuinely viewed by management," promising to confront the issues at the bargaining table. Mather's Mariners had been part of the problem, tanking through 2018 and 2019 to set themselves up for the future. "The game is heading in the wrong direction," Mets shortstop Francisco Lindor said. "You're rewarding teams for losing." On another spring day, Lindor evoked the Major League Baseball of his youth. "Back in the day, guys were stealing bases, hitting home runs, making good plays," he said. "Pitchers were going eight, nine innings, and the relievers were closing like Mariano Rivera. It was just, overall, a better-played game, more rounded. I still think this generation is really good, but right now it seems like it's a home run, a strikeout or maybe a double."

Born nine months before the 1994 strike, Lindor pined not for some distant past. His opinion is widespread among current players, who celebrate and decry the influence of data on their game. On both counts, they are correct. The more advanced the information has become, the easier it has been to implement its guidance. "Increased data complexity, almost counter-intuitively, has enabled more intuitive conversations with coaches and players," said Doug Fearing, the former director of research and development for the Dodgers. To people like Fearing, the evolution is exciting. To vigilant fans, too, there's ample allure in the modern game. Players' peak performances are better and more quantifiable than ever. But the economics of professional sports hinge on mass, not specialized, appeal.

Forty years ago, the people pioneering the study of sabermetrics, the use of statistical analysis to pursue truths about baseball, never expected their work would one day be adopted by every one of Major League Baseball's teams. They believed they were writing for an alternative audience, not the billionaires who own and operate these franchises. For a long time, they were. Then came *Moneyball*, the book, eventually the movie, and the rapid assimilation of such thought within front offices. Eight months after the book's 2003 release, the Dodgers hired Paul DePodesta, the prominently featured Oakland Athletics assistant general manager. Within a few years, most major league teams included sabermetric elements in their decision-making processes. Within a decade, it was the most common operating philosophy, rebranded as analytics.

Whatever the measures are called, few, if any, teams use them more than the Dodgers. Through 2020, two dozen employees with multidisciplinary degrees worked out of a converted club-house at Dodger Stadium, ideating ways to quantify and predict success. The research and development department produces systems and models designed to answer every possible query about the game and log anything unanswerable for future study. Using the team's proprietary platform, "42," named for Jackie Robinson's retired jersey number, staffers can check on the team's trove of data wherever they are.

The franchise has come to define this fractured era. Long one of the sport's model organizations, they fell into disrepair in the aughts when they were purchased by Frank McCourt, a man with little liquid capital but a grandiose vision to use the team to fund his indulgences. He began with DePodesta, who had experience operating a team on the cheap. Five years later, McCourt's plan sputtered when he and his wife, Jamie, separated and began a protracted court fight over their shares of the team. He fired her as CEO, she filed for divorce, and MLB soon forced Frank to sell the team. Because television rights contracts were skyrocketing, he made the sale price back fivefold. After recruiting Magic John-son for local goodwill, a consortium of Guggenheim financiers won the bidding. They orchestrated massive, expensive trades to recapture the sullen fan base, then, two years in, hired exalted executive Andrew Friedman to run baseball operations.

Friedman came for a bounty from the Tampa Bay Rays, Oak-land's rival for the title of poorest team around. Nine years earlier, Tampa had hired him to run its historically hapless team that was still without a winning season in eight tries. It took three seasons for Friedman to assemble an upstart winner that raced all the way to the World Series. The 2008 Rays' best players were Carlos Peña, the first baseman the A's jettisoned amid the 2002 season chronicled in *Moneyball*, and Evan Longoria, a rookie third baseman. One week after debuting that April, Longoria signed a contract extension that tethered him to the Rays for nine years yet guaranteed him only $17.5 million, not one tenth of what he proved to be worth over that span. "This is obviously fairly unique," Friedman said at the time. "The economics of the game and us being a low-revenue team, we have to think differently and take chances such as this to keep our nucleus in place as long as we can."

From 2008 to 2014, the Rays paid Longoria and fellow breakout star Ben Zobrist a total of $45.3 million while the two players logged 76.9 Wins Above Replacement. At the start of that period, each win was commonly estimated to be worth at least $4 million on the open market. By the end of it, the estimate approached $8 million. By those metrics, Friedman's acquisition and subsequent signing of the two players saved Tampa Bay anywhere from $300 million to $600 million. More accurately, his extending of the two players' contracts made employing them in the long term feasible for the Rays. In that span, the franchise went 627–508, a .552 winning percentage. They made the playoffs four times and the World Series once, all while carrying one of the sport's slightest payrolls.

More than a decade after he signed it, Longoria said he did not regret agreeing to his extension. It had given him financial security for life. "Now, things might have been a little different if you had told me, 'Fast forward 10 years and everybody is viewing the primes of guys' careers from 21 to 26 or 22 to 27, or whatever it is,'" he said. "That might've made me stop and think a little bit." After rival teams copied Friedman and agents caught on, the going rate for extensions increased. "Not that we didn't before, but I think players understand their value better now," Longoria said. "And the age range has changed. Players understand they're being evaluated based on the prime of their career being younger." Friedman moved on to a new method: ceding youngish stars just as their salaries were peaking in exchange for unproven but promising prospects. That worked wonderfully, creating a self-sustaining system when timed right.

The man Friedman hired to manage the Rays, Joe Maddon, noted the team also benefited from starting its run just as MLB "was putting the kibosh on steroid use and amphetamine use." "After that," he once told the *Los Angeles Times*, "we were ahead of everybody else with the metrics and defensive shifts and data." That's right; Friedman was behind the shift Showalter so resents. Theo Epstein, the wunderkind executive who helped two long-troubled big-market teams win the World Series in the post-*Moneyball* era, told NPR in 2020 that he took some responsibility for the sport's decline. "Because the executives like me, who have spent a lot of time using analytics and other measures," he said, "have unwittingly had a negative impact on the aesthetic value of the game and the entertainment value of the game." In 2021, Epstein became an MLB consultant tasked with reversing that impact.

One week after Friedman left for Los Angeles, Maddon fled to work under Epstein with the Chicago Cubs. Together they severed a curse. While he worked in Florida, Maddon cultivated a reputation as an analytics savant. After a few seasons in Illinois, it became clear Maddon functioned more as a conduit for Friedman and Epstein to convey their ideas to players. In his next managerial job, with the Angels of Anaheim, Maddon began to reckon with the deleterious impact of the trends he helped accelerate. He did not do so to any acute extent. He surmised that deadening the baseball itself would solve the problem, and he expressed pleasure when the league disclosed plans to do just that. "I think part of the disinterest in the game today is that it's been reduced to small patterns of striking people out, accepting walks and trying to hit home runs," Maddon said in February 2021. "When you change the ball, we can go back in time to where we had a better brand of baseball."

The next month, he again cited his proposal as a cure-all for the sport's ills. "If the ball doesn't travel as far, a lot of the things you're looking for will just occur because hitters will have to adjust," he said. "Pitchers will adjust. Defenses will adjust. Everything will adjust. Speed will become more prominent. All the things you're looking for will just happen. The game will just come back, I think, to almost what we had grown up knowing." By April's end, it was clear the baseball was not traveling as far and all those things weren't just happening. "I don't like legislating hardly anything," Maddon said then. "I'm much more that things change based on people making adaptations and adjustments based on what they're seeing."

Whatever MLB did to its baseballs in 2021 was not exactly a deadening. Firsthand reports indicated the seams rose higher, but it's possible the league only removed from circulation some lighter, live baseballs that, *Sports Illustrated* showed, contributed to surplus home runs in 2020. In moves that better reflect the league's understanding it must modify its product, aggressive and imaginative rule-change experiments continued in the minors, peppered into each level one at a time.

In Triple A, the bases grew from fifteen square inches to eighteen, making stolen bases and infield hits slightly easier to achieve. In Double A, four infielders had to remain positioned on the infield dirt, reducing defensive shift possibilities. Lower, pitchers had to step off the rubber before attempting a pickoff throw. Even lower, they could only step off twice. In one low-A league, an automated ball-strike system replaced home-plate umpires' primary purpose. In the other low-A league, on-field timers enforced limits during pitching changes and between pitches and innings. Later in the season, that league began testing technology that allowed catchers to electronically communicate signs to pitchers. Two partner independent leagues attempted even wilder changes, one without MLB input: designated pinch-hitters and pinch-runners, a sudden-death home-run format to resolve nine-inning ties, a hook rule that removes the designated hitter when the starting pitcher exits, and, maybe most significantly, a mound one foot farther from home plate.

Craig Wallenbrock detested the changes. "We jumped the gun on trying to correct the game," he said. Wallenbrock has been involved with high-level baseball for more than a half-century; he long ago grew to respect the game's cyclical nature. But in assigning blame, or credit, for baseball's evolution over the last decade, Wallenbrock warrants mention. He sparked the resurfacing of Ted Williams's age-old ideas on hitting, which then spread from his select few pupils throughout the sport. To match the plane of the approaching, downward-trending pitch,

Wallenbrock advocated a controlled swing with a slight upper-cut. Such a stroke, the thinking went, would allow a hitter to attack fastballs and breaking balls just the same.

It worked for Williams, who publicized the concept in his 1970 book *The Science of Hitting*, and it worked for many of the hitters Wallenbrock advised, mostly privately, outside of professional teams' purviews. It worked so well that thousands of others tried to replicate it, to sometimes destructive effect. His slight uppercut became a sizable uppercut in the popular imagination. His emphasis on an on-plane swing that netted hard contact, often in the air, became the public's obsession with those outputs.

The more success his famous pupils had, the less control Wallenbrock had over how others heard him. He coached pre-teen boys his way, then heard back from their excited fathers that they had hit a baseball off a tee at a league-average exit velocity. "I'm sorry, but that's all bullshit, and that's what I'm against, that type of crap," Wallenbrock said. "I was misinterpreted on launch angle and exit velocity." Still, Wallenbrock had it on good authority that corrections were about to come from within the game when the league chose to act.

For decades, Wallenbrock operated either in the background of Major League Baseball or outside it, always calling Southern California home. He coached in junior college, he scouted, and he taught hitting on his own. But since 2016, Wallenbrock has been a hitting consultant for the Dodgers, working at first with mostly major leaguers and transitioning over time to minor leaguers. Minor league camp was just ramping up when the sport's 2020 shutdown began. Coaches were starting to reemphasize the value of moving runners over, of fouling off tough pitches, of making contact with runners on third and fewer than two outs.

"It's old stuff, but we feel it's very important in the game to-day. We were gonna move in that direction and make strong emphasis on it in our minor-league system," he said. "And we were gonna be the leaders in that. Once a winner starts doing that, then everybody else wants to copy it. The Dodgers start winning a few more pennants, and other teams start going back to playing small ball, some of the old varieties of the game." He is right that others will follow whatever the Dodgers do, or at least try. Especially offensively, the Dodgers are their sport's pacesetters. "They are so far ahead of the industry on hitting," said one person who worked in a rival front office. "It's wild."

The Dodgers' February 2020 trade for Betts will not be remembered as a return to fundamentals. The deal will be cited as a fleecing, a misguided salary dump on behalf of the Boston Red Sox. It was made possible because Friedman wielded the Dodgers' financial advantage differently than the Red Sox ever had. During his first five years on the job in Los Angeles, Friedman promised only seven players more money than the $35 million the Dodgers pledged him.

Every decision he made was governed by the guiding principle of optionality, a term co-opted from Wall Street, where he had his professional start. The idea is to render no decision absolutely necessary, to preserve as many possible choices as long as possible. It manifests in many ways, most notably in the Dodgers' relative lack of desperation. Desperate teams make decisions they will regret. Because of Friedman's patience and ownership's resources, the Dodgers stand perpetually ready to seize on opportunities created by another team's desperation.

"That's the benefit the Dodgers had with the Guggenheim hedge fund. It's nice having money," said Trey Magnuson, a Dodgers scout who has worked for the franchise since 2000, spanning three ownerships. "We were able to fill our roster with some bigger names while we allowed our player development to grow our kids. Now we're getting into the fruit of the labor of all that. Our minor leaguers that we didn't have to give up in trades to make us competitive those years are now producing."

What differentiates the Dodgers from this era's other titans is the balance they have maintained. Their most successful area scout doesn't even glance at advanced statistics or biomechanical data for the prospects he recommends the Dodgers draft. Some of their top R&D employees arrived in the organization glaringly unaware of time-honored baseball concepts. Yet they leave room for insight from all comers and employ people who specialize in integrating it. Players respect Friedman in spite of his spending history because he and his staff often make them better.

"We've taken guys like Max Muncy and Chris Taylor that were somehow not developed properly or even ruined in other organizations that represented bad thinking processes," Wallenbrock said. "All of the sudden, they are really good players in the Dodger organization. But I think more and more, we won't get guys like that, because teams are gonna realize that they have a good player in a Muncy or a Taylor and they're gonna be able to develop them themselves."

Even if teams cannot develop those prospects themselves, they have become reticent to deal them to the Dodgers. In making his annual rounds calling executives to ask about their prospects, ESPN's Kiley McDaniel noticed in 2021 that teams have become especially eager to mention when the Dodgers or Rays are interested in a player. "We aren't sure why," he quoted one staffer saying, "but they asked for him." McDaniel described a scenario in which the Dodgers or Rays asked for a "mediocre player" in trade talks, and his team balked because they suspected the team knew something they didn't. The player soon improved.

As their peers learned how to better develop their own players, or at least to respect the Dodgers' eye for outside talent, the Dodgers focused their acquisition scope earlier in players' careers. They don't need to coerce another team into parting with the next Muncy or Taylor. They can find him themselves, like they might have with Zach McKinstry, a slap-hitting small-college shortstop who transformed into a powerful utility player two years into his Dodgers career. It is the combination of strengths and the consistency of purpose that makes it impossible to predict the end of their reign. "It's kind of the perfect storm of sustainability," said Alex Wood, a 2020 Dodger, citing the resources, region, front office, drafting, player development, and fan base. "There's not many teams," said Clayton Kershaw, "that have gone all in, year after year, like we have, to try to bring home a World Series."

One longtime rival executive sees it as a permanent state. "I don't think they're ever gonna stop being a top-ten team in player evaluation, player analysis, and money," he said. "Those three top-tens are always gonna be around, and that's a hell of a combo to start with." The only thing that could stop them, the executive suggested, was a new CBA that fundamentally changed the business of the game.

The last CBA did that. During the 2017–2021 agreement, the average salary decreased 6.4 percent, according to an Associated Press study. During the three preceding CBAs, all of similar lengths, salaries rose 17.9 percent, 25 percent, and 29 percent, respectively. The median salary in 2021 was $1.15 million, down a half million, or 30 percent, from the record 2015 figure. The AP counted 902 players included on opening-day rosters or injured lists; the 100 highest paid of those players earned 52.4 percent of the sport's salaries.

For many players, the 2017–2018 off-season signified the turning point. Twelve days after the Dodgers lost to the cheating Astros in Game 7 of the World Series, the league held the general managers meetings at the Waldorf Astoria Orlando. Every November, top executives convene for the low-key precursor to the high-profile Winter Meetings. Agents also come to pitch their clients. On his way to a meeting with one team, one agent walked by an open ballroom where, according to the signage, Manfred had just given a presentation. Left on an overhead projector was an introductory slide about the league's economics going forward. The agent considered sneaking a further look but thought better of it. "I imagine there was something in there almost like Joseph Stalin's five-year plans," the agent said.

A new economic strategy was in place. One month before spring training, more than 80 percent of major league free agents had not agreed to contracts. "Maybe we should go on strike and fix that," Dodgers closer Kenley Jansen said. "Maybe not. I think it's a thing we maybe address to the union." Union leaders had insufficiently fought for the luxury-tax thresholds to increase during the 2017–2021 CBA, and the crop of available players was weaker than usual. The Dodgers and other big-market teams took the opportunity to reset their tax multiplier in preparation for future classes.

As camps started, so many established players remained unsigned that the MLBPA put on a training camp for them. Their peers took notice. One, Angels outfielder Justin Upton, had opted against becoming a free agent at the off-season's start, sensing the turning tide. The last time he had been a free agent, two years earlier, at least seven teams had offered him a one-year contract within a one-week span, he said. He termed that trend "really, really, really sketchy and weird," but stopped short of calling it collusion. Owners have a long history of colluding against players in free agency. Since an arbitrator ruled teams had practiced collusion for three off-seasons in the 1980s, the union has aimed to avoid haphazardly using the word.

Rather, Upton blamed the decline of free agency on the spread of data. As sabermetrics spread through the game, he said, players ceased to be players and became instead run-generating instruments. "That's how players should feel about this," he said. "When you carry yourself in the clubhouse, just know that the people upstairs see you as a statistic."

Clear as the typical Los Angeles afternoon, the statistics showed that most players were well into their decline by the time they reached free agency. As clubs followed the data and limited their outlay on all but the top-tier free agents, who were both better and younger, the league also instituted bonus caps in the draft and on the international market. Players with fewer than three years of service time continued to have no say in their compensation. That left the fraught land of salary arbitration as the last hope for players to gain ground in the fight for pay. "No one likes arbitration," Muncy once said on former teammate Ross Stripling's podcast. "It's a bad thing. That's what sucks about this game. It's a team game that's full of so many personal objectives."

The system is generally detested, but exceptions exist. Ed Edmonds is Professor Emeritus of Law at Notre Dame, a longtime law library director, sports-law expert, and baseball fan. For more than three decades, he has kept exhaustive records of every MLB arbitration case: figures exchanged, cases heard, the arbitrators who heard them, the rulings they made. He believes baseball's final-offer system, in which an arbitration panel must choose either the figure presented by the team or player, has been effective, because it minimizes posturing and forces compromise. Or it did, until a new strategy—file-and-trial—took hold in the late aughts. Teams practicing file-and-trial refuse to do any negotiating once they exchange figures with their players, forgoing the final weeks of discussions. "File-and-trial unbalanced the system," Edmonds said. "I think it's a pro-team strategy."

Teams gradually introduced self-imposed deadlines under the influence of Houston Astros president Tal Smith, who had for decades run an arbitration-consulting business where he handled up to a dozen other teams' cases. Late settlements after weeks of research bedeviled his fee-arrangement structure, and he suggested his clients set a deadline for a few days after the sides saw each other's "hold card." In 2008, the Astros tried it with two players. It's unclear if another team or two did so, too. In 2009, Friedman took it a step further in Florida: the figure exchange was now the cutoff. The Rays won both their hearings, and he stuck with the strategy, which he preferred to call "file to go." Friedman argued that the relatively even split in decisions through the system's first few decades was evidence that arbitrators would, well, arbitrarily pick sides to preserve their "really cushy job," and that the subsequent tilt in decisions toward the teams' side was evidence they were more incentivized to settle. "When you don't," he said, "more often than not, the team has a better argument."

When agents voiced their disdain, it only emboldened Friedman. "Andrew liked to say that the reason he knew it was a good strategy for the teams," said former Rays executive James Click, "is because the agents hated it so much." It particularly preys on inexperienced or unprepared agents, who, afraid to lose a hearing and a client, settle for less than the situation warrants. "It's smart," one representative at a prominent agency said of file-and-trial. "There's a fucking ton of bad agents out there." Speaking on an MLB.com podcast, Click noted that the Rays earned a reputation for not revealing their best offer until twenty-five or thirty minutes remained until the deadline. "That's an unfortunate part of human nature, but we deal with it," he said.

In time, everyone had to deal with it, because everyone followed Friedman. Before the 2019 season, influential CAA agent Jeff Berry even proposed a counter in a widely circulated memo obtained by ESPN. He suggested all agents agree not to negotiate until the sides exchanged figures, trying to force clubs into action. Berry did not succeed. By 2020, every MLB team reportedly employed at least a modified version of file-and-trial, refusing to sign one-year contracts but occasionally agreeing to multiyear deals after the artificial deadline. "If you were really cynical," Edmonds said, "you would say that this is an example of collusion, that word has gone out from MLB: All of you need to adopt the file-and-trial strategy." Edmonds is more a realist than a cynic. He understands a gap exists between groupthink and what constitutes provable collusion. Under US antitrust law, parallel behavior among competitors cannot itself trigger a violation. Under the CBA, teams are permitted to work in concert on arbitration.

On official orders or not, each owner benefits by falling in line. One successfully suppressed salary begets dozens more, because the system runs on comparisons. One player's decision to settle can cost his peer a million bucks hours later. Baseball's arbitration system was designed to encourage compromise, and file-and-trial does not befit the founding spirit.

Compromise, of course, will be required for the sport to continue, or at least for it to improve. Friedman succeeds in part because he convinces players he is compromising with them when he is attaining what he wants. Consider the 2019–2020 offseason, when players believed the league was pushing teams to hold arbitration hearings to reset precedents. Taylor and Muncy, the late-blooming stars the Dodgers discovered, both filed figures after they could not come to terms with the team. Under the file-and-trial policy, both would head to always-contentious arbitration hearings unless they agreed to multiyear contracts. The Dodgers signed both to multiyear contracts. "You think that's a coincidence?" asked Wood, who also signed with the Dodgers that winter. "He gave the finger to the league and took care of two guys that had been terrific." Friedman also secured the players on terms that proved deeply favorable to the team.

In his seminal book *Lords of the Realm*, John Helyar argued that collusion might finally have ended on October 15, 1988, the night Kirk Gibson launched his one-legged home run to win Game 1 of the World Series. "Nobody who witnessed that scene—a fist-pumping Gibson rounding the bases, his teammates mobbing him at home, Dodger fans filling the night with a roar—could ever again say that no free agent was worth it," Helyar wrote in 1994. When Friedman became a GM at twenty-eight, he cited the book as a favorite.

Perhaps, six years after the 2020 World Series, it will be clear that Betts's winning performance had the same enduring impact. Maybe baseball will survive. Maybe players will learn the thrills of a balanced skillset. Maybe teams will learn to hold onto their generational talents, cost be damned. Probably, the Dodgers will still be at or near the top.

# Chapter 2

ABOUT A CENTURY AGO, AROUND THE START OF the Great Migration, a white man named Bob Terrell sold a Black man named Jim Miller 104 acres of farmland outside Paducah, Kentucky. The property has stayed in the family ever since. Miller and his wife raised their children on the farm, and their daughter, Birdie, married a man named George Reeves, who also hailed from a farming family. In 1941, they bought the land from her father and built a brick-sided four-room house where they raised their nine children.

They grew tobacco, wheat, corn, and grapes. They raised cows and hogs. All nine of their children had children, and by the mid-1960s, dozens of Reeves descendants worked the farm. When they weren't tending to the animals or picking tobacco, they were playing sports: basketball, football, and, mostly, baseball. George Reeves carved a diamond into the dirt and his progeny played, daily in the summers and on Sunday afternoons all year as the weather allowed. So many kids roamed, they could form two full lineups with substitutes.

On that land, Diana Collins learned the game and the competitiveness her family holds dear. There was not much else to do on breaks from farm work. There were no toys, only a hand-crank ice-cream machine, decks of cards, a few sets of marbles, and baseball bats and gloves. So she played and played on the field fashioned by her grandfather, then starred on the softball team at the high school in town. In 1986, at twenty-five, Collins moved to Nashville, the neighboring big city. She is a skilled bowler, and in one of her many bowling leagues in town, she met Willie Betts, an Air Force veteran. They married, and, in 1992, had a boy they named Markus Lynn Betts—MLB for short. They called him Mookie.

As a toddler, Mookie Betts regularly accompanied his parents to the bowling alley, where they'd set up a playpen next to the night's lane. By age three, he could competently push a ball toward the pins. Baseball came a bit later. At five, local Little League coaches deemed him too small to play, so Collins fielded her own tiny team. Betts wore Teenage Mutant Ninja Turtles suspenders so his extra-small pants did not slip. The team came in last place, and Collins never coached again, but her son proved to her coaching peers that he deserved a roster spot the following season.

Collins took Betts to the family farm on vacation, only for play, not for work. He was uncomfortable around animals, and she was uncomfortable subjecting him to the grunt work she performed in her youth. "I knew when I was a little girl that I wanted to go to school so that I didn't have to do that work," she said. "And I knew I didn't want Mookie to endure picking tobacco, holding tobacco, chopping tobacco, smoking tobacco." Still, like his mother, he picked up on the farm the family's currency of competition, constantly challenging everyone around in everything around. Nobody ever let him win, and his response to defeat was to concentrate harder. "We tried to teach him: 'You've gotta work for what you want,'" Collins said. "If you wanna be a winner, you gotta practice hard, learn the game, better yourself. Nobody's gonna give you anything."

He learned every game there was. By age eight, Betts's bowling team won a state championship. By ten, he was a standout baseball and basketball player. When he was eleven, he had one cousin, Terry Shumpert, leaving Major League Baseball and another cousin, George Wilson, entering the National Football League. Both had grown up on the Paducah farm around Betts's mother. Shumpert faced a decision that spring. For fourteen years, he had been a big leaguer, rarely a regular and never a star, but usually a big leaguer. When he did not make the 2004 Red Sox roster out of spring training, he sensed those days might be done. He could go to Triple A Pawtucket and try to earn a midyear call-up to what looked to be a great team. Or he could sign with the Pirates, who offered him a spot on their Triple A team in Nashville, not far from Paducah and minutes from Collins's house outside town.

Shumpert signed with the Pirates. All summer, he brought his son, Nick, and Betts to Herschel Greer Stadium with him. Betts adored it there, shagging flies in the outfield, roaming the grounds. Back at home, Collins forged a strike zone out of cardboard boxes. Betts would practice in front of it for at least a half hour most nights. "Opportunities to be in different settings are what allowed him to progress," Collins said. And her willingness to withhold praise. "We never told Mookie he was doing everything right," she said. "You always need to be able to reach for something. If you tell a child they're doing everything perfect, what are they gonna be aiming for next?"

In the summer before his senior year of high school, Betts began to attract interest from major league scouts. His size remained a concern. One scout saw Betts changing into his uniform while walking from the parking lot before a game. He noticed that Betts struggled to cinch his pants so that they stayed on his frame. Another evaluator saw a "high ass," the sort he believed bespoke a still-growing body. The Red Sox drafted Betts in the fifth round, after their longtime area scout Danny Watkins grew enamored with his athleticism and competence across various sports. It helped, too, that Betts demonstrated superb reaction time when Watkins administered him a NeuroScouting test at his Nashville high school. The Cambridge company, then in its infancy, developed a means to quickly test athletes' neural processing abilities. The Red Sox and Andrew Friedman's Rays are thought to be the software's earliest adopters; Betts's rise was a testament to its accuracy and an influence in its spread across the sport.

Betts's first professional season, 2012, was a qualified success. He walked more than he struck out, controlling the strike zone. But he weighed 155 pounds and he hit for no power. At summer's end, he returned to Nashville, desperate to develop strength and obtain a haircut. When he told his barber his goals for the off-season, his barber mentioned he knew someone who could help. So began Betts's ongoing relationship with Deon Giddens, a former Arena Football defensive back who trains amateur and pro athletes in Nashville. Together, they added twenty pounds to his five foot ten frame before spring training, employing workouts lifted from football playbooks: power and hang cleans, tire flips, and weighted-box work.

But Betts began the next season using an exaggerated leg kick, striving to hit homers, and it disrupted his timing. He thought he was playing so poorly that he confided in teammates he planned to quit baseball and pivot to college basketball. While he was hitting .157 at April's end, that statistic oversold his struggles. Again, he was controlling the zone, with nineteen walks to just nine strikeouts. George Lombard, who would become his first-base coach with the Dodgers, was a coach and mentor then. Many afternoons, Lombard said, he met with Betts to assure him he was doing just fine. "Mookie, you're a really good player," Lombard told him. "Just trust yourself."

Betts trusts himself by letting his insecurity guide him. His friend and longtime teammate Brock Holt described an undercurrent of panic always available to him as motivation. "Whenever he's not performing at the highest level, he feels like something's off," Holt said. "I think deep down he knows he's gonna be fine.

But that's just what he's always done." Betts is a glutton for punishment. "He won't tell me this, but I think he secretly likes me kicking his ass," Giddens said. "He beat himself up if he didn't do things the way he expected," said Tim Hyers, who was twice Betts's hitting coach, in the minors and majors. "He challenged himself. Sometimes it came across as too hard on himself. But that's just who he is: If he sees something to do, he wants to do it to perfection."

Betts sensed that his self-critical behavior bothered some teammates. As Holt said: "He's kind of frustrating, at times." After the fifth three-homer game of his career, in his fifth season, several Red Sox remarked on the ridiculousness of his achievement. Betts told them to stop, arguing it was standard to have such a game once a year. That did not go over well, for the all-time career record is six. (Betts tied it in 2020.) Three men who managed five hundred career home runs, including Boston legend David Ortiz, never once managed three in one game. Presented with the facts, Betts apologized to his teammates. "He said that, but he didn't mean it," Holt said. "He meant to just say he was getting lucky."

Back in May 2013, Betts eased his leg kick and dominated the rest of the minor league season, maintaining control of the zone while adding power. Over the final month, he hit .404, earning an invitation to the Arizona Fall League. Against many of baseball's best prospects, almost all of them older, he held his own and captivated top talent evaluators, among them Friedman, who was still running the Rays. By then, Friedman had eyed Betts for almost two years, since he spoke with Theo Epstein in the fall of 2011. Epstein had just left the Red Sox for the Cubs, and he mentioned to Friedman the exceptional athleticism and work ethic observed out of Boston's fifth-round pick that year, Betts. Friedman started following his career. "You were drawn to the way he separated himself," said Buck Showalter, then the Orioles' manager, who introduced himself to Betts at the Fall League. "He was just engaged in every part of the game. He was very cognizant of what was going on around him, situations. [When] the ball was hit to him, you never saw him have that panic movement."

Only those close to him understood his inner panic. Everyone else was transfixed by his athletic ease and varied skillset. After that autumn, he rose quickly. The following June, Betts became a big leaguer at twenty-one. Because Dustin Pedroia was entrenched at second base and the Red Sox were desperate for a boost, they expeditiously converted Betts into an outfielder. In one of his first games, he threw out a runner at home but overshot the cut-off man, allowing a trailing runner to advance. Between innings, he apologized to Red Sox outfield coach Arnie Beyeler. "How many players do you know that's gonna do that?" asked Chili Davis, the Red Sox hitting coach at the time. "I don't know any in the big leagues right now." Betts did it often. He would make a play, then ask the nearest coach if he did it right. "He always wanted that affirmation, early in his career," Beyeler said. "But, nine times out of ten, he was doing it right."

On several occasions when Betts was not hitting well, Davis ordered him to stop practicing in the hours before a game. Even if he took a dozen ideal swings, he'd keep going, eventually err, and then try to correct that error. "It's like you're waiting for that bad swing to show up," Davis told him, "then you'll have something to work on." Anticipating how he might fail, Betts would set up a tee far above his strike zone and repeatedly swing at it. Davis redirected some of his energy from a persistent preemptive search for bad habits to a steadier reinforcement of good habits. "When that kid is focused, he's tough to beat," Davis said. "I guarantee you, the older he's gotten, his focus has gotten so much better, which is why he's consistently becoming a better and better player every year."

During 2017 spring training, Davis asked Betts what he wanted to achieve in the coming season. "You know how you have those really good weeks, and then you have two, three really bad weeks, and you're kind of up and down, up and down?"

Betts replied. "I want to minimize the two or three really bad weeks. Maybe it's two or three really bad days instead." Davis was dumbfounded. Betts, all of twenty-four, had already learned a lesson many players never do. "Smartest answer I ever heard," Davis said after two decades of playing and a decade of coaching.

Betts also learned to occasionally indulge his desire to work himself into near oblivion. That state calmed him. On the second day of 2018 spring training, a new Red Sox assistant hitting coach, Andy Barkett, asked Betts how he could help him. "I need somebody to listen to me," Betts said. It took months for Barkett to understand what he meant. Betts had heard so many coaches tell him, like Lombard and Davis did, that he needn't fret about hang-ups within his swing. He was asking Barkett not to do that, not to tell him how he should feel. "The way his swing works, he's not Mike Trout with 250 pounds coming at you," Barkett said. "He's got to feel that synchronicity every day, that connection to the ground. And when he does, great things happen."

And when he doesn't, he hits until he does. On July 20, 2018, the Red Sox began the second half of their season on a muggy evening in Detroit. Three days earlier, Betts had led off the All-Star Game. After reworking his swing in the image of new teammate J. D. Martinez's, he led both leagues with a .359 first-half average. But he didn't feel right that night. To find his form, he asked Barkett to throw to him in the Comerica Park batting cage before the game and in between each of his at-bats. So Barkett threw, hundreds of times, from Betts's preferred distance of thirty feet, as the best hitter in baseball toiled out of sight.

Barkett eventually stopped them, not out of concern for Betts's condition but for his own. His arm ached. "It was hot as hell in that cage, and he was wearing me out," Barkett said. When he arrived at the ballpark the next afternoon, Betts told the coach he felt good. The normal routine would be just fine for that night's game. "I remember thinking, 'OK, we're off the mania cycle,'" Barkett said. When he returned to his Florida home for the off-season, Barkett began to see a chiropractor. It was Betts's doing, he said.

More consistent habits mixed with occasional hitting indulgences and new technology sprung Betts into another tier of excellence. He finished 2018 with the sport's best statistics as his
Red Sox raced to a World Series title and he won his first MVP
award. He held his connection to the ground, not in the way his
ancestors had but in the way Martinez championed: using force
plates to quantify the start of his kinetic sequence. The plates
measured how much vertical, horizontal, and transverse force
hitters incorporated from the ground into their swings. Betts
learned to check his output whenever he was searching, comparing himself with his baseline.

When the Red Sox faltered to begin 2019, Friedman thought—
dreamed?—he might have a chance to acquire Betts in a sell-off.
As the July 31 trade deadline approached, Friedman reached out
to Boston general manager Dave Dombrowski, who didn't dis-
miss the thought. Then the Red Sox won five of six against good
clubs, and Dombrowski opted to stand pat. The run didn't last.
Neither did the general manager. Red Sox principal owner John
Henry made clear he wanted his payroll to retreat under the
sport's luxury-tax threshold. To supervise the shedding of salary, he targeted Chaim Bloom, Friedman's Tampa Bay protégé.
When Bloom called Friedman ahead of his Boston interview,
Friedman floated the idea that they could collaborate on a big
trade. He suspected Bloom would get the job, and he wanted to
plant the seed.

Bloom got the job. One week before Christmas, they began to
discuss the trade in earnest. Two weeks later, they settled on outfielder Alex Verdugo as the centerpiece. For another month, they
debated the rest of the package. For an elite team in pursuit of
a late, great addition, the Dodgers were in an unusual position:
They had so much major league talent and not enough space for
it all. So they were more inclined to trade established players
than prospects. The Red Sox sought prospects, not players with
a few years left of team control before they reached free agency.
To make a match, the teams roped in a third organization, the

Minnesota Twins, who were willing to part with a prospect for a player who'd improve their 2021 chances.

As the deal was originally devised, the Dodgers would send Verdugo to Boston and right-hander Kenta Maeda to Minneapolis. From the Red Sox, they would get back Betts and left-hander David Price, plus half of the $96 million due to Price until 2022. But the Red Sox disapproved of the medical reports on the pitching prospect, right-hander Brusdar Graterol, the Twins were sending them. After a week, the teams reworked the plan into separate trades. Instead of getting Graterol from the Twins, the Red Sox received two prospects from the Dodgers: celebrated infielder Jeter Downs and a lesser catcher. The Dodgers then took Graterol, an outfield prospect, and a draft pick back from the Twins in exchange for Maeda.

Whatever the particulars, the deal made a mockery of the competition. The most talented team added the sport's second-best player without ceding a star. Increasing the insult, the Dodgers stole Downs from the tottering Cincinnati Reds. After five years of wretched play, the Reds decided they would actually try to win in 2019. To do so, they were willing to take on salary, but only in the short term. Top free agents were not on the table.

Conveniently, the Dodgers employed three players due to earn significant sums the following season, then become free agents. While Matt Kemp, Yasiel Puig, and Alex Wood had all been productive in 2018, each man had clearly plummeted from his past peak. Kemp and Puig were marketing stars, but the Dodgers wouldn't suffer without their services. The Reds agreed to take all three and package two prospects, Downs and right-hander Josiah Gray, if the Dodgers sent some cash and took back pitcher Homer Bailey's contract.

The transaction saved the Dodgers about $6 million in player payments and untold millions more in future luxury-tax charges, because the tax increases after consecutive threshold crossings and resets after any year under it. From a financial perspective alone, it was a fine deal. It also replenished the Dodgers' farm system with two players the system was designed to prevent them from obtaining. The Reds had obtained the rights to both prospects with recent top draft picks awarded through a "competitive balance" provision in MLB's collective bargaining agreement.

Since 2012, the league has annually gifted picks after the first or second round to teams in the smallest markets and with the least revenue. The Dodgers, of course, are not eligible to receive those picks. But the league cannot stop teams from trading the Dodgers the products of the picks. Soon after they joined the Dodgers, both Downs and Gray rose to be ranked among the sport's top one hundred prospects. These were the players small-market teams like the Reds needed to develop to compete with the Dodgers; instead they were giving them to the Dodgers in exchange for regressing, expensive veterans. They were perpetuating the cycle of competitive imbalance.

When the Red Sox determined they needed to trade Betts and Price, no other team had both the prospects and budget space to take on most of their 2020 salaries. The rising Padres, the Dodgers' chief competition in trade talks, insisted on Boston taking back a cumbersome contract in any agreement. The Dodgers were willing to pay the players and foot the tax bill, in part because the tax rate stood to be 10 percent lower after they skirted the threshold in 2019. (Ultimately, they did not pay it in 2020, either, because Price opted out of the shortened season due to coronavirus concerns. That came in handy in 2021.)

What Betts brought to Los Angeles was, by most measures, obvious. Over the four preceding seasons, he had hit .305 and swatted an average of twenty-nine home runs per year. He had walked nearly as often as he struck out. He had stolen an average of twenty-four bases per year at an exceptional 86 percent success rate. He had won a Gold Glove every year. "He just embodies so much of what I really value in players," Friedman said.

It was, by others, subtle. Betts encapsulated what the Dodgers had been lacking. Because of his diversified skillset, he never went a week without contributing something of value, even within his worst slumps. Consider the first moments of the 2018 World Series, when Betts fought back from a no-ball, two-strike count against Clayton Kershaw to slap a single into center field. A pitch later, he stole second. A pitch after that, he scored the first run. Betts did little else that week, but he started the series-shaping rally.

Betts is the human embodiment of optionality, always available to boost the team in one facet or another. He could connect on a home run. He could beat out an infield single. He could unleash an unreasonably accurate throw. He could make a leaping, or diving, catch. He could steal second base, or he could score from first on a single, as he did to finish his final game with the Red Sox. He could demand his teammates establish a new, higher standard of effort, as he did before his first game with the Dodgers.

He contemplated speaking up in that manner in Boston, often enough that he repeatedly mentioned his desire to coaches. He'd vent about what he should say to teammates. They'd encourage him to say something. And then he wouldn't. "You could tell he wanted to be that guy," said Tom Goodwin, a coach on those teams. "Maybe he just didn't feel like he could because of some other veterans we had on our team."

After their Arizona meeting, Showalter watched Betts play from the opposing dugout seventy-nine times over five years. He came to see Betts as the salve to the bore that "three true outcomes" baseball has become. "The game is getting so robotic, and that's why Mookie catches your eyes, because there's nothing robotic about him," he said. "If I was a fan, out of all the people in the game, that's the guy I'd be drawn to."

His play presents as authentic because it is intentional and because it is efficient. "Mookie has the ability to use every ounce of force and strength that he possesses," Giddens said. "That's what separates him, and you can see it in the way he moves. It's crazy to see somebody with his frame produce that much power."

Even Betts still finds it strange, or claims to. In between bench-press sets one off-season morning, he remarked to Giddens that he cannot possibly hit home runs in batting practice, no matter how hard he tries. "But as soon as you turn the cameras on," he said, laughing at himself, "I can." Giddens knew this was not true but smiled and said nothing, prompting Betts to begin his next set. He has learned to cooperate with Betts's self-flagellation. "In his mind," Giddens said, "he's never at the mountaintop."

But he finds exhilaration in the climb. No one exhibits more joy than Betts when he is at his best, roaring when he leaps to rob a home run, hammering his chest when he snares a line drive in the gap. And when he is struggling, he does not exude anger but a forlorn focus, storing his frustrations within as motivation. It is part of his formula. "With all the sports I've done and all of the levels of focus I've had to go through," Betts said, "I've had to zero in on one thing at a time."

To sustain that approach, boundaries are essential. He forbids his family from bringing up baseball in conversation with him, and he limits his exposure to the game when away from the ballpark. In an increasingly white-collar industry, it is a decidedly blue-collar approach to the pursuit of greatness, reminiscent of the farmers from whom he descends.

Wilson, the NFL veteran in Betts's family, now owns the land where Betts's mother was raised. He plans to open a farm-to-table restaurant and a bed and breakfast on the property while retaining the familial history cultivated there. In 2019, the family published a bound book commemorating and delineating its tree, dating to Jim Miller's generation, incorporating nearly two hundred people. The book commemorates the high achievers the lineage has produced. As Black Southerners, every family member is taught in childhood that they must outwork their peers to find the success they desire.

"We don't have to sugarcoat it: That's the reality of it," Wilson said. "That's just what you gotta do. You gotta be willing to work harder and do more to be able to get that opportunity to show your worth. We just want the opportunity. If you give us that, we'll prove you right because we're gonna work harder and longer than anybody else is willing to. That's been instilled in us for generations, and it continues to be the case. It's sustained our family for this long, for four generations. There's no reason why we shouldn't expect it to sustain us for four more generations."

Betts is but the highest profile, highest paid of the many hardworking descendants of what the family calls Reevesville. "His story, and his mom's willingness to pour herself into her son, is just a true testament of what achievement is about, what family is about," Wilson said. "He is talented and he is fundamentally sound. But more than either of those, he was always willing to do the work that was necessary to be a great baseball player."

# Chapter 3

TEN MINUTES PAST 10 P.M. ON OCTOBER 9, 2019, Clayton Kershaw said he had never felt worse. He was thirty-one then, already a certain Hall of Famer. He had won his sport's highest individual honors. He had not won a World Series, the distinction he most craved. Nine times in his twelve seasons, the Dodgers drew close. Each time, they failed. Often, he felt responsible. The blame both burdened and spurred him.

Two hours earlier, Kershaw had jogged in from Dodger Stadium's home bullpen to extricate Walker Buehler from a two-on, two-out situation. Buehler, twenty-five and the team's ace in waiting, was the rare young pitcher who had proven himself in the postseason, but the Dodgers babied him more than they ever did Kershaw at that age. In the fifth and final game of the National League Division Series, Buehler stymied a punishing Washington Nationals lineup for most of seven innings. But his day was done when his career-high 117th pitch spun into the dirt. Upon his entrance, Kershaw faced a favorable matchup in the left-handed-hitting Adam Eaton. He dispatched him on three pitches to preserve the Dodgers' two-run lead, clapping his hands as he walked off the field, awaiting more duty.

The eighth inning was a more treacherous assignment. The Nationals sent up two of the world's best hitters: Anthony Rendon and Juan Soto. Both quickly swatted sliders into the bleachers. Rendon's drive barely cleared the left-field wall; Soto's game-tying smash left no doubt. As soon as Soto made contact, Kershaw reflexively sunk into a crouch, his eyes locked on the backstop. He knew it before he saw it, but he willed himself up and around to watch. Soon, he turned back to ask umpire Alfonso Márquez for a new ball, but Dave Roberts, his manager, sooner came to take it from him.

Kershaw staggered back to the Dodger Stadium dugout and sat with the uncomfortably familiar feeling of fresh October failure. For seventy-five minutes, he hardly moved. He layered on a jacket. He looked up at the damage on the field, but mostly down at his cleats. When the Dodgers' season was officially over, he trudged into the clubhouse with his teammates. His rookie catcher, Will Smith, hugged him and told him how much he admired him. Amid another embrace, the club's rookie video coordinator, Chad Chop, said he'd still give him the ball "every fucking day." It was both men's first time witnessing a Kershaw postseason misstep. Seasoned teammates stayed away as Kershaw sat at his locker and stared at his iPhone until a Dodgers staffer ushered him to where reporters waited.

Television cameras crowded all around him, Kershaw still wore the cap he had worn all season and the team-issued undershirt he had torn into a V-neck. He volunteered that "everything people say is true right now about the postseason," referring to the widespread criticism that he choked come October. "But I'm not gonna hang my head," he continued. "I'm gonna be here next year, trying to do the same thing." Watching from his Wisconsin home, Kershaw's best friend and former catcher, A. J. Ellis, recognized a hurt he had never seen. "He was just empty," Ellis said. "It all poured out of him in that moment."

That was a Wednesday. By the weekend, Kershaw asked Brandon McDaniel, the Dodgers' director of player performance, to do what they had been discussing for months and book him an appointment at Driveline Baseball. In other words: Kershaw told McDaniel he was willing to change. "That," Ellis said, "was the beginning of him trying to discover a new way of doing things."

Within professional baseball, Driveline was no longer new. It had been around for a decade, widely accepted for perhaps half that time. Founded by an iconoclastic college dropout turned card counter turned entrepreneur named Kyle Boddy, the facility became synonymous with a data-driven approach to pitching development. Their weighted-ball program attracted their first attention, much of it negative, for many in Major League Baseball long looked askance at anything out of the ordinary. In time, too many Driveline devotees found success for its methods to be ignored or belittled.

Located in a suburban Seattle business park, Driveline houses a biomechanics lab conducting motion-capture study, pitch analysis, and pitch design. Together with Trevor Bauer, they popularized the use of high-speed cameras to examine the intricacies of a baseball in flight. Now, amateurs flock there each spring and summer, professionals each fall and winter, to be coached by spirited young men with baseball backgrounds and scientific bents.

On the morning of October 17, Kershaw and McDaniel arrived at the facility, a glorified warehouse. Driveline had blocked off the area to curious outsiders, so Kershaw saw only four men when he walked inside: Rob Hill, Bill Hezel, Bryan Leslie, and Anthony Brady. Three of the four men were in their twenties. Two of them would soon be hired by major league teams. None of them received much advance notice of Kershaw's visit. All of them signed nondisclosure agreements that protected what they would cover that day, and all of them quickly introduced themselves. "All right," Hill said, pulling out his iPhone and recording the rest of the meeting in the Voice Memos application. "What are we trying to lock in today?"

Kershaw told Hill he wanted to undergo the full assessment they gave any arriving pitcher. Hill said OK and began the routine. He asked Kershaw to strip down to his underwear, and he affixed motion-capture devices across his body. After Kershaw threw, the staffers showed him the results on a screen. Besides clearing the space, the young men had not done much preparation for Kershaw's arrival. They preferred to respond in real time to whatever new clients voiced. "It was a normal assessment, how we pretty much do anybody," Hill said. "We just got a little bit more granular when we got to the pitch design sort of stuff."

Given the NDAs, details about what they discovered are scarce. But on a podcast called *Cutternation*, Hill noted that Kershaw's focus was on his off-speed pitches. That most likely refers to his slider, which scouts said had degraded in 2019, so much so that it was intermittently indistinguishable from his fastball. Because Kershaw threw three pitches—fastball, slider, curveball—he needed all three to be distinct.

The curveball is his most famous pitch, the only one Vin Scully nicknamed. The slider, he happened upon in the Wrigley Field outfield after making the majors. But it became his most important offering, his differentiator. At its best, the pitch looked exactly like his fastball until milliseconds before it reached the hitter, when it decelerated and darted down, dodging the opponent's bat barrel. It traveled seven or eight miles per hour slower than his fastball. By some measures, Kershaw's slider was the most effective pitch in baseball from the day he debuted it. But as Kershaw aged and lost velocity from his fastball, his slider suffered an unusual fate: it lost bite but not velocity, leaving it too similar to his fastball.

That day, Kershaw didn't say all that. But he did repeatedly ask the Driveline employees to explain why they recommended what they did. "It was really, really cool to see how invested in his career he was, how many really, really good questions he had," Brady said. "It humanized him."

When Kershaw left, Hezel told his colleagues he was going on a walk to clear his head. Hill stood in place and smiled. "What just happened?" he thought. "It was pretty wild," he said a year later. "But, looking back, it just makes so much sense to me now, knowing him more, and knowing how the game is going, why he would do that. The real question is, why wouldn't someone do that?"

Hill got to know Kershaw better because, on Halloween, Hill became the Dodgers' pitching coordinator of technical development. The visit had gone so well that McDaniel had offered Hill a job the Dodgers created for him. While continuing to work for Driveline, he would conduct similar assessments with dozens of pitchers across the Dodgers organization. "Democratizing baseball's new-age analytics and training to everyone," he said, explaining his goal. "The idea is raising every single person's floor, which allows us to raise the ceiling."

As one of the richest organizations in professional sports, the Dodgers are not exactly democratizing baseball. Gone are the days when Dodger Stadium ticket prices stayed the same for eighteen years. But the franchise's willingness to entrust their most prized pitcher to Hill demonstrated that the path to industry influence has been disrupted beyond recognition. Kershaw's entire professional career had been supervised by the same man: Rick Honeycutt, who played twenty-one major league seasons and coached fourteen before retiring, at age sixty-five, after the 2019 season.

When he met Kershaw, Hill was twenty-four, eighteen months removed from throwing his last game in front of twenty fans for a tiny NAIA school. He logged a 17.36 earned-run average in his final collegiate season. He had never been drafted, never been seriously scouted. Driveline was his only connection to professional baseball. But he studied the relevant data, and he intuitively understood how to communicate it to pitchers who were leagues better than he ever was.

Kershaw was known for his regular-season excellence, his postseason disappointments, and his insistence on a rigid routine. As he aged and his body began to fail him, he accepted that he needed to change. "It's just amazing that this guy has the track record he has," said Connor McGuiness, the Dodgers' assistant pitching coach, "and he's taking advice from a twenty-four-year-old kid." It started with advice from an elder.

After the 2017 season, Kershaw's friend Chris Young had trained at Driveline while pursuing one last major league run at thirty-eight. Young, now the Texas Rangers general manager, felt Driveline helped him and suggested Kershaw pay a visit. Kershaw's former teammate Alex Wood specifically recommended he work with Hill, just as Bauer, Kershaw's future teammate, had once recommended Hill to Wood.

Kershaw had declined their overtures over the 2018–2019 off-season. On the recommendation of another future teammate, Max Scherzer, he instead traveled to Cressey Sports Performance. The Cressey facility, in Florida, was named for and operated by Eric Cressey, whom the Yankees hired in 2020 to be their director of player health and performance. His programs are influential in the industry, if not as historically radical as Driveline's. Kershaw kept pitching well in 2019, but his velocity continued to decline. With it went his margin for error. Particularly problematic was the shrinking gap between his fastball and slider. The NLDS defeat convinced him he needed to engineer a solution. "It was something I identified with," Hill said. "Instead of getting small and shrinking and wanting to hide from the world, he doubled down on himself, sticking to his word of coming back with his head held high. I admired that so much."

Kershaw's teammate, the longtime closer Kenley Jansen, visited Driveline twelve days after him for another assessment. He, too, liked what he heard, and he brought it up to reporters when he arrived at spring training in February. Kershaw did not mention it when he spoke about his off-season, but it was too tantalizing a bit of gossip to stay secret forever. In mid-February, scouts started to whisper that something was different about Kershaw that spring. When I heard the rumor, I asked Andrew Friedman if it was true. He said it was, and profusely praised Kershaw for being open to improvement after what was still, he maintained, a great season.

When I asked Kershaw about it, he asked who had told me that. I said Friedman had talked about it. "I'm gonna have to yell at him," he said. I laughed and asked what he could say about what he had learned on his visit. "I could say a lot," he said. "I'm just trying to decide if I want to." He decided he did not.

"I'm not confirming or denying anything, but I will say that what Driveline does is not necessarily just a weighted-ball program," Kershaw said. "They're smart in how the body works, and how to create the most efficiency with your body, and how to create the most power with your body. They have ways to apply that. I think you can glean different things from different usages of it. Some guys are going in there maybe because there's more in there and they're trying to figure it out. Some guys maybe lost it. It's definitely a good tool. I think everybody thinks of Driveline, 'Oh, you throw weighted balls,' but it's a lot more than that, which I learned. It's cool."

He noted then that the Dodgers had since hired Hill and McGuiness, another young man with an unconventional track record. "Baseball's changing," Kershaw said. "It just kind of goes with the new wave of pitching. At the end of the day, you still have to compete. I would consider myself more on the old school side of things, but that doesn't mean you can't learn from stuff." McGuiness disputed that claim, pegging Kershaw in the middle of the pendulum, capable of tilting toward either side from equilibrium. Of course, he only met Kershaw before the 2020 season.

Kershaw came of age in another generation. Major league teams scouted him in the spring of 2006 with eyes and radar guns, not statistical models or high-speed cameras. He had his first pitching lessons only the previous fall, as a high school senior in the moneyed Dallas suburb of Highland Park. As Ken Gurnick once chronicled at MLB.com, a man named Skip Johnson shifted up his arm angle. That enabled Kershaw to keep his weight back and better incorporate his lower body into his delivery, improving his velocity and command. Johnson told him to pretend that his hands and legs were connected to one string and move them in unison. Fifteen years later, the imaginary string remained. So did Kershaw's signature hitch, which predated Johnson.

The 2005 Dodgers were the franchise's worst team this century. It was a good time to be bad. Three pitchers who went on to win multiple Cy Youngs ranked among the top talents available in the 2006 draft, and the Dodgers had their pick of the litter with the seventh selection. Not two years later, two months after he turned twenty, Kershaw made his major league debut. He added the slider, refined his command, and began to torment the league. By 2011, at twenty-three, he was the world's best pitcher. He won three of the next four Cy Youngs, finishing second to fluke knuckleballer R. A. Dickey in the lone outlier. But Kershaw often slipped in the playoffs, when fatigue annually overran him.

Each fall, Dodgers reliever J. P. Howell felt an urge to pull aside every pundit critical of his teammate and interrogate them. "Do you know how exhausted this man is?" he envisioned asking. He knew. The two left-handers worked out at the same time every afternoon. In June, Kershaw completed his routine with ease. In October, he moved more slowly. "It's not that his energy was down; it's that his body was physically beat," Howell said. "It's not like you can just strap it on and be tough. It's like his leg isn't strong right now because he's so exhausted and it's just not going to fire right." The two men never discussed it, but Howell saw what he saw.

Kershaw was not forced or coerced into such a state. Rather, he repeatedly opted to overextend himself. In September 2012, he called Ned Colletti three time zones away and demanded to pitch the next day despite a hip injury. Colletti, then the GM, deferred to the pitcher. In 2013 and 2015, Kershaw reached regular-season innings totals that may never be matched. Then, before every playoff series, he met with club officials and insisted that he pitch on short rest to maximize his availability. "I work all winter to be able to tell you what I'm telling you today," Colletti remembered him saying. The Dodgers let him do it. Sometimes it worked. More often, it didn't. "He was dragging," Howell said, "and he wouldn't show it to an opponent, to his teammates."

2015, Friedman's first season running the team, brought the first signs of regular-season downfall. Mediocre teams thrashed him early, and Kershaw owned a below-average 4.32 ERA on Memorial Day. When forecasted rain washed away a scheduled game in Colorado, Ellis thought he'd use the free evening to compare the footage from Kershaw's early-season starts with that of the previous season. Inside an emptying Coors Field visiting clubhouse, Ellis set up a side-by-side analysis along-side pitching coach Rick Honeycutt and video coordinator John Pratt. They began to examine it all, Ellis later remarked, as if Abraham Zapruder had shot the footage. Suddenly he felt a weight behind him.

He turned around. Kershaw was right there, livid. He glared only at Ellis and ignored the others. "What are you now, the freakin' pitching coach?" he asked. "It's time to play catch." While they threw, Kershaw said he did not want Ellis watching any more of his film. He promised that he was fine, that he would figure it out. He did. Foreshadowing what was to come, his slider had lost a bit of its vertical movement, and Kershaw recovered it by slightly altering his grip. But there was more to the story.

Before he was caught, Ellis had been paying particular attention to what Kershaw did in each count: 0–0, 1–0, 0–1, 1–1, and on. The next day, he recounted to reporters his evening in the video room. "Come to find out," Ellis said, "he's the same guy." That was exactly it. Opponents were smarting to Kershaw's tried-and-true sequencing. He essentially did the same thing every start: fastballs early in counts, low and inside. Sliders to the back foot of right-handed hitters and down and away to left-handed hitters. Occasional curveballs to mix it up. "I think you're seeing the National League adjust to him a little bit," Ellis said. "I think you're seeing a guy who's sticking with his process, and I'll take my chances with that in the long run." Ellis did not mention his confrontation with a certain large left-hander.

Around that time, Friedman and his deputy, Farhan Zaidi, tried to persuade Kershaw to change his sequencing. They showed him evidence that hitters had caught on to his patterns. He refused and remained angry into June, losing three straight starts for the first time in his career. He called the first of those, against his hometown Rangers, "the most frustrating game I've ever pitched." In July, he mixed it up and strung together his best stretch ever. Over his final seventeen outings, he completed an average of seven and one-third innings and allowed an average of one earned run. That postseason, he actually pitched well. But the Dodgers lost the decisive game by one run, undone when, during a defensive shift, no one thought to cover third after a runner advanced to second.

Halfway through a dominant 2016 season, Kershaw's back began to ache after a four-run, six-inning outing in Pittsburgh. "Sometimes I think we all forget that he's not perfect," Roberts said that night, before he knew his ace was hurt. Four days later, Kershaw was diagnosed with a herniated disc and administered an epidural. Building back toward a return three weeks later, he experienced a setback. It took him seventy-five days to make it back. When he did, he was as good as ever, and he extended the Dodgers' season with a heroic NLDS relief appearance. Then he bore the loss in their final game, thrashed by the World Series–bound Cubs. "Most guys," Friedman said, "would not have come back at all from what he suffered."

The next two years yielded the same outcome. Kershaw continued to lose velocity but pitched well whenever he wasn't hurt. The Dodgers perished in the World Series. Kershaw's $215 million contract gave him the right to opt out after 2018. So that he wouldn't, the Dodgers agreed to lengthen his deal by another season. The day the extension was announced, Kershaw conceded outside doubt was a significant motivator. He said he was eager to prove everyone wrong for believing in his decline. He noted that many older pitchers had maintained their velocity better than he had, and he alluded to off-season work he could do to recapture it. (Jacob deGrom, only three months younger, threw about as hard as Kershaw as recently as 2016. Since 2018, he has been throwing much, much harder.)

That off-season's work generated only an earlier playoff exit. So, to the Dodgers, the news that Kershaw wanted to go to Driveline was doubly good. It meant he might get help, and it meant he was more receptive to outside advice. "I'm pleased with not only where he chose to go, I'm pleased with the way he is now," Roberts said. "Clayton is open to information. He's been so great at doing something one way. But when you're talking about Driveline, changing up his workout regimen— that's growth. And that's how great players, in my opinion, remain great: adjusting. And it's hard to be great and to be open to adjusting."

The next time I saw him, Kershaw was upset. He believed I had misled him about how I had learned he visited Driveline. Friedman hadn't first disclosed it to me, he said. Someone else had, and Friedman had only confirmed it. I said that I never said Friedman was the first person to mention it to me; he said I made it sound like that. We argued about the nature of sourcing in journalism for a couple minutes. "There was a better way to handle that," Kershaw said as we parted ways. *ESPN* writer Wright Thompson, who witnessed our discussion, asked him why he cared so much about keeping it a secret. "I don't want people to know what I do every off-season," he said. "I guess to answer the question . . . I don't really know. I just don't like it. I feel like I don't want people to know."

Yes, Clayton Kershaw likes to be in control. To observe him was to learn this. He holds his teammates' admiration, but he expects them to approach competition like he does, and he demands they leave him alone on his start day. New players sometimes ran afoul of that requirement. In 2015, clubhouse clown Kiké Hernández laid on Kershaw's designated stretch table before one start. When Kershaw entered the training room, he screamed, and Hernández scampered to the next room. Kershaw most let loose on team flights, when he'd proudly pass what teammates describe as especially foul-smelling gas.

Otherwise, he was serious, intent on maintaining what he had, and, later, recovering what he lost. He was not a robot. He regularly experimented with new grips while playing catch. On extremely rare occasions, he broke out new pitch sequences in games. But until it became obvious that he couldn't, he always decided to stick with what got him where he was. "I think one of the worst myths professional baseball players tell themselves is, I just gotta get back to who I used to be," Ellis said. "We tell ourselves this because we want to find the quick fix, get the quick result, and we remember that success we had. But what we don't account for is that we're five years older. Our body has changed. The environment around us has changed. The league has changed. The hitters have changed. We have got to find new ways, while sticking to our core principles. For Clayton, it's first-pitch strikes."

Kershaw always prioritized beginning each at-bat with a strike. It confers him control of the encounter. In 2016, 2017, and 2018, he led all starting pitchers in first-pitch strike percentage. After a 2019 dip, he returned to the leaderboard in 2020 by sourcing the strikes in a new manner. He ceased with the occasional curveball, targeted the outer part of the plate with his fastball, and located some sliders in the zone. Hitters swung at his initial offerings less, but he got more strikes out of them.

He also acceded to the Dodgers' request to shift infielders behind him. In 2016 and 2017, the team shifted only 3 percent of the time a right-handed hitter batted against Kershaw, and 15 percent of the time he faced a left-handed hitter. In 2020, those shares were up to 87 percent and 83 percent, respectively. "After a little bit of arm wrestling with the organization and himself," Ellis said, "he's come to grips with the fact that in this third or fourth quarter of his career, some of his same fundamental principles will be in play, but he's willing to take a big look at things."

When the 2020 season began, opponents described a different pitcher. In his first start, he surprised right-handed hitters expecting familiar fastball locations. "The four-seams away he was throwing me in the first inning, he hasn't in the past thrown me a lot of those," said Christian Walker, who had hounded Kershaw in recent years. "They seemed like they had maybe a little bit more finish through the zone." Walker was right; both Kershaw's stuff and his sequencing were obviously different. His fastball was up more than one mile per hour from 2019, his slider and curveball a little faster, too. This was significant. Over the preceding four seasons, only 2 percent of pitchers his age or older had added even 1 mph to their fastballs, according to Beyond the Box Score research.

On his best days, Kershaw paired that increase with an extra bit of bite on his slider. Suddenly, hitters could not adjust to the slider at the last millisecond like Rendon and Soto had. In 2020, hitters barreled Kershaw's slider at half the rate they did in 2019. The expected slugging percentage off the pitch plunged 100 points, from .381 to .281. As the postseason approached, Kershaw expressed guarded optimism about his capabilities. "I'm hopeful that some of the things that I've done, because I've been sort of beat up in the past," he said, "has prepared me to kind of maintain what I've got going right now."

On October 1, 2020, Kershaw pitched his first postseason game since his nadir. His postgame countenance relayed how far he had come. As he waited to take reporters' questions through Zoom, Kershaw discussed nut butters and children's snacks with the waiting Joe Jareck, the Dodgers public relations senior director. (Because genetics have a sense of humor, Kershaw's son Charley has a peanut allergy.)

Kershaw had changed. The hurt shifted his perspective; the openness made him better. In his final regular-season start, Kershaw had detected a variation in the results his slider obtained. The pitches that most major leaguers had missed all season, the Angels had fouled off, and the pitches most major leaguers had fouled off, the Angels put into play or let pass. He dug into the data, which showed his velocity, movement, and arm speed all had decreased. To counteract it, McDaniel supervised Kershaw through additional arm-care exercises, focusing not on preparing for his playoff debut but on recovering from his last outing. On the eve of his season's biggest game to date, Kershaw did what, until October 2019, he never would've done. He amended his routine.

It worked. Kershaw's metrics ticked back up to their regular-season norms. The Brewers swung at nearly three-quarters of his sliders and missed almost half of them. No team had erred with so many swings in any of his twenty-five previous playoff starts. His catcher, Austin Barnes, remarked that his sliders seemed to float under the Brewers' bats all night. Kershaw wryly reflected on his improvement. "Maybe, in years past, I've been known to be pretty stubborn, so I just kind of do the same things no matter what in between starts, no matter how I'm feeling," he said, his teeth now visible in an emerging smile. "I think that might not be the best idea, at times."

# Chapter 4

S AM FULD MIGHT HAVE BEEN THE FIRST PROFES-
sional ballplayer to read *Moneyball*, in the summer
of 2004, as he recovered from shoulder surgery
soon after he signed with the Chicago Cubs. He made the major
leagues three years later. For the next eight seasons, he observed
the influence of data on his favorite game. Fuld was a uniquely
qualified judge, the embodiment of a stereotypical jock and nerd
commingled in one modestly sized man.

On the field, he repeatedly risked his body with daring defensive plays. Off it, he interned at a statistics company and pursued
a master's degree in the discipline from Stanford, his alma mater.
He manned the outfield for the two most innovative teams of
his time, the Oakland Athletics and Tampa Bay Rays. But as he
saw it, front offices used data to drive their acquisition decisions.
Players did not apply data to their games.

"The analytics age, for a decade-plus, was purely from a
decision-making standpoint, a value standpoint," said Fuld, who

became the Philadelphia Phillies general manager after retirement. "Now, it's taken over the game, in terms of being able to impact players on an individual level."

It changed, he believes, in 2014. One balmy late-spring evening seven years later, Fuld stood in foul territory at Dodger Stadium and gestured to the source. One person, he said, initiated the step change from front offices exclusively employing analytics to players wielding them to improve themselves, and in an hour's time he and his resplendent red beard would stand, oh, fifty yards away: Justin Turner. "Maybe he didn't use a ton of information, necessarily, to turn himself from a utility player into a year-in-year-out All-Star," Fuld said. "But the underbelly of that change was rooted in analytics: You could do more damage if you hit the ball in the air."

Turner met the man who taught him to hit the ball in the air a few feet from where Fuld stood. With six weeks left in their forgettable 2013 season, the New York Mets met the streaking Dodgers in Los Angeles. Mets outfielder Marlon Byrd invited Doug Latta to watch batting practice at Dodger Stadium and introduced him to Turner, then a reserve infielder.

Until he met Byrd, Latta might have been better known among amateur swimmers than professional ballplayers. He had frequently published treatises on plaster care, algae, and gas chlorination in *California Pool Owner Magazine*. A licensed contractor but a self-taught hitting coach, he had long worked alongside Craig Wallenbrock, the preeminent private hitting coach. Unlike Wallenbrock, he specialized in working with amateur players. Like Wallenbrock, his primary implement was video. Latta taped every swing at his unadorned Northridge facility, the Ball Yard, and reviewed the footage between sessions.

While Turner's reinvention is remembered as an analytics triumph that spawned the league-wide manhunt for technological gains, the humorous truth remains that his was a charmingly low-definition endeavor. Turner hatched a generation of data-driven redesign; his was more data supported. Latta is no statistical fiend, no tech devotee, just a lifelong fan who understood what many baseball insiders lost sight of: hitters were better served hitting the baseball into the air.

Byrd found Latta by chance while banished from baseball, serving a suspension for performance-enhancing drugs. They hit together every day for three months. During the career year that followed, Byrd repeatedly told Turner and other teammates about Latta's teachings. As he later explained to *Swing Kings* author Jared Diamond, he did so against the Mets' wishes. Not that anyone heeded his advice anyway.

The week after they left Los Angeles, the Mets traded Byrd for prospects. The next day, Turner for the first time sampled his suggestions. The most obvious difference was an extreme leg kick Turner utilized to start his swing. He had used a leg kick at times, but never as high as what Byrd advocated. Everything else flowed from there. Turner transferred his weight earlier to connect more forcefully with oncoming pitches. He tried, too, to lower his hands to hit them higher. Throughout his life, Turner had aimed to let the ball travel before he made contact. Now he would try to ambush it as early as he could.

In his first at-bat with the new approach, he doubled against Phillies ace Cole Hamels. A few days later, Turner reverted to his old, punchless swing. He went back and forth once more before he crossed the Rubicon along Lake Erie. The first night of a weekend series in Cleveland, Turner whacked his first homer of the year, against Cody Allen, a dominant reliever. The next night, he doubled off the wall against Vinnie Pestano, a college teammate. The next afternoon, he homered again, against future All-Star Danny Salazar. Turner struck out four times that series, his season high, but he was sold on the damage he did with his new swing. He has recounted the weekend countless times, in clubhouses to new teammates, to reporters, to anyone inquiring. He often omits the double and peppers in the story of walking through the Jack Casino, blocks from the ballpark, unable to stop thinking about who he could be.

Turner didn't relate the story publicly for years, but in every retelling since he excavated it, his tone changes when he switches from narrating the facts to describing his awe at his sudden power. It always captures the marvel of a man learning he is capable of more before anyone else realizes it. "You knew something was different," Pestano said. "But who'd have thought that trajectory would have started right then?" Not the Mets. Two months into the off-season, they declined to tender him a contract for 2014, saving about $800,000. "Don't assume every non-tender is a function of money," general manager Sandy Alderson told reporters, hinting that the Mets were not, in this case, their typical thrifty selves, but ready to move on from a player they perceived as lazy.

Other teams were mildly interested. In fact, Turner's September batted-ball data popped off of the Tampa Bay Rays' spreadsheets. While Andrew Friedman's front office did not go so far as to research what drove the improvement, they found the data attractive enough to warrant a minor league contract offer. Turner garnered similar interest from the Minnesota Twins and Boston Red Sox, but he hoped for more, and he worked for it.

At season's end, Turner had called Latta. He spent that off-season the way Byrd had spent the last, hitting at the Ball Yard for three or four hours, four or five days a week. He was relearning how to hit, replacing twenty years of muscle memory. Byrd was almost always there, rotating into the cage. Latta sat atop an upturned bucket and soft-tossed them pitch after pitch. After Turner left his first session, Latta asked Byrd if Turner understood how good he could be.

Three hundred games into his major league career, Turner owned a career average of .260. He had established himself as a steady utility infielder, the type teams had been stashing on their benches for decades, the type that would've once been assured of employment into his mid-thirties. By common measures, Turner had been a nearly average hitter. Considering that he had not even been trying to hit home runs, he was stunningly successful. He had reached the peak of what his old swing would allow. Turner had no power, no set position, and little speed. The odds had always been against him.

He was comfortable with that. Turner grew up outside Los Angeles in working-class Lakewood, a post–World War II planned community constructed in record-breaking time. His was a baseball family. His father, John, had played baseball in his youth alongside Rick Vanderhook, the future Cal State Fullerton coach. Through that connection, Justin Turner became a Titan bat boy. He absorbed the game's pacing and made himself fundamentally sound enough to earn a place in the program after high school.

He fit just right. As a freshman, he stood five foot ten, weighed maybe 165 pounds, and beat out a shorter senior to start at second base. Fullerton prided itself on thriving as the undersized underdog compared with USC and UCLA. For generations, every coach preached the same mystique, no matter how talented they were. "We were always overlooked, and that really helps a team, when everybody's got that common goal of proving everybody wrong," said Pestano, a fellow bat boy turned teammate. "Those are the cornerstones of Justin's entire career."

Turner led off for the Titans, all the way to Omaha and the 2003 College World Series. In the third inning of an elimination game against Stanford, he set up to bunt. Shadows surrounded the infield, and a wandering fastball he never saw instead hit him in the left cheek. Turner crumpled to the dirt. The Cincinnati Reds scout who signed him learned Turner's name that day, specifically after he returned to the Fullerton dugout following a medical examination, his face bloodied and bruised. "That kid's a grinder," thought the scout, Mike Misuraca, a former major league pitcher. "That's the type of kid I used to love to play with."

Months later, an MRI showed that Turner had fractured his ankle when he fell. The news only emphasized Misuraca's impression. He saw more of Turner when he started scouting Southern California the next year. The 2004 Titans, the eventual champions, were filled with future major leaguers, most of whom scouts rated higher. Turner lacked their tools but kept up with his teammates statistically, and Misuraca noticed that he always did what needed doing: skying sacrifice flies, moving runners over, even bunting. "I had to do it to survive," Turner said. "I never hit for power. I never hit home runs. If I wasn't successful at situational hitting, I probably never would've gotten to the big leagues."

The public perception of his game matched his internal view. "Turner is a pure baseball player with outstanding instincts, a love of the game, and an ability to turn every ounce of his potential into production," read his scouting report in *Baseball America 2008 Prospect Handbook*. "He likely never will hit for much power, but his ability to produce for average while doing all of the little things gives him a chance to make it to the big leagues as a second baseman or utilityman."

Turner made it at twenty-four, in September 2009, after hitting .300 or better at six minor league levels and .289 at a seventh. The Reds had drafted him in the seventh round in 2006, paying him a paltry $50,000 bonus. Cincinnati soon traded him to Baltimore, which sooner placed him on waivers. The Mets claimed him, but they, too, in time deemed him fungible.

On January 25, 2014, Turner drove down from his Los Angeles home to Fullerton. One Titan tradition is an annual alumni game, held on the eve of the college season, before current professionals begin spring training. Turner was a frequent attendee. He always took part in the pregame festivities and performed in the storied trick plays that kicked off each game.

Several prominent ex-players made the trip to meet the 2014 Titans, the preseason favorites. That morning at Goodwin Field, Turner was a professional without a place to ply his trade. He explained his situation to Fullerton's most accomplished alum, All-Star third baseman Tim Wallach. After his seventeen-year playing career, Wallach had turned to coaching. Earlier that off-season, he became the Dodgers' bench coach.

When Wallach watched Turner take batting practice that day, he noticed the difference in his swing. So did the other alumni present. "Holy cow," thought Eddie Delzer, a comically undersized left-hander who, twenty years earlier, pitched the team to a national championship against a pitcher eight inches taller and ninety pounds heavier. "Look how effortless it is compared to before." Wallach called the Dodgers general manager, Ned Colletti, and connected the two men.

It is fair to say Colletti had a weakness for veteran utility infielders. In fact, he already had interest in Turner, and, the day before Wallach saw Turner, Colletti had signed another utility man, a onetime great, Chone Figgins. This was not a problem. The previous season, Colletti had employed three, at times four, at once: Nick Punto, Skip Schumaker, Jerry Hairston Jr., and Michael Young. All four were leaving the team that off-season.

To replace them, Colletti offered Turner a guaranteed contract worth $1 million, pending a physical examination. Turner accepted. But the physical revealed left knee problems, and the Dodgers reworked their offer into a minor league contract worth the same, only not guaranteed in the event he didn't make the opening-day roster. He agreed anyway. As a National League team, the Dodgers offered more room for him to play. Turner once said on *The Chris Rose Rotation* that he looked it up: Colletti's trusty utility men had batted far more often than their equivalents on the interested American League teams.

And the Dodgers were his hometown team. Turner was born twenty-four miles from Dodger Stadium at Long Beach Memorial Medical Center. On October 15, 1988, Turner, aged three, watched on his grandmother's couch while Kirk Gibson hit the most famous home run in franchise history. Decades earlier, she had visited Chavez Ravine to track progress on Dodger Stadium's construction. Twenty-nine years after Gibson, Turner hit his own game-winning playoff home run there to help the Dodgers inch toward the World Series. Minutes afterward, he said on television that he thought about imitating Gibson's fist pump on his way around first base, but decided to wait for the World Series to repeat the theatrics. He waited years.

When he signed the initial deal, Turner was not nearly as open about his swing change as he would become. "Even the Dodgers," Latta said, "didn't realize what they were getting." Most teams still frowned on work with private hitting coaches. Some still do. Turner faced discouragement from coaches that first spring, but he performed well enough to make the manifest for the team's season-opening goodwill trip to Australia.

After the sixteen-hour flight, Turner, his future wife Kourtney, and Colletti met in the lobby of the team's Sydney hotel and decided to play a few hands of blackjack at its casino. As they squandered their money, they built trust, enough that, a month later, Colletti could confront Turner. He had started slowly, and his clubhouse behavior—including playing plenty of *The Settlers of Catan* with reliever Brian Wilson and reserve outfielder Scott Van Slyke—belied his struggles. "We need more," Colletti said he told Turner. "I know there's more in there."

Turner was not the type to linger on one bad night, week, or month. The same perspective made him a natural leader after he became a star, but, as the roster's twenty-fifth man, it was unwelcome. Unsuccessful bit players are not supposed to have fun. But at Fullerton, Turner had taken sports psychologist Ken Ravizza's classes and soaked in his teachings. He learned flushing his failings on his way out of the clubhouse each evening best prepared him for the next day's game. "I really think that's what he is about: Winning the next pitch," the late Ravizza once told the *Los Angeles Times*.

Soon after the conversation with Colletti, Turner found his way. He hit his first homer on his first visit back to the Mets' Citi Field, over Memorial Day weekend. From that day forward, he hit .386, still as a part-timer. The Dodgers were unconvinced Turner's body could handle more play.

Sometime that summer, once it was clear he would be coming back, Dodgers strength and conditioning coach Brandon McDaniel gauged Turner's interest in training with him full-time over the off-season. If he was, McDaniel said, he, his wife, and their infant son would move out from Omaha and make Los Angeles their permanent residence. Turner said he was.

The Dodgers' season ended on October 7, with an NLDS loss to the Cardinals, probably Clayton Kershaw's most crushing postseason defeat until the 2017 World Series. Turner batted twice in the series, both times as a pinch-hitter. One week later, McDaniel sat in the passenger seat of a U-Haul motoring along Interstate 80 near the Nebraska-Colorado border. His father-in-law at the wheel, McDaniel checked MLBTradeRumors.com around midday. There was big, relevant news: Colletti was out, and Friedman was in. They pulled over while McDaniel called his boss, Dodgers vice president of medical services Stan Conte, with a question: Should they turn around?

They continued west. McDaniel met Turner at Dodger Stadium every weekday between 8 and 9 a.m. and trained him until the early afternoon. Their first session was October 17, the same day Friedman held his introductory press conference. When Friedman met Turner in the weight room, he quipped that he was glad Turner had not chosen the Rays the previous year.

For the first six weeks, they focused on conditioning. The left knee that cost Turner his guaranteed contract continued to cause problems, and the team's medical staff concluded he could lessen the burden by losing weight. "I just wanted to get a good base under him," McDaniel said. Soon came kettlebell work, followed by weightlifting.

In January, McDaniel started throwing Turner batting practice on the days he wasn't hitting with Latta. In February, they proceeded to Arizona for spring training, and Turner was hitting and moving better than ever. In May, Friedman traded incumbent Juan Uribe to clear space for Turner to become the Dodgers' primary third baseman. His lighter, more agile frame made him a better defender. "I've seen a lot of players become better hitters," Colletti said. "I've seen very few players in their mid to late twenties become better defensively. He became really good."

Not too many sustained as much offensive growth as Turner, either. When the Dodgers met the Mets in that fall's National League Division Series, Turner was their cleanup hitter. He reached base eleven times in twenty opportunities. The Mets won, but the New York media pressed club officials about giving up on Turner. One night during that series, McDaniel suggested to his pregnant wife, Andrea, that they name their son Turner. He maintains he was joking. She liked the name.

Now, Turner McDaniel is in elementary school, and his father is the Dodgers' director of player performance, supervising the team's strength, conditioning, and nutritional recommendations. "JT changed my life," McDaniel said. "Like, if he gets hit by a pitch, he doesn't play in '15, and he doesn't become Justin Turner, there's no credibility."

His success might have boosted Latta's credibility even more. The coach soon began to work with famed sluggers Adrián González and Ryan Howard. In recent years, he has counseled hitters young and old, including top Red Sox prospect Jarren Duran, longtime Giants outfielder Hunter Pence, and hitters across the world. Not all of them use a leg kick as pronounced as Turner's, or one at all.

Latta does not believe in a uniform swing. He believes in hitting principles: balance, time in the zone, and an attack angle that produces air balls, as he calls them, where damage is done. "Efficiency was the defining idea," Latta said. "And it still remains that. It's not about chasing exit velocity or launch angle." But he does love a good leg kick. "It's kind of a pitcheresque move," he said, "and, if you ask me, kind of a sexy move." In fact, before Latta ever worked with Turner, a nine-year-old named Maddox Latta, Doug's son, did it. He graduated from high school in 2021 still using it.

More than he shaped McDaniel's and Latta's careers, Turner transformed the Dodgers' trajectory. "There have been so many things he has done behind the scenes," Friedman said, "that have contributed to the success we've had." The Dodgers describe Turner as insistently vocal about two tenets of his altered approach: getting in front of the ball, and hitting it into the air. Turner began to demand teammates do push-ups when they hit grounders in spring training. He challenged others to swing and miss under breaking balls in the batting cage, sneakily teaching them to lift the ball. He was less vocal about situational hitting, but he modeled it every day. He often took a daily round of batting practice in imagined pressure situations, sometimes suggesting others do the same.

Now, at his slimmest weight since college, Turner looks more like the prototypical try-hard utility man than he ever did when he filled that role. He swings with a significant enough uppercut that he dirties the back of his uniform every night. In the on-deck circle, he exaggerates his follow-through to mimic what he wants to feel in the batter's box. The pine tar he applies to his bat barrel for grip smears, always between the second and third letters of his last name.

But it is his past that renders Turner an effective leader. Like Betts, he learned to hit first, then hit for power. And he understands what it is like to begin as a part-timer, and worse, an up-and-down player between the minors and majors. Betts, for example, never experienced either, but the Dodgers ask many of their young players to accept that status. Turner offers them counsel. He'll collaborate on crossword puzzles with fringe relievers called up for one day. In spring training, he'll tell prospects it's better to be down 0–1 in a count than 0-for-1 in a game, and tell them so often they make it their minor league mantra.

Turner was the first Dodger to spend his off-seasons training at Dodger Stadium. (Before the ballpark's 2013 renovation, the weight room was not designed for the modern athlete aiming for fitness goals.) Now, up to a dozen players and more prospects cycle through in a typical winter, led by Turner. He is one of few Dodgers to make his full-time home in Los Angeles, living where the exclusive Hollywood Hills give way to the expansive San Fernando Valley. He appears in events across the metropolis more than any other Dodger. Before Betts arrived, he functioned as the de facto team captain.

It is rare in the modern game for a player and team to be tied together so deeply, rarer still for such a connection to form when the player debuts for the team as late in life as Turner did for the Dodgers. He was nine months from thirty when he signed the team's minor league contract offer. At that age, on that pact, it was more likely his MLB career was over than it was that he was embarking on a partnership that would last at least nine years and pay him nine figures.

There is precedent for a career-changing conversation to occur at an alumni game. In fact, the game at tiny Haverford College set Dodgers executive Josh Byrnes on the path to twice becoming a GM, when a fellow alum, agent Ron Shapiro, met and recommended him to his son, Mark, a Cleveland executive. There was less precedent for the changes Turner was making to his game at the same time. There was only Byrd. Now there is an entire industry.

The launch-angle revolution, misinterpretations and all, began with a bet Turner placed, not on the blackjack table but on himself. His old swing made him a big leaguer. He risked cutting short his career for the chance he would become better.

Friedman, the man who would become his boss, was a betting man himself. Once, NJ Advance Media reported, he boarded a gambling cruise to the international waters outside New York City. When the boat owners ran out of money, scared travelers started selling their chips for dimes on the dollar. Friedman bought them up, and, back at shore, recouped full value from his purchases. He harbored the ultimate respect for Turner's gamble. "A lot of guys feel like, OK, this level I'm at, I don't want to take any chance of it diminishing, even if I have the potential to access a lot of upside," Friedman said. "Even the psychology to do it is really impressive."

# Chapter 5

UNTIL 2008, THE TAMPA BAY RAYS HELD THEIR spring training in a World War II–era ballpark bordering the actual Tampa Bay. That last year at Al Lang Stadium, their first after exorcising the pesky "Devil" from their name, senior vice president of baseball operations Andrew Friedman and manager Joe Maddon held a clubhouse meeting announcing changes for the coming season, the two men's third in charge. In both preceding campaigns, the Rays had been Major League Baseball's worst team. In its decade of existence, the franchise had never won more than seventy games in a season. They hosted home games in a soulless dome 7,500 feet west of the St. Petersburg waterfront, built on spec twenty years earlier. Ventilation inside the old spring stadium was so bad, Maddon said it aggravated his allergies.

In that outmoded space, Friedman revealed the team would embark on an unprecedented undertaking in 2008. For a century, major league teams had exclusively utilized shifts when defending left-handed sluggers. The Rays, he said, would broaden that. The Rays would not only shift against Red Sox designated hitter

David Ortiz, but against any left-handed hitter who pulled the vast majority of his grounders. Data gathered the last two years guided the decision. "This is gonna work at least seventy-five percent of the time, maybe even more," Rays in the room remember Friedman saying. "But we definitely like our odds at the end of the year, if we're consistent with it." Pitchers did not like theirs. "The overall census was, 'Who's gonna be that twenty-five percent?'" said right-hander James Shields. "It was beef," said left-hander J. P. Howell. "There was a lot of pushback. Everyone was like, 'This is cute, a guy trying to reinvent the wheel. Get him out of here.'"

It was an uncomfortable experience for Friedman, who was then thirty-one and still fighting a lifelong fear of public speaking. Little from his four years at Tulane sticks out in his brain more than the feeling of anxiously awaiting presentations in crowded lecture halls.

Daily infield practice, Friedman explained with help from Maddon, would change. Fielders and pitchers were to spend a portion of each session rehearsing how to move within a shift. Friedman noted that he had an open-door policy; players could discuss this with him at any time. "No one had ever heard of that," Howell said. "Some of the old guys were offended by it."

Others liked it, and Friedman spoke in private with members of both parties. A decade later, he did the same to convince disbelieving Dodgers, namely Clayton Kershaw. Friedman has always been more comfortable in small-group settings. The skeptical Shields estimated he met with him nearly a hundred times over their seven seasons together, Friedman often sketching an infield onto a whiteboard and explaining the math. Shields recalled consoling Friedman after tense defeats. "Andrew, it's OK, man," he'd say. "We got another game tomorrow." More than a decade later, Shields chortled at his memories. "There were a lot of times," he said, "he took a loss harder than I did."

That trait helped the shift take hold. Friedman won over some Rays with video proof and others with his competitiveness. Howell was sold when he entered the clubhouse after a relief appearance one night at Tropicana Field. In the cafeteria, he encountered Friedman engrossed in the television broadcast of the ongoing game. The Rays put on a shift in an important situation. A pitch jammed the opposing hitter, who barely managed to make contact. The ball traveled through the hole where the shortstop normally stood. Friedman flung a water bottle across the room. "That's badass," Howell thought. He became a disciple convincing the dubious. "I tried to smooth it over, because it was a dicey move at the time," he said. "If I heard bad-mouthing about it, I'd say, 'You gotta give it a chance, man. It may work.'"

It worked. There was no public data on defensive shifts until 2010, but in terms of defensive efficiency, or the percentage of balls in play converted into outs, the Rays went from baseball's worst team in 2007 to baseball's best in 2008. The team itself went from worst to near-first, all the way to the World Series. There were other factors; the team employed much better infielders in 2008. Only in the Fall Classic did the nation notice what Tampa Bay was doing. Minutes after the Backstreet Boys crooned the Game 1 national anthem, the Rays broke out a shift for Phillies second baseman Chase Utley. The FOX broadcast remarked on the perceived oddity. "Maybe they thought Ryan Howard was the hitter," color analyst Tim McCarver said in reference to Utley's hulking teammate. Utley tried to bunt into the void, but failed to keep it fair. Then he swung away and smashed the game's decisive home run.

Friedman did not enjoy employing defensive shifts. Nor does he today. The hits the maneuvers prevent, the mind moves on from in seconds. The hits they create tend to linger, in his case for weeks. But Friedman's teams continue to lead the league in shifts. "One of the most challenging aspects of the shift is that it's a terrible quality-of-life play," he said. "I just deemed winning was more important than that." He was referring to his own quality of life, but in contributing to the decline of balls in play, the shift has had adverse effects on the fan experience. Few actually enjoy it. Most players, too, detest it. "It's your fault," Dodgers hitting coaches frequently remind Friedman, who frequently and unsuccessfully reminds hitters to bunt when they see extreme shifts.

When reporters asked Maddon that October why his team had shifted against Utley, he cited information the Rays had been receiving all year. "If you look at a spreadsheet and you notice that balls are not hit in a certain area," Maddon asked, "why do you cover it?" (Utley surely understood. By 2008, according to statistician John Dewan's *The Fielding Bible*, he was changing his own defensive positioning between batters more than his second-base peers.) In the coming seasons, the Rays stopped covering those areas, and everyone eventually copied them. By 2021, an average week of MLB games featured as many shifts as the entire 2011 season.

Baseball Info Solutions, Dewan's company, has supplied the data that informs clubs' choices since 2006. In the early days, a host of interns watched recorded games on thirteen-inch televisions in a Pennsylvania basement and logged every ball put in play. On the rudimentary BIS website waited—and still waits today—a password-protected stockpile of information on every major leaguer's last 120 grounders and short liners. When at least 75 percent of a left-handed hitter's contact was aimed to the right of second base, a bit of red text popped up on screen: "Shift candidate!" That, of course, was the same number the Rays reported to their pitchers. The site showed similar information for right-handed hitters, but with an 80 percent threshold, to account for the difficulties inherent in leaving first basemen alone on the infield's right side.

For years, Dewan publicized his belief that shifting would be smart. He never expected teams to actually heed his advice. "This is so cool," he blogged in May 2012, after other teams started to shift in the Rays' image. "Have I died and gone to heaven?" He correctly predicted that the league would eventually adopt shifts within counts, like NFL teams change their defense depending on the down and distance. Some readers were less thrilled. "Though I'm glad for Mr. Dewan if he considers this a professional triumph," wrote the first commenter, sbromley, "all I could think about was that this means the future of baseball will be even more home run/walk/strikeout oriented. In those terms, it's depressing."

Indeed, Friedman's success with the Rays foretold much of how baseball would change in the twenty-first century. Their prosperity on a budget became a case study in an oft-required business textbook, *Management*, by Ricky W. Griffin. It was Tampa Bay, too, that first hoarded pitchers who specialized in fastballs with apparent rise, deceiving hitters when thrown up in the strike zone. The Rays did this just as the tenets to the launch-angle swing were spreading, misinterpreted, across the sport. Uppercuts were common, and hitters were poorly equipped to attack high fastballs, particularly those that spun so much they appeared to rise. Soon, high fastballs were everywhere and strikeouts were up.

It all began in 2008. "You know when this thing started?" Shields asked. "When we were winning. Nothing gets recognized unless you win." In at least one way, the 2008 Rays were the real-life version of the 2002 Athletics hyperbolized in the film adaptation of *Moneyball*. Despite its location inside a stadium named for a soda-company subsidiary, the Tropicana Field home clubhouse did not contain a soda fountain. Interested players had to wander out onto the stadium's service level, dollar in hand, to procure their preferred factory-sweetened beverage from a vending machine.

But unlike the real or dramatized Billy Beane and the A's, Friedman was around the Rays' players all the time. Friedman played in their fantasy football league. He competed in their clubhouse contests. He ribbed and accepted ribbing. "I always felt like he was real," said Evan Longoria, the franchise player. "It was never like, 'Andrew's the GM,'" said left-hander Cesar Ramos, a Ray from 2011 to 2014. "It was always, 'Andrew's one of the boys.' That goes a long way, and I think that's why the Dodgers have had a lot of success. He's still one of the boys without a jersey."

That went, too, for Friedman's lieutenants, particularly Chaim Bloom, whom players most often saw. The inner circle of

Bloom, James Click, and Erik Neander were all baseball-crazed kids who joined as interns and ascended. Neander, in fact, began in the Baseball Info Solutions basement. All three now run their own teams. During their shared St. Petersburg experience, they spent the preponderance of their waking hours together, blurring the lines between personal and professional. They say it spurred their growth. "The trust in that environment was enormous, and I think it enabled us to learn more, learn faster," Bloom said. "There's always a lot you're trying to figure out in this game, and we were going to figure it out together."

Friedman was first, figuring it out on his own for a time and unsure he could. At his introductory press conference, he sported something approaching a mop top, an ashen face, and a nervous smile. He described the session as an "out-of-body experience," an anxiety overload. "It was literally throwing me in the deep end," he said. He knew none of these people. It was worse than college. At her Texas home, Barbara Robins Friedman, his mother, displays a photograph that captures her son's blanched look.

Quickly, Friedman determined that his success would hinge on players seeing for themselves how passionate he was about their sport. "I resisted the temptation to try to prove that I belong," Friedman said. "In 2006, I wasn't even convinced I belonged." Friedman had worked in baseball for about five hundred days when the Rays owner, Stu Sternberg, offered him the opportunity to run the team's baseball operations. Friedman said he wasn't ready. Sternberg said he would ask again in a few weeks. When he did, Friedman again said no.

He was coerced when Sternberg said he would be asking him to rule on baseball-operations decisions even if he did not accept the job. The two had been building a rapport since a mutual friend, Goldman Sachs alum Matt Silverman, introduced them in 2003. Silverman and Friedman advised Sternberg on constructing a bid for the Rays, in which his group would assume debt accrued by the founding owners.

When the bid was approved, Sternberg brought the two men to St. Petersburg. When he became the managing general partner, in October 2005, he fired the incumbent GM, named Silverman the team president, and offered the de facto GM job to Friedman, who was twenty-eight. Sternberg's decision lacked precedent. Theo Epstein and Jon Daniels had recently been hired as GMs at the same age, but both men had been working in baseball for several years. Friedman had been trying, to no avail, to find work in baseball since college.

Before his senior year, his father, soon to be the chairman of the Harris County–Houston Sports Authority, even arranged a meeting with longtime Houston Astros executive Tal Smith. The stated purpose was to help Friedman decide if he should accept an offer to be a Wall Street analyst after graduation, or keep pursuing an entry-level front office job. "I went to get his advice, but it was less to get his advice and more that hopefully he'd be like, 'Hey, we want to hire you,'" Friedman said. "That did not happen." Smith warned Friedman about long hours and low pay. The finance experience, he said, would differentiate him from baseball's Brobdingnagian candidate pool. It was, as Friedman said, "incredibly valuable, sage advice that didn't land with me for years."

To handle his first arbitration cases a few months into the job, Friedman hired Smith, who, in his time, had been something of a baseball revolutionary himself. In the summer of '69, Smith, then thirty-five, tested a new way of processing the reams of data the Astros collected each year. Using an IBM keypunch device, he filed away information on every player selected in that year's amateur draft. Soon, every scouting report, on amateurs and professionals, went into the machine. Smith is certain his was the first mechanization ever undertaken in an MLB front office. "It was very, very basic, and fundamental, a far cry from what is available today," he said. "But at least it was a start of trying to use some kind of computerization to process all this information and arrive at conclusions."

Two intrigued teams, the White Sox and Mets, visited the Astrodome to examine Smith's attempts. More of the others, he said, expressed unease about his methods. "There was a lot of opposition by the old school, people who were not willing to accept or didn't understand initially what was involved," he said. When Smith left for the Yankees in 1973, the Astros abandoned his system. He restarted it upon returning to Houston two years later, finding more acceptance as the game's statistical evolution accelerated. (This was the same season, 1975, the radar gun came to baseball. Bill James was about to begin publishing his *Abstracts*.) Smith started providing his reports to other clubs, who chipped in on the cost. It was the genesis of his successful consulting business.

When Smith spoke to Friedman the second time, the would-be mentor understood that the Rays were about to embark on a technological operation his younger self, let alone the vintage old school, could not have fathomed. "I sensed that Andrew was not going to be bound by the routine or the ordinary way to do things," Smith said. "He's got a unique perspective that things can always be done differently. That's probably what separates him from everybody else."

His first spring, Friedman told a *New York Times* business reporter that the market would drive all his decisions. "I love players I think that I can get for less than they are worth," he said. "It's positive arbitrage, the valuation asymmetry in the game." He learned not to speak that way around players, but arbitrage and innovation distinguished his tenure. Once the Rays became a relative juggernaut, Friedman turned down repeated overtures to leave the Tampa Bay incubator, including from the Angels and, when Smith was fired, his hometown Astros. Houston instead hired another outsider who had not been in baseball long, only months more than Friedman: a former McKinsey & Company consultant named Jeff Luhnow.

After the 2014 season, the Rays' worst since 2007, Friedman made the leap. The Dodgers offered him $35 million to become their president of baseball operations, essentially their GM. It was Sternberg who refashioned the titles of baseball executives to resemble corporations. The convolution has a function. With the Dodgers, it meant Friedman could hire a No. 2 to be, technically, the GM, providing that person, Farhan Zaidi, a promotion from his previous job and easing his exit. It also meant that, after Zaidi left to become the Giants' president of baseball operations, the Dodgers continued for years without a GM. That did not stop them from employing multiple men as "special assistant to the GM."

At his first Dodgers press conference, Friedman felt within his body but on edge. To begin, he looked down every few seconds to read from a script. When the floor opened to reporters, one asked if he believed clubhouse chemistry mattered. Friedman's resulting grin might have been his purest of the day. "I think," he said, "winning matters." Within weeks, he had traded two of the Dodgers' most popular position players, Matt Kemp and Dee Gordon, in a series of deals that netted prospects, stopgap veteran shortstop Jimmy Rollins, and young catcher Yasmani Grandal, the rare player to test positive for performance-enhancing drugs and not deny it, and, rarer still, earn a public censure from a teammate. "You want to talk about a guy who is unproven and had a good couple months on steroids, go ahead," fellow catcher Nick Hundley told the *San Diego Union-Tribune*. Chemistry did not appear to be Friedman's focus.

In those early weeks, Friedman met at least twice with Ned Colletti, his predecessor, once in the stands at an Arizona Fall League game. Regime changes rarely happen with rosters as talented as the Dodgers. Colletti's last two teams had won the West but failed to make the World Series, and Colletti warned him the team's clubhouse culture had to change for the team to take the final step.

The two men had very little in common besides their jobs. For one, Colletti made himself scarce in the clubhouse. "I didn't live down there," he said. "I visited it for business purposes." Their differences spanned the sartorial and the deep-seated.

Colletti wore cowboy boots daily. For a time, Friedman rotated his footwear between unicorn start-up Allbirds' purportedly eco-friendly sneakers in several colorways. Colletti patronized deep-dish pizza places deep in the Chicago suburbs. Friedman frequented omakase-style sushi restaurants. Colletti grew up in poverty outside Chicago, living many years in what he has described as a garage. Friedman grew up in the Houston upper crust, with season tickets behind home plate at the Astrodome. His father later tried to buy the Astros. Colletti's first job out of college had been, decades earlier, as a sportswriter, making $15,000 annually. Friedman's father likes to say that his son left money on the table to leave Wall Street and work in baseball.

As a GM, Colletti preferred to spend his money on proven veterans. In such signings, he hit about as often as he missed, an above-average rate. In fact, Friedman proved to be worse at picking out free agents who would stay ripe for a few years. But he spent most of the Dodgers' considerable funds on young talent, and there he almost always hit. In Tampa Bay, Friedman found he could cede young stars just as they started to earn significant sums and receive promising prospects in return. By the time he got to Los Angeles, other teams had caught on, but by then he could afford to pay those players to stay.

Friedman used data to make decisions, supplemented by scouts. Colletti based his decisions on the opinions of his most trusted scouts, among them baseball lifers Vance Lovelace, Rick Ragazzo, and De Jon Watson. "Here, the bottom line is, it's always going to be scouting first," Alex Tamin told the *Los Angeles Daily News* at the inaugural Society for American Baseball Research analytics conference, held in March 2012. Tamin was then the Dodgers' director of baseball contracts, research, and operations, the organization's most stat-fluent employee.

The week after the conference, McCourt agreed to sell the team to the Guggenheim group. Stan Kasten, a longtime NBA and MLB executive, took over as the team president. Kasten later said that the Dodgers' commitment to analytics had been "near the bottom" relative to their peers. "Andrew will be helpful there, but he's not a one-trick pony," Kasten said. "Over time, we expect to become that homegrown, player-development organization. We are on our way, and I think, along with that, with being homegrown, with being younger, you end up with a payroll that's less."

Indeed, Friedman instituted the franchise's most immediate, significant change in player development, hiring former player Gabe Kapler to run the farm and two-time GM Josh Byrnes to supervise it as senior vice president of baseball operations. There were few noticeable novelties within the major league team. Shifts were one. Beginning on opening day, staffers taped a sheet of paper next to Dodger Stadium's dugout bat rack before each game. It contained guidance about how to position the defense against the opposing team, recommendations varying for each pitcher and hitter.

Those who knew Friedman knew more was coming. The manager, Don Mattingly, and the entire coaching staff were all Colletti hires. The lineup was among baseball's oldest. In the winter, few players trained at Dodger Stadium, and prospects were left to their own devices. None of that would last. "He was sitting tight," said Howell, by then a Dodger. "Not that he wasn't going for it, but he was doing a lot more observing than normal. He was doing the math, in his head, lining things up. He wanted to have a nice, smooth transition, see what he had, up close and personal, and then start making a run."

Friedman's first season coincided with two significant MLB changes: a new commissioner, Rob Manfred, and new statistics. On his first day, January 26, 2015, Manfred expressed an openness to banning the shift, alluding to but not naming Friedman. "I mean, we have really smart people working in the game, and they're going to figure out way[s] to get a competitive advantage," Manfred told ESPN that day. "I think it's incumbent on us in the commissioner's office to look at the advantages that are produced and say, 'Is this what we want to happen in the game?'" Manfred did not act. He did celebrate the introduction into every major league stadium of the TrackMan radar system, packaged on broadcasts and on the league's website as Statcast.

TrackMan tracked everything on the field, from pitches and throws to hits and sprints, and the league publicized metrics based on the new data: perceived velocity, launch angle, spin rate, and many more. The Dodgers tried to take immediate advantage. They brought several spin-rate specialists to camp in 2015. "You don't have to give them a name," left-hander Ryan Buchter, one of them, later told FanGraphs. "You just bring in the numbers from the TrackMan, give them ten guys and they'll pick off of their stats. They don't care what they look like or anything."

The Dodgers also mined for inefficiencies among injured players. Friedman's first off-season in charge, they signed more pitchers who had succumbed to Tommy John surgery than any other team. "It's obvious with all of us being signed that they're confident in what they can do," said Brandon Beachy, one of the pitchers returning from surgery. "I don't know the logic behind it or the basis for it or what they're planning to do differently, but it's intriguing." Said Brett Anderson, another: "They think they can either figure out why it happened and prevent it from happening going forward, or they figured out it was just fluky things. As a cohesive unit, you have to think you can figure out stuff other medical staffs haven't." They didn't, at least not then. Most of the pitchers injured their arms again. That summer, the Dodgers hired Dr. James Buffi, who had pursued groundbreaking research on the sources of arm injuries.

Near summer's end, the Dodgers engineered specialized camps at their Arizona facility for prospects whom they wanted to develop specific skills. Alex Verdugo and Cody Bellinger attended strength camp, where they added mass to their skinny frames. Edwin Ríos and Willie Calhoun, bulkier both, went to metabolic camp, or, in the players' parlance: fat camp. Edwin Drexler and Robbie Garvey, sprinters who could not hit, went to speed camp, where they focused on base running. The speed camp was the least successful; the club conceived of it with the hope that someone could develop into a pinch-running option on the big-league postseason roster. But the underweight prospects gained weight, and the overweight prospects lost it.

The Dodgers soon embarked on even more experiments. Green position players who had the hand-eye coordination to hit, but not the experience, attended hitting camps. Raw pitching and catching prospects matriculated in what the club called Game Calling University, where they learned the basics of pitch sequencing while reviewing video from major league games. Most draftees reached professional baseball having rarely had a say in what pitch they threw; college coaches often imposed their whims from the dugout.

When 2016 spring training ended and the real prospects reported to minor league affiliates to begin their seasons, the Dodgers held back eleven marginal pitchers who agreed to follow a ten-week weighted-ball program designed by Driveline. The idea was to pit the players against each other in a demanding regimen, including weight training not typically prescribed during seasons. They did not pitch in games. They did not even throw off of mounds. "This is before it was accepted across the industry to do velocity programs, and really focus equally on strength and conditioning for pitchers," Kapler said. "At the time, pitching coaches felt uncomfortable with that."

The majority of players finished the program throwing noticeably harder. The Dodgers used two products as trade chips, and, in 2017, expanded the Driveline partnership, by then known simply as the "gas program." Right-hander Tony Gonsolin became its biggest success story, for, six months later, he threw several pitches clocked at 100 mph, 6 mph faster than anything he'd thrown before he enrolled. "Of course, there's literally twenty other guys that went through the same program with him, and then didn't have the results that Gonsolin did," said Kyle Boddy, the Driveline founder who led the players in their fueling pursuits. "But I guess that's exactly the point, right? You don't know who exactly is gonna pop, who's gonna experience the benefits."

After Year 2, the Dodgers ceased formal ties with Driveline but incorporated the velocity-development program into their recommended training for all minor league pitchers. "This is why I think he's so good: He paid us to render a service," Boddy said of Friedman. "And then we deliver the service, and then through rendering a service, he evaluated who was going to get on board, and he evaluated the results of the program. But he also had a plan to fold what he felt was the best of the program into everyday Dodger life. And that, I think, is really commendable, because the program lives on with the Dodgers, in a different form."

Many experiments did. As it became clear that the efficiency of a pitch's spin mattered as much as how much it spun, the Dodgers set up a spin station at their spring-training facility. Pitchers threw hockey pucks so they could see immediate feedback on their spin efficiency. A perfectly thrown puck would reach its destination without issue. A misthrown puck would wobble and miss its target. When he witnessed this in 2018, a new minor league pitching coach, Connor McGuiness, mentioned it to his brother, who then created a company that worked to patent a puck that looked like a baseball. By early 2019, with Friedman's blessing, Dodgers pitchers were practicing with product prototypes. By July 2020, McGuiness was on the major league staff, and Clayton Kershaw was mixing the final product, called CleanFuego, into his off-day catch routine. CleanFuego spread to twenty-eight teams that year and the final two the following year. But the Dodgers were first.

Rival executives speculate that their small-budget backgrounds have shaped Friedman and Byrnes's success in Los Angeles, and Zaidi's there and in San Francisco. In Tampa Bay, Oakland, and San Diego, the triumvirate's last stops, it was often a better bet to attempt another development method than sell low on an unsuccessful prospect or player. "We've gotta build resumes," Byrnes used to say. "We're not gonna buy resumes." Because they can afford to, executives who trained with bigger-spending teams tend to give up on players sooner.

After his first few years on the job, Friedman has said, he feared that the Dodgers were not advancing quickly enough. He was certain the Rays were still ahead in some races. "It's a difficult thing to know what you don't have and still be working towards that," said Doug Fearing, one of Friedman's earliest hires as the director of research and development, the only Tampa Bay employee who came with him. "But at the same time, I think we did catch up very quickly." Of course, financial supremacy helped, but the Dodgers continued to search for tiny edges in locations no one else thought to look.

In September 2018, the Dodgers called up catcher Will Smith without formally calling him up. It was an unprecedented maneuver, for which they sought out and received MLB approval. It was Friedman's idea, according to staffers who heard it. Throughout the month, Smith shadowed almost everything the rest of the roster did. He traveled with the team, ate with the team, and sat in on daily meetings with pitchers. He just did not receive major league pay nor suit up in uniform and play, instead watching each game from the video room adjacent to the Dodgers' dugout.

The scheme did not cost the Dodgers any service time to Smith's name, and it expedited the learning curve he was sure to experience as a debuting catcher. A free agent at season's end, Grandal essentially trained his replacement, not quite begrudgingly but not exactly cheerfully. "I didn't know how the players were gonna take it, the me being there but not being there," Smith said. "It was kind of weird. I wasn't nervous, but I didn't know what to expect. And, after a day or two, it was great."

September 2018 was not the ideal month for an apprenticeship, because the Dodgers found themselves in a pennant race for the first time during the Friedman era. The team's game-planning coach and designated catching mentor, Danny Lehmann, said Smith obtained a sense of the daily anxiety and pressure circulating in an MLB clubhouse. He just didn't have as many free hours to tutor him as the club envisioned. "[2019] would've been much better, just because of our situation with the standings," Lehmann said. "But he got an inside look." The

Dodgers considered giving another prospect, Gavin Lux, the same view in September 2019, until they decided he could help them come October. They called him up for real instead.

By 2019, the Dodgers' clubhouse contained every possible technology players would want: top-of-the-line Woodway tread-mills; Kistler force plates to measure ground-force interactions, like Mookie Betts used in Boston; a Win Reality virtual-reality hitting lab that allowed hitters to see each day's opposing pitcher throw to them; a float tank; a cannon-looking strength-training system made by Proteus Motion that used electromagnetic brakes to generate fluid resistance; Power Plate, a whole-body vibration system that resembles a futuristic scooter; and several Synexis BioDefense Systems, which are said to convert ambient humidity into dry hydrogen peroxide and thereby reduce viruses and bacteria. "What in the world is going on over here?" journeyman outfielder Terrance Gore thought when he saw everything for the first time. "After a while, it clicked to me what these guys are actually doing: Everything is for a purpose."

A US Army Chemical Corps veteran of the Cold War invented the Synexis technology. The Dodgers first installed several Synexis machines at Dodger Stadium in 2016 and soon began traveling with four to install in each visiting clubhouse upon arrival. In 2021, the company claimed its systems could eliminate all but three-hundredths of 1 percent of coronavirus particles from the air within an hour, based on a laboratory study it conducted using MS2 bacteriophage, a coronavirus surrogate. The Synexis website quoted the Dodgers head athletic trainer, Neil Rampe, in praise of the machines. "It felt like there was a competitive edge this year, that it's one less thing you have to worry about," he said. "Going into 2020, we look like geniuses that we already had this installed."

The tripling of his budget did not alter the ferocity with which Friedman pursued gadgets or bargains. It merely expanded his reach. One agent described a case in which his client had a two-year offer from one team and a three-year offer from the Dodgers for slightly less money. Friedman repeatedly

played up the additional service time the Dodgers deal promised the player, noting that it would get him a year closer to
the ten-year pension maximum that guarantees players more
than $220,000 annually if they begin collecting at sixty-two. The
agent pointed out that the other offer guaranteed more money
now, not decades from now. "He's a very smart guy," the agent
said. "Maybe a little too smart."

Those were the minute pursuits. Always operating in the
background was the Dodgers' sweeping development machine.
"You have the old-school scouting, you have the new wave of
player development, and then you have the desire," Boddy said.
"Where I think Andrew excels is the ability to build a system
around all of that, incorporate all the feedback, and then make
other decisions around it. It's a really multidisciplinary approach." The first fruitful sign arrived in June 2015.

# Chapter 6

I N LEXINGTON, KENTUCKY, IN THE MID-AUGHTS, A single mother and her preteen son started betting on the horses at the iconic Keeneland Race Course. A neighbor in the business gifted them surplus copies of *Blood-Horse*, *Thoroughbred Times*, and *Daily Racing Form*, the home of the popular Beyer Speed Figures. The boy analyzed all the available data: recent race results, race conditions, career earnings, quality ratings. He converted them into confident determinations. "He would pick the horses. I would place the bets," said Karen Walker, his mother. "We may or may not have split the earnings."

In their area, time at the track was part of a balanced childhood. At Henry Clay High, an inordinate amount of students scheduled doctor's appointments after lunch during the short spring and fall racing seasons. Parents dropped by to ferry them the ten miles to Keeneland. The track was the town healer, the joke went: "Dr. K." Walker's boy was so engrossed, she believed he would grow up to be a horse trainer.

He was a precocious, restless child, the sort who drew a squiggly line through math assignments he deemed beneath him. She learned it was best to keep him engaged, and, at the track, he always was. When he spotted top trainer Todd Pletcher at a concession stand, he ran over to introduce himself. But it was the data, not the people or animals, that most captured his imagination. "He was way into the numbers with horses way before baseball," she said.

A decade later, Walker's boy, Walker Buehler, became one of the first data-fluent pitchers to emerge in Major League Baseball—and a microshare owner of Authentic, the bay colt who won the 2020 Kentucky Derby and Breeders' Cup at Keeneland. Buehler's knowledge of the numbers empowered his unlikely success. Throughout his childhood, his body better resembled a jockey's than an archetypal pitcher's, and he lacked the familial baseball background that is the norm in major leaguers. His grandfather built him a mound, but he was insecure about his baseball knowledge, so Buehler learned his first pitching tidbits from a VHS tape produced by the famed coach Tom House. He easily copied what he saw on television; it turned out he had unusual kinesthetic awareness. "You could just describe what you think the mechanics should look like," said John Wilson, his first coach with pro experience, "and he could just do it."

Walker still had no idea how good her son was until the summer of 2010. At a Perfect Game showcase in town, scout after scout complimented her on her son's "nasty" curveball. "I kept thinking, 'What's wrong with his curveball?'" Walker said. A personal injury attorney, she knew enough to play it cool and look up later that the term "eleven five" meant his curveball spun between those numbers on a clock. "From there, it kinda went fast," she said. Buehler had just finished his sophomore year of high school. He accelerated from hoping he'd play in college to believing he could, after college, become a professional.

Pro scouts grew enamored with the ease of his delivery. Vanderbilt, the rare prestigious university with an equally esteemed baseball program, started recruiting him. He headed there, two hundred miles from home, registering 152 pounds at his first weigh-in. In Lexington, Buehler had been the best player in at least a hundred-mile radius. "He was throwing ninety-five," said Dodgers catcher Will Smith, who grew up in nearby Louisville. "No one really threw ninety." Smith was overstating the numbers but correct on the margin. In Nashville, teammates towered over Buehler and threw harder than him. He suggested that he developed a Napoleon complex as a result.

In Division I baseball, there are weekend starters, a designation reserved for each team's top three, and midweek starters. Buehler did not become a weekend starter until his final season, but he became one of the team's most outspoken players as a freshman. On fall Wednesdays, he recruited a group of pitchers to the football field for a field-goal throwing competition from progressively farther distances. He challenged his teammates daily, taunting them, proclaiming his superiority. "He knew he would be dominant," said Tyler Beede, the No. 1 starter during Buehler's sophomore season. "I think he was just unsure of how to present that to people at first."

He often meshed better with the team's coaches. Head coach Tim Corbin learned he could be more direct with Buehler than other players without hindering him. "That's what I loved about him," Corbin said. "You could come right at him, and he'd come right at me." Pitching coach Scott Brown came to expect an explosive quip whenever he saw a smirking Buehler approaching from another room. "There's a candor that exists between us that I enjoy," Brown said. "You could see it in his aura and the way he walks around. He goes there."

His mother foresaw that. "That's who Walker connects with, and always has: older people," she said. He was the first grandchild from either side of the family and, therefore, the temporary center of their universe. After his parents divorced and his father moved to Ohio, he spent most of his time around his grandparents and his mother, in frequent debate. "You got a teenage kid and a solo practitioner single mom," Walker said. "Arguing, in our house, was an art."

At Vanderbilt, Buehler raised the stakes on every conversation. Teammates teased him about his stature, amazed at the velocity he unleashed despite it. By his junior season, Buehler weighed about 165 pounds but could touch ninety-six miles per hour. "I don't get it, personally. I never have," teammate Carson Fulmer said years later. "The guy looks skinny. He doesn't look strong if you look at him." But by then Buehler had already learned what it took most peers many more years to grasp. Velocity was not a divine gift but a bodily equation. In the simplest terms, force is the product of mass multiplied by acceleration. "Well, Walker's got a lot less mass," Brown said. "But he has a lot more acceleration." Buehler learned to create enough acceleration to counteract his weight deficiency.

The seeds of that pursuit source from high school, when he worked with another local ex-pro, Kentucky graduate Ben Shaffar. When Buehler experienced arm pain, they started searching photographs of top pitchers' deliveries for a solution. (It was a different time.) They looked beyond Tim Lincecum, the shorter, lithe right-hander to whom Buehler was most often compared, and settled on emulating Justin Verlander, trying to match his exceptional arm acceleration to produce velocity without pain. Their work produced results and, in time, the trust that made Shaffar his pupil's local confidant. "He had his grandfather. But in those horrible years of high school for all of us, he really didn't have a younger male role model in his life," Shaffar said. "I think I also served as much, for him, as a life mentor, someone he could confide in."

Understanding their bond, Buehler's mother successfully pushed his high school to employ Shaffar as its pitching coach. By the time Buehler got to college, he possessed the confidence and obsession that thrust him forward on his mission. "He really fell in love with the whole idea of just throwing the shit out of the baseball," said Kyle Boddy, the Driveline founder. Boddy met Buehler on campus in January 2015, when Boddy gave a preseason speech to the Commodores pitchers.

Before Boddy spoke, Buehler stood up and challenged him concerning the claims within his book *Hacking the Kinetic Chain* about the development of velocity. Buehler had read much of it, intrigued, but he disagreed that everyone could benefit from the techniques therein. They argued for an hour, settling on the idea that the book was a guidepost, not a one-size-fits-all prescription. "Knowledge is power," Buehler said. "That's why I ask those questions, to try to figure out for myself so I can adapt it for me the best way I can."

The two men continued to talk after that afternoon. To this day, intermediaries are known to send Boddy video clips of Buehler trash-talking him, middle fingers raised, at random. "Most of the stuff that he says is eminently embarrassing and really true," Boddy said. "He's just a ridiculous human, in a lot of ways."

In every way but his frame, Buehler emerged as the ideal draft prospect. He had best-in-class confidence. His delivery appeared effortless, yielding easy velocity. He threw three competent secondary pitches for strikes. He helped his team win the College World Series as a sophomore, dominating on the largest amateur stage. The Dodgers' area scout Marty Lamb, a Lexington resident, had eyed Buehler for years. He stopped dreaming on him during his draft-eligible spring because he figured another team would select him before the Dodgers' first choice, twenty-fourth overall.

In that belief, Lamb had company. Vanderbilt pursued a repeat title in Buehler's final season. On the way into an anticipated super regional, Lamb ran into Buehler's mother, who introduced him to her parents as a Dodgers scout. "Well, I don't know why you're here," Dave Walker said. "He's not gonna get to ya'll anyhow." But he did. Buehler's velocity was down that night, and the sharpness in his secondary pitches had vanished. Because of fears he would require an arm operation, Buehler fell to the Dodgers' choice. They happily selected him.

Baseball was unique among major American sports in that, until 2020, it held its draft before top college players finished their seasons. Two weeks after the Dodgers drafted Buehler, Lamb settled in to watch him pitch in the College World Series. Buehler debuted that day a new throwing motion in which he brought the baseball over his head before releasing it. He knew additional deception could counteract the velocity his injury had sapped. Lamb was impressed. "The confidence to be able to change your delivery on the biggest stage he'd been on at that point?" he said. "He's on a different wavelength."

Soon, Buehler traveled to Los Angeles to undergo a physical examination, a prerequisite for signing with the team. Tests uncovered a significant tear to the ulnar collateral ligament in his throwing elbow. "I was 165 pounds, and throwing a little bit too hard for my body," Buehler said. Dr. Neal ElAttrache recommended he undergo Tommy John surgery. The operation meant he wouldn't pitch for at least a year, and the lost leverage shaved a few hundred thousand dollars from Buehler's slotted signing bonus.

Buehler signed and had the surgery, then reported to the Dodgers' Arizona training facility to rehabilitate his arm. He had just turned twenty-one, and he was alone for the first time, far removed from his Vanderbilt world where he roomed with a revolving door of teammates. The early months of Tommy John recovery present more of a challenge to a pitcher's mind than his body. It drives many young men to drink to excess. It drove Buehler to strengthen his figure. "He was kind of on an island out there, and it really sharpened him mentally and obviously physically," his mother said. "His physical transformation through that rehab, from head to toe, was stunning. He'd always been this scrawny little green bean. The muscles that he built, particularly through his flank, was unbelievable."

Buehler gained almost fifteen pounds, mostly muscle, much of it in his shoulders. He hoped it would protect the rest of his arm from succumbing to another surgery. "A year's a long time, man," he said. "It humbles you and it drives you: I'm not doing this again." He also started throwing harder, an uncommon but not unprecedented byproduct of the procedure. In his first outing back, Buehler threw his fastball 99 mph. The improvement both thrilled and scared club officials.

During his isolation, Buehler made two friends. As usual, both of them were older: Bronson Arroyo and Dr. James Buffi. Arroyo was a veteran sixteen years Buehler's senior who was working his way back from his own Tommy John surgery. He and Buehler trained together at Camelback Ranch. Yasiel Puig, tasked with recovering there from a hamstring strain, sometimes showed up, and trainers were always around to lead exercises. But most of the conversations were solely between Buehler and Arroyo. "It's almost like he came up to me saying, 'Oh, I see you're building a house over there. I'm building one too, and I want you to take a look in,'" Arroyo said. "But he wasn't bashful about it. He wasn't worried that I was gonna look at his house and be like, 'Man, that's a piece of crap.'"

The Dodgers had acquired Arroyo and his expiring contract to make the money work in a labyrinthine three-team trade, not to actually pitch for them. No matter. He showed up daily to rehabilitate, and Buehler peppered him with questions about forging a career in baseball, about earning money and staying healthy and handling playoff intensity. Arroyo sensed and appreciated his curiosity and confidence. "He was coming off Tommy John, and he wasn't that focused on his arm," Arroyo said. "He was looking outward, trying to foresee how he should play his chips to make this thing work."

Buffi also joined the organization that summer, fresh off a four-month stint working for Driveline. He was one year removed from finishing his PhD in biomechanics, which he earned with what he described as an "extremely theoretical" study of how the arm's muscles protect pitchers' elbows as they pitch. He had almost no experience interacting with actual professional pitchers. After he completed human-resources basics, one of his first assignments was to ensure Buehler's arm did not burst again as he worked his way back from surgery. "Talk about throwing me into the fire," Buffi said. He helped script the strength training Buehler performed. He asked him not to throw at 100 percent all the time, to which Buehler said he wasn't.

Buffi is an inquisitive type. He wants to know why everything works, but while he worked for the Dodgers he learned that others often don't. It was difficult for him to gauge how much a pitcher wanted to know of what he could teach, to ascertain how long they were willing to listen to him. He appreciated that Buehler, effectively his first neophyte, made it very clear. "He was very much like, 'Here's the thing that I need. Give it to me. I don't need all this extraneous stuff,'" Buffi said. "He was much more targeted with really understanding what information that was going to be useful to him."

Those who know Buehler, even those who don't know about his history with horses, attribute that to his intelligence and his affinity for data. Buehler learned how to pitch in a manner much different than Kershaw or Arroyo. The equations underpinning pitching have been in his head since high school. But he had never interacted with a PhD-level biomechanist. That first summer, he and Buffi spoke regularly. Buehler's ulnar collateral ligament became tighter after Tommy John, as is common, but he strove to understand why. Buffi explained to him the scientific theories behind the muscle and tissue adaptations.

"Those were some of the most impactful conversations of my career," Buffi said. "It seems like it was really helpful for Walker, too." Even as an academic, Buffi was not immune to Buehler's teasing. He detected right away the pitcher's extraordinary self-assurance, just as he noticed his wit. "Those two things," Buffi said, "are a diabolical combo."

By the time Buehler was a teenager, the combination made his legal advice attractive to his mother. "Let's put it this way: I have run and continue to run hypotheticals by Walker to this day," she said. He is always willing to offer his opinion, and he regularly brings up unconsidered angles. "Combined, the intelligence, the smart-aleck, and the competitive nature kind of created Walker," his mother said. "It goes way beyond baseball. It's who Walker is."

The Dodgers understood that. In February 2017, manager Dave Roberts asked Buehler to introduce himself to his Dodgers teammates before a spring-training workout. "My name's Walker Buehler," he began, trying in vain to curb himself. "I'm from Lexington, Kentucky." Roberts had barely met Buehler, but he knew enough to know the young man could supply some entertainment. He told Buehler's teammates that this small, skinny pitcher with a boyish face had received a signing bonus of nearly $2 million.

Then he asked what pitches Buehler threw. "I throw a fastball," Buehler said. "Last year, my average was 97.1 mph." The room erupted while Buehler identified the rest of his pitches. No one remembers what he said about those. Several men who were in the room still cite, to the decimal, how hard Buehler threw his fastball in 2016.

Buehler leads the team, if not the league, in memorable lines. "He's just always talking shit," said Smith, his catcher. "It's, like, a psychological thing," said infielder Gavin Lux. Buehler even does it with Friedman, his boss. "That trait can be annoying," the president said, "but with him it's endearing." Buehler learned long ago he could get away with speaking his mind as long as he expressed matching vulnerability. "I've just always believed that if you say something outlandishly arrogant, even if you wholeheartedly believe that, it comes off poorly to everyone," Buehler said. "But if you learn how to make fun of yourself too, then you're getting back to equal."

In August 2019, Dodgers head athletic trainer Neil Rampe was searching for a player inside Miami's visiting clubhouse. He needed to administer treatment before the team's postgame flight to Atlanta. In the restroom, he encountered several players, including Buehler, who had been that day's losing pitcher. In a four-hour slog, baseball's worst offense had torched him for five runs over four innings. He saw an opening for a joke. "Hey, Neil," Buehler began. "You got anything for my fucking ego in there?"

Only professional athletes and those within their orbit would find some of the following endearing. In June 2016, Lux, then eighteen, arrived at the team's Arizona complex to play in the rookie league, settling into a locker near Buehler's. "Dude, I heard you're nasty," Lux told him. "I want to face you in a live

BP." Lux maintains he intended to be complimentary, but Buehler interpreted it as a challenge. "He thought I was talking shit," Lux said.

Nine months later, they arranged a tense tussle. With teammates all around, Buehler pumped fastballs approaching 100 mph, and Lux could only tap a weak comebacker. "Lux is like, 'Congrats, I don't care,' and Buehler is motherfucking him," recalled left-hander Caleb Ferguson. "And everybody's like, 'Walker, this kid's a [teenager]. You played in the College World Series. What do you get out of this?'" Motivation. "At this point, if he didn't act like he was the best at everything in the world," Ferguson said, "people would be worried."

Buehler once introduced himself to a new, slightly overweight teammate by saying, "What's up, you piece of garbage?" Within weeks, that teammate, David Freese, learned to love him. "I think he makes interactions comfortable, in a very weird, unusual way," Freese said. "He's a respectful human being, he really is. He's smart, he's aware." The way Freese understood it, a confrontational tinge to conversations soothed him. "It allows his mind to be at ease in certain situations, because he's just so observant," he said. "I see him as a thinker. I think he's always turning in his own brain about stuff."

By the time he turned twenty-five, Buehler said, he had uttered hundreds of barbs that people did not want to hear. "But that's not gonna change the way I look at things," he said. "And I generally avoid people I don't like, and hang out with people I do like and like me."

The day Buehler made his first major league start, teammate Kiké Hernández offered an equivocal endorsement of his personality. "We kind of like his attitude, sometimes," Hernández said. The day Buehler propelled the Dodgers into the playoffs six months later, Hernández saw no need for equivocation between glugs of celebratory Champagne. "We have zero problem with Walker being the cocky motherfucker that he is," he said. "He can be as arrogant as he wants."

Earlier in his career, Buehler leaned into that perception. "If you wanna feel great all the time," he tweeted, "enjoy your 76-mph fastball." His former coaches have taken to quoting that line. "One of the things that he believes strongly in is when he's gonna pitch, he throws as hard as he can," said Brown, his college pitching coach. "There's no reason for him to throw balls slow, in his opinion."

By 2018, his future teammate Trevor Bauer, a peer in that pursuit, had taken notice. "I've seen the velocity that he throws with," Bauer said. "You don't throw that hard unless you're actively trying to throw that hard." That was his public statement. Privately, he fretted over his own obsolescence. "This is the fucking guy that's gonna make my career useless," Bauer repeatedly told Boddy. If a superior athlete mimicked Bauer's approach to pitching development, he feared he would be left in the dust.

Buehler's rookie season got people talking. In his third start, he finished two-thirds of a combined no-hitter. In his fourth, he faced the Reds, his childhood team. "It feels like that's the way Lincecum's fastball used to feel," Joey Votto said. In his sixth, facing the Rockies, Buehler pitched two innings after taking a 108-mph line drive to the ribcage. "Most pitchers usually get taken out," Nolan Arenado said. "To see him stay in there and continue to pitch shows you what he's made of, shows you he's not afraid." Like Votto, Arenado referenced Buehler's deceptive fastball. "Ninety-six is ninety-six; it's hard no matter what," he said. "But it was playing really hard."

That first summer, Buehler amazed teammates with how little he prepared for opponents. He relied on what the coaches and catchers suggested and declined most of the team's offers to provide supplementary statistics. He was easing into the majors. By the subsequent spring, he requested immediate printouts presenting the spin data from each of his starts. They were often at his locker before he arrived; he'd brag to teammates when he hit another milestone.

This was but the next step to how he approached information in college. "A lot of people are envious of the way that he can be both not attached to results and super serious about getting better," said Beede, his ex-teammate. "It's tough to have that balance, but he has a good way of handling it." Chad Martin, a retired pitcher from Lexington who trained alongside Buehler over his early pro off-seasons, pithily captured that balance. "He's this perfect combination of meticulous along with not giving a fuck," he said.

He could both bounce back quickly from failure and learn from it, an elusive medley. "People look at you and they say, 'He's so easygoing. He's always in a good mood. How does he brush that bad start off so easily?'" Arroyo said. "Internally, that's not what's going on when you're getting your butt kicked. But you know that's the most efficient way to be. You can't be super-emotional all the time, wasting that extra energy. He always seems to have had the perspective of what matters the most in a season. He knows that the tide turns quickly. That's part of what makes him so good."

One afternoon in September 2018, four days after the best start of his rookie season, Buehler plopped onto a brown leather couch outside the Dodger Stadium clubhouse and examined the tide. He had pitched the Dodgers into playoff position with eight shutout innings in St. Louis. Roberts had called it the best pitching performance by a Dodger all year. Buehler trained his gaze past it. "That game I just threw, I'm not going to remember that fucking game when I'm retired," he said. "I'm just not. I'm going to remember playoffs. I'm going to remember World Series."

Another afternoon, in February 2020, Buehler squared off against Clayton Kershaw on the ping-pong table. The challenger against the ace became a tight, tense game. A reliever pulled up a chair to watch and wait his turn against the winner. Cody Bellinger noticed the action from across the clubhouse, stopped, and smiled. "This," he said, "is phenomenal ping-pong." Buehler raced to an early lead. When Kershaw tied the score at 17,

Buehler praised his serve. Kershaw quickly surged ahead, and Buehler served to stay alive. On game point, Kershaw gently returned a sharp serve. The ball tipped the top of the net, and for a few milliseconds its destination was unclear. It then bounced on Buehler's side of the table. He couldn't return it before it bounced again.

Kershaw could only laugh. Buehler could only leave the premises. He was known to exclaim expletives upon suffering similar losses. This defeat, he handled with relative grace. "I mean, it's early in spring," he said later. "My first game, I'm not as mad about it. But if I've been playing a lot and I play like shit, I'm gonna be upset. Same when I throw. My biggest thing is not living up to expectations for myself."

Those who learned him learned that. "You can appreciate the arrogance," pitching coach Mark Prior said, "if you know the work behind it." Before 2020, the Dodgers challenged Buehler to make one more jump. Prior, once a young star much like him, delivered the message. "You've established yourself as one of the best pitchers in the game," Prior said. "Now, can you put yourself in the upper echelon?" For most men not named Kershaw or Prior, it takes years to progress from great to elite. Prior pointed to Gerrit Cole, who needed three years and a change of teams to complete that jump. "Took him a little while," he said. "Started building, and then all of the sudden, [in 2019] you're like, 'Fuckin' A!'"

The organization eagerly awaited Buehler's fuckin' A year, which arrived in 2021, just after he declined a long-term contract offer. With its first draft pick, the Dodgers regime had obtained the precise type of superlative performer the system was supposed to prevent them from acquiring for anything less than top dollar or a terrible season. The Dodgers paid the latter price when they earned the right to draft Kershaw seventh overall in 2006. Come 2015, the only talent-acquisition advantage their poorer competitors had over them was better draft positioning. Beginning with Buehler, the Dodgers erased it.

# Chapter 7

HISTORIC COLLECTIONS OF TOP DRAFT PICKS ARE years in the making. The Tampa Bay Rays built and built toward a World Series run in 2010, spending far more money on players than they ever had, more money than they typically do today. Whether or not they won, they knew their veterans would flee as free agents at year's end, they would reap compensatory picks for each, and they could pull back 40 percent on payroll.

So it was that the Rays boasted a record-breaking collection of picks in the 2011 draft: ten of the first sixty selections, twelve of eighty-nine. Andrew Friedman referred to it as "among the most important days in the history of this franchise." Gifted a decade of perspective, we can say with certainty that the Rays bungled their bounty. With their dozen picks, they drafted as many men who were convicted of murder as made the major leagues: one. Brandon Martin, the thirty-eighth overall pick, was sentenced to life in prison for a triple murder. Blake Snell, the fifty-second, became a good pitcher. They could have used any of fourteen selections on Mookie Betts, who went 172nd. That is why Friedman does not gloat about what the Dodgers did in 2016, the year they came the closest they will ever get to the Rays' largesse.

When Josh Byrnes, the Dodgers' scouting and development chief, ran the Arizona Diamondbacks in 2009, they stockpiled seven of the first sixty-four picks. They found a center fielder in future Dodger A. J. Pollock, so it went fine, but they missed the Hall of Famer in their midst: Mike Trout. They might have selected Trout, too, if their scouting director hadn't seen him one last disappointing time when rain canceled his planned excursion to watch another prospect, future major leaguer Steven Matz. And anyway, Byrnes guessed after the draft that their best selection would somehow emerge from one of their later selections. Sure enough, they selected Paul Goldschmidt 246th overall. He provided twice as much value as the dozen players Arizona picked ahead of him combined. That is why Byrnes does not gloat about what the Dodgers did in 2016. Executives learn that randomness reigns in every draft.

That never stopped Friedman from trawling for edges. In 2011, he hired Dave Eiland, whom the Yankees had just fired as their pitching coach, to scout the best available pitchers. The idea was to blend their data with Eiland's traditional acumen—and anything he picked up from his last job. "Maybe they used me a little bit to see how the Yankees did things," Eiland said. "Andrew uses all the tools in the toolbox." The Dodgers don't have a bigger-budgeted rival, but Friedman still asks special assistants to do similar work.

Besides the impossibility of projecting teenagers' futures, Friedman and Byrnes faced one significant problem: for as many picks as they had, none fell within the top fifteen selections. The MLB draft is more like the NBA's than the NFL's, increasingly so lately. The elite prospects are better bets to advance to the majors than they once were. That's one part of what makes the Dodgers' 2016 draft class so remarkable. They had more early picks than usual—including twentieth, thirty-second, and thirty-sixth overall—but none high, and far fewer than the Rays' assortment. Yet ten of their first eleven selections debuted in the major leagues fewer than five years from draft day. Only ten of the year's first fifteen overall picks debuted by that anniversary.

The Dodgers dreamed of collecting even more early selections. They issued qualifying offers to three players the previous off-season. No player had ever accepted the offer, and, under the terms of the old CBA, any player who declined one netted his old team a compensation pick upon signing with another team. But one Dodgers recipient, Brett Anderson, accepted his offer, and another, Howie Kendrick, received so little interest from competitors that the Dodgers re-signed him at a discount rate after he rejected his. But in agreeing to terms with the Arizona Diamondbacks and quickly finalizing his pact, Zack Greinke gave the Dodgers the thirty-second pick. Because compensation is allocated in chronological order, the brisk completion proved valuable. Fellow right-hander John Lackey's deal with the Chicago Cubs was reported a few hours earlier but finalized a few hours later. Lackey's old employer, the St. Louis Cardinals, received the thirty-third pick.

Twentieth, the Dodgers chose Gavin Lux, who became their second baseman. Thirty-second, they selected Will Smith, who became their catcher. In the third round, they took right-hander Dustin May, a potential ace who succumbed to Tommy John surgery in 2021. In the ninth round, they tapped right-hander Tony Gonsolin, another key starter. And in the thirty-third round, after precisely 1,000 players had been named, the Dodgers drafted Zach McKinstry, now a utility player. Already they have unearthed five quality players from one draft, at least four with All-Star potential.

Long before the owners willed compensation picks into existence once free agency sheared their profits, the Dodgers collected what is widely considered the most productive draft class of all time. In 1968, they signed eleven future big leaguers who combined for a record 235.6 Wins Above Replacement, by Baseball-Reference's calculations. It is unlikely this crop will surpass that. But those were different times. The draft occurred in three phases, spread throughout the year.

For one team in one modern draft, it is triumphant to descry even two regular major leaguers. In 2016, the Dodgers found many more. In one way, they did it like Oakland did it in the 2002 draft chronicled in *Moneyball*, using historical draft classes as a guidepost for what prospects could become. Only the Dodgers bored further than betting on collegians instead of high schoolers, as the Athletics attempted. By 2016, most teams prized position players who were close to MLB ready and already excelling, ideally in college, thereby reducing their bust risk. Perennially picking in the back half of the first round, the Dodgers deprioritized fixable elements of players' profiles. By necessity, they focused on prospects who managed despite clear flaws and appeared amenable to guided instruction. In assessing tractability, two traits were key: athleticism, creating the possibility of improvement; and aptitude for focused practice, to actually enact prescribed changes. A statistical model attempted to account for it all.

The cycle that produced the Dodgers 2016 class began before Friedman even arrived in Los Angeles. Most amateurs are eligible to be drafted after high school, then not again until their third year of college, but scouts keep their eyes on underclassmen two or three seasons from draft eligibility. For high schoolers, showcases begin even earlier. The Dodgers ramped up 2016 preparations three months after the 2015 draft. Scouting director Billy Gasparino rejiggered the scouting map and conducted the scout-by-scout reviews that the team calls postmortems. It's a trick adapted from Daniel Kahneman's *Thinking, Fast and Slow*, one of several books about decisions that circulated through Friedman's front office. Various departments now perform the postmortems after all kinds of transactions.

In September 2015, such sessions were new in the Dodgers organization. Gasparino, a Friedman hire, set up a call with every area scout. Marty Lamb, responsible for Ohio, Kentucky, and Tennessee, was nervous to draw the first one. The team's incumbent scouts had been fretting about what the regime change might mean for them. "You've got Friedman coming over, and the analytics," Lamb said. "We're like, 'Uh oh, are we even gonna have jobs?' We didn't know what to expect." Across the sport, scouts suspected that new data-driven front offices would let their contracts expire and be rid of them. In some cases, those fears proved warranted. *The MVP Machine*, by Ben Lindbergh and Travis Sawchik, chronicled the Astros shedding roughly two-thirds of their scouts between 2009 and 2019.

On his call with Gasparino, Lamb talked through why he liked Buehler and Matt Beaty, another future major leaguer for whom he had vouched in the 2015 draft. Lamb thought their conversation went fine. He was maybe a bit brusque, but these were, as scouts like to say, baseball guys. They could be crusty, right? Two days later, Gasparino called again, this time without notice. "I was a little confused about if you were mad at me, mad at what we were doing, or didn't like it," he said. This caught Lamb off guard, but they talked through it. In time, the boss won over returnees with a personal touch. When Lamb's wife spoke to Gasparino for the first time, she promised to help her husband with his phone etiquette. As Lamb emerged as the organization's most successful scout, it became a running joke between the two men.

Pre-Gasparino, the Dodgers scouting department had been an old-school stronghold. "Our office was turning into a more new school, and it was the question of how do these two dynamics merge together," said Trey Magnuson, another veteran staffer. "Do they butt heads or do they massage each other to help each other out?" Gasparino had worked as a stockbroker for two years, but before that he was an infielder in the Rockies organization. He was a baseball guy. The Dodgers did let go of many experienced scouts near the end of the 2015 season, including the advance scouts who studied upcoming opponents. But they filled many of the vacated positions. As of 2020, the Dodgers had eighty-six scouts on staff, the fourth-most of any team, according to that year's *Baseball America Directory*.

The Dodgers drafted and developed sixteen players who began 2021 on their forty-man roster or injured list. Improbably,

Lamb was the signing scout for six of them. He also assisted in the scouting of a seventh and, two regimes earlier, drafted but could not sign an eighth, David Price. "This is a strong word to throw out there, but he's a bit of a savant," said Stephanos Stroop, a minor league pitching coach who has shadowed Lamb to scout several prospects. "We all hope that we see the best in people, but I think he sees a guy and truly sees what they really can be and what they realistically can do. Some people worry about industry value, what other people think. He is secure in his beliefs."

Lamb is a scout's scout. After a decade on the job, he was promoted to crosschecker. He asked for his old job back after a year. That was more than a decade ago, and he has done it uninterrupted since. He dips. He drives a pickup truck. Scouting has changed, but he has stayed the same. While he is friendly with rival scouts he works alongside, he tends to stand alone. "With most scouts, you can generally tell who they really like, who they're getting after," said Nate Birtwell, who for several years scouted the same area for the Diamondbacks. "With Marty, you have no idea. How he pulls off the straight poker face all the time with these guys is pretty impressive." Some see patterns in his targets. Former Dodgers catcher A. J. Ellis was one of the first players Lamb ever signed, in 2003, for $2,500. For the next seven off-seasons, Lamb threw him batting practice in their shared hometown of Lexington. "There's definitely a certain type that Marty tends to see really clearly," Ellis said. "He really gravitates towards the high-IQ position players, those really athletic pitchers."

This century, teams have reduced their scouting spend and turned to video study to replace the lost hours. Fear they or their friends could be fired drives many scouts to share intelligence, once an unthinkable act. "A lot of the guys now, yeah, it's competition, but you're almost willing to share information a little more these days, with how the industry's gone," Birtwell said. "It's so much reliance on analytics and data that it's just a little bit more of a 'Don't let your buddy get burned' kind of thing."

It's a vicious cycle, for that altruism homogenizes their work and attenuates any competitive advantage.

The Dodgers, Lamb very much included, approach the draft with old-school secrecy. Maybe it is paranoia. Maybe it is warranted. But they take great pains to disguise their interest, including ceasing all contact with prospects themselves in the weeks preceding the draft and sending staffers from faraway regions to scout in street clothes. They employed these techniques on many players in the class of 2016, particularly in the middle rounds. It would not be feasible to hide the array of evaluators they send to scout top prospects like Lux.

The boy bearing the name and face of a teen-movie protagonist was big on the Indian Trail High campus in Kenosha, Wisconsin, and he secured a favorable arrangement for his senior spring semester: lunch and study hall back to back. He'd drive the six miles to Carthage College on Lake Michigan and take batting practice with the coach there: Augie Schmidt, his uncle. Schmidt had been the second overall pick in the 1982 draft, a remarkable talent who never made the major leagues because failure drove him mad. He managed to instill in Lux both his love for the game and the ability to bounce back better than he ever could. Schmidt invited scouts to watch batting practice. They came in droves.

It was there that Magnuson, one of the Dodgers' longest-tenured employees, fell for the first player he would ever sign. Magnuson grew up obsessed with baseball in the 1980s, when his home state of Montana had no high school teams, let alone college programs. Desperate for a way into Major League Baseball, he started selling group tickets for the Dodgers weeks after Y2K, a few years out of college. He was amazed at the mass of humanity in the stadium each night. "It was surreal," he said. "The amount of people at Dodger Stadium would be the second- or third-largest town in Montana."

Once a week, Dodgers employees gathered at the Los Angeles Police Department Academy, just outside the stadium grounds, to play pickup basketball. On the court, Magnuson met and befriended a few scouts, who invited him up to the "draft room," the repurposed eighth-floor suite where players' wives typically spent games. For years, Magnuson attended draft meetings on an informal basis, taking time off from his actual job.

Then a young baseball-operations employee named A. J. Preller left for the Texas Rangers and brought some staffers with him. Magnuson moved up from salesman to scouting coordinator, where he handled logistics for Dodgers scouts traveling the world and opposing scouts coming to examine the Dodgers. This was 2007. Frank McCourt still owned the team; Juan Pierre, a man nearly incapable of hitting homers, was one off-season's big acquisition. Over seven years, Magnuson got to know a number of old-school scouts. Then Friedman replaced Ned Colletti, and the Dodgers' and Padres' scouting directors swapped jobs, Gasparino going to Los Angeles and Logan White to San Diego.

Gasparino asked Magnuson for his opinion of the incumbent scouts before offering him his first scouting job, in a region the organization had not been canvassing: Montana through Minnesota, plus all of Canada. Surely, Magnuson would lap the other area scouts in miles traveled; three scouts split Southern California alone. But some Southern California high schools produce more prospects than entire Northern states. Magnuson accepted and moved back home. A year in, he added four Midwestern states, including Wisconsin.

By the time he first saw Lux, in October 2015, several rival scouts already recognized the kid's elite hand-eye coordination and athleticism. There were two primary concerns: he played weak competition, and he still had the body of a boy. Magnuson quoted Red Redding to describe him. "A stiff breeze," he said, "would blow him over."

Lux started filling out his frame over the winter. By the time Wisconsin warmed enough to host baseball games, district coaches were calling him the greatest player the area had birthed since Schmidt. Magnuson liked what he saw in afternoon batting practice, and what he heard from Lux's mother, Heather, in the stands at his games. He came to believe the boy possessed the right blend of confidence and modesty, reflected in his healthy perspective to learn from, not be hurt by, failure. The team uses psychologist Carol Dweck's term for this: "growth mindset." Fortunately, Lux also tested well on the Dodgers' NeuroScouting software, like Betts five years earlier.

The Dodgers compared him not to cold-weather Wisconsinites but to past prospects across America, especially those who played shortstop and hit left-handed. "We feel this type of player does very well historically in the draft," Gasparino said at the time. "We just thought it was an undervalued or underappreciated skill set. Left-handed-hitting shortstops that are athletic and can hit, usually overachieve more than underachieve." Lux himself said he had heard frequent comparisons to Chase Utley, the standout Phillie turned Dodger who fit most of those criteria.

The Dodgers could not rely on historical precedent as much with Smith, for they were betting he could be a new type of catcher, smaller and more agile. As the draft approached, they considered him more of a mid-round pick. He lacked a consistent track record, and he disappointed in the all-important Cape Cod League the summer after his sophomore year. But Lamb, his area scout, spoke to Smith's coach there, who endorsed his preparation.

Then, two weeks from draft day, Byrnes became enamored at the ACC Tournament in Durham, North Carolina, when Smith homered twice in Louisville's first game, delivered a key pinch-hit single in the second, and walked in the third. The majority of the school's roster would eventually be drafted, but Smith stood out. The Dodgers weren't the only ones who adjusted their expectations. The Cardinals had the thirty-third and thirty-fourth picks, and they, too, planned to select Smith. If Lackey's deal had been official before Greinke's, St. Louis would have had him.

May was a classic draft bet, a tall Texan teenager who threw hard and looked like he might amass muscle over time. Hundreds of similar prospects have failed to reach their potential. A select few have surpassed theirs. Gasparino told scouts the team was uninterested in high school right-handers unless their deliveries demonstrated above-average athleticism and they succeeded with strikes, not purely by overwhelming opponents. May found the zone. He also clocked the highest-spin breaking ball at a tournament in the fall of his senior year, attracting the attention of area scout Josh Herzenberg. When May began his senior season continually throwing his fastball in the nineties, Herzenberg alerted his superiors. Several trekked to Texas to see him. The Dodgers bet a million bucks on May, and he repaid them in three years.

In July 2015, a new Dodgers scout named Paul Cogan attended the Northwoods League All-Star Game in a tiny riverfront town in Wisconsin. Most of the involved amateurs were underclassmen hoping to get drafted the next year. During pregame drills, Cogan timed one athletic-looking outfielder's sixty-yard sprint at 6.5 seconds—elite speed. On the roster he had in hand, he matched the uniform number to a name: Anthony Gonsolin. Later, Gonsolin walloped six home runs in a home run derby and entered from the bullpen to throw an inning of promising relief.

A Google search showed he had gone undrafted a month earlier, after his junior season at Saint Mary's College, not far from Cogan's Northern California home. Cogan was astounded that no scout knew Gonsolin and embarrassed that he didn't. "I could not believe that somebody didn't draft him," he said. "I really don't know why the industry did not see what I saw. It was clear talent." The industry didn't see what he saw because it didn't grasp the entirety of Gonsolin's skillset. To other evaluators, he was an outfielder primarily, a competent one, but not special enough to drum up draft interest. "Gonsolin is the perfect example of why you've got to give a shit about old-school scouting," said Kyle Boddy, the Driveline founder who later played a role in Gonsolin's development.

Two months later, the Dodgers hired a longtime Bay Area college coach, Tom Kunis, to scout the region. Cogan told Kunis about his discovery. Kunis, too, fancied Gonsolin's athletic ease. "It wasn't too hard to see the athlete, the competitiveness," he said. "You knew it was gonna get better. It was implied." Several teams were willing to draft Gonsolin late. As a senior, he had little leverage and would have to sign for a minimal bonus. So on the two scouts' recommendations, the Dodgers plucked Gonsolin in the ninth round, well before other clubs considered him. He signed for $2,500. Teams are allotted a pool of money to split between selections from the top ten rounds, so taking Gonsolin in the ninth freed the Dodgers to preserve more money for May, who had far more leverage.

Magnuson found McKinstry by accident. He was scouting his college teammate, a more talented left-handed pitcher, when he noticed a young shortstop who happened to be draft eligible as a sophomore. McKinstry's lack of power was an obvious problem, but Magnuson appreciated his contact ability and athleticism. In his mind's eye, he saw a second coming of Pierre, the man he had once watched from the Dodger Stadium offices. "He was a slap, hit it to left field, and bust his ass down the line kind of a kid," Magnuson said. "He was always in a crouchy little stance." When Lamb, the trusted scout, came across McKinstry at a conference tournament, he, too, offered an endorsement. The Dodgers did as the two men recommended.

Until 2018, McKinstry performed like late-round roster fodder. The Dodgers shuffled him around various affiliates to fill temporary holes, sometimes only for a few days. Top prospects are never handled that way. The obvious problem remained: McKinstry's tools were not so great that they could compensate for his power deficiencies. So, that spring training, the club set out to add loft to his swing. He worked for weeks with consultant Craig Wallenbrock and director of player development Will Rhymes to cement the changes, then started the season at a low level to see if they worked. They did, and he ascended. Magnuson called it an ideal example of scouting and player development working together. "It's not purely scouting, it's not purely PD," he said. "It's a good mixture of both, to find the right player."

The ingredients were impossible to separate, as some Dodgers scouts were also Dodgers coaches. The franchise did not invent this concept. A baseball lifer named Tom Kotchman has been doing it since 1990, first for the Angels and now the Red Sox. It started as a way for him to see his children more, but he found it so helpful he continued. "It resets your eyes," he said. "I don't know how people scout all year round. It brings the two a little more together when you have someone that's doing both." Kotchman and another lifer named Rob Mummau were among the few men known to split those duties. Right after the 2016 draft, the Dodgers sent Herzenberg, the North Texas area scout, to Utah to coach rookie ball, and Kunis, the Bay Area scout, to Rancho Cucamonga to coach Class A. After the 2017 draft, they flipped roles, and North Florida area scout Scott Hennessey traveled to Tulsa to coach Double A.

When the scouts returned to the amateur circuit from their coaching sabbaticals, their peers would tease them. "Oh," they'd say, "I thought you were a hotshot coach now." But the stints had significant impact. Kunis, who in his first two years signed three pitchers who became major leaguers, none of them first-rounders, said he needed a gauge in those early years, a "threshold" for what a Class A player resembled that he could compare with a current collegian. "It just became easier to scout," Herzenberg said. "Because if I understand the foundation of what our hitting coaches at the highest level are looking at, what they believe is going to succeed, I'm just going to look for that blueprint, so we can hand it to them, and they'll just become good Major League Baseball players. It felt simple at that point."

It wasn't exactly that simple, but Herzenberg saw more clearly why, out of two similarly graded players, one thrived and one failed. Dual-role employees like him also served as connectors to the rest of the organization. In both 2017 and 2018, the Dodgers brought hundreds of employees to the World Series at Dodger Stadium. Many of them had never or rarely met, requiring repeated introductions. "But if you were sitting next to Tom Kunis," Magnuson said, "he would develop the conversation with player development and you. It felt like an easier transition."

That's an organizational hallmark. Most involved in the 2016 draft attribute most of its radical success, relative to other years, to luck. Gasparino has come to believe there was a honeymoon effect at play for the first full year his new hires worked together. "Our *Wisdom of Crowds* approach is always in place," he said, "but it just felt like it was a little more pure that year." The previous year, he said, had been chaotic. The next year, their risk-taking flopped.

With their 2017 first-round selection, the Dodgers chose Jeren Kendall, an athletic, power-hitting center fielder with one glaring flaw: an inability to make contact. When he connected with a pitch, he often produced good results. He just did not connect enough. Kendall entered his final season at powerhouse Vanderbilt as a consensus top-five prospect. On the surface, he fulfilled expectations, launching fifteen homers and stealing twenty bases in sixty-two games. But his seventy-four strikeouts, his most yet, troubled teams—and Kendall himself.

He had his eyes checked three times. He argued to inquiring scouts that, yes, he had a deficiency, but it was better than other deficiencies, like athleticism or fitness. His draft stock sank. "That's why I think the Dodgers are perfect for me, because I struck out seventy times my junior year and they still took me in the first round," Kendall said. "Everybody else was like, 'This kid just can't hit.'"

Everybody else was right. In the first 250 games of his professional career, none above Class A, Kendall hit .223 and struck out almost a third of the time he batted. As soon as he entered the Dodgers organization, Kendall became the best defensive outfielder across it. He maintained above-average power and exceptional base-running ability. If he could trim a third of his strikeouts, he'd become a star. He just couldn't. Of course, other teams had seen the same strength and speed and defense. They recognized the potential, but his college contact rates had sufficiently scared them away from a first-round investment. "He's just got so much talent, man, it's hard," said Walker Buehler, his college teammate. "He'll do stuff that nobody in the world does, and then he'll punch out four times. It's weird."

The Dodgers tried a variety of tactics to reduce the weirdness and induce more contact. They began by letting him struggle his way, figuring it would render him more open-minded. It didn't. Kendall accepted instruction, but not without his own input. "It's a two-way street," he said in June 2018, a year after he was drafted. "I have my opinions, and they have theirs. I have an idea of what my career is going to be, and what I want it to be, and so do they."

Kendall's swing was "suboptimal," as Friedman put it. But the Dodgers waited to provide more instruction until Kendall told them he was ready. That came after the 2018 season, and it did not work. Repeating the same level using a hybrid of his swing and their swing, Kendall hit for more power but struck out 10 percent more in 2019, 10 percent more often than any major leaguer struck out that year.

Kendall's talent has not evaporated. He could still learn how to make enough contact to become a viable major leaguer. "You could poll ten guys in our organization and say, 'Hey, who's the most talented player we have?'" one Dodgers official said in 2021. "A lot of them will still say Jeren." But the odds are against him. The Dodgers declined to protect Kendall from the 2020 Rule 5 draft. No other team was willing to carry him on their roster for a year to control his rights for the next five. He is, to date, a squandered pick, evidence that the Dodgers sometimes fail, spectacularly so, in their draft pursuits. Their second-round pick in 2017, a right-hander named Morgan Cooper, fared even worse. Because of a series of injuries, he made his professional debut forty-seven months after the draft. One month later, four years and a day after drafting him, the Dodgers released him.

Unsurprisingly, the Dodgers aim to draft like a financial adviser might formulate a portfolio, balancing higher-risk players with a few safer selections. But they don't ever behave so cautiously that they select, say, a reliever, in the first round, like the White Sox did in 2016. Diversification is paramount, not necessarily confined to one class. "The exact yield from any re-spective draft, we don't try to be that precise, appreciating that we can't," Friedman said. "I mean, we'd like to." The 2016 draft was so fruitful that the Dodgers' 2016–2017 haul would rank highly.

Two problems plague many scouting departments in the an-alytics era. First, scouts often feel at odds with coworkers from other departments, particularly when draftees don't develop as envisioned. "It's like that Spiderman meme," one scout said, "just pointing fingers at each other." Dodgers officials do not recount such scenarios.

Second, scouts who work for the many teams that deploy drafting models are often unaware how their opinions factor into the decisions their employers make on draft day. Dodgers officials do recount those tales. To prevent leaks and because the draft unfolds in unpredictable ways, scouts enter each year uncertain if their recommendations will be followed. But to fos-ter understanding, Dodgers research and development staffers attend pre-draft workouts alongside scouts at Dodger Stadium, putting a face to their models that spit out statistics-based player recommendations every spring. "They give that to you early enough," Magnuson said, "so that you're looking at these play-ers in person." They're all in the Dodgers' "42" database, not that scouts are required to be fluent in its contents.

Lamb has arguably been the most successful amateur scout of the last decade, and, accounting for draft order, the Dodgers one of the three or four most efficient drafting teams in that time. Even they, Lamb said, never discuss specific statistics. Nor, he maintained, does he investigate them. "I'm not saying that ar-rogantly, and I know it's sort of lame," he said. "I mean, I know what some of those numbers mean. I just don't look at them. I figure, they do their deal, we do our deal, and then they blend them together."

His peers peg some of his claims as gamesmanship. "My guess is," Birtwell said, "he understands some of the data and analytics more than he might be willing to admit." At the very least, Lamb has tested every position player in whom he took an interest on the Dodgers' NeuroScouting software, like the Red Sox had with Betts. And he has been steered to search for the sort of players the Dodgers and the data prefer: athletic, up-the-middle defenders who are willing to rethink their swing under the organization's umbrella. Others can take it from there. In 2019, the Dodgers started employing some strength and conditioning coaches as part-time performance scouts to travel around and file reports on amateurs just like an amateur scout might. The difference was the reports covered only the player's athleticism, not his hitting or pitching ability.

"We understood, if we target the underlying tools, the underlying abilities these players have to make consistent contact and play a premium position, over time the player-development group is gonna be able to tap into the untapped potential of their other tools," Herzenberg said. "The Dodgers' player development staff has been really good over the years in understanding that just because a guy has a high floor—Will Smith, for example—doesn't mean he has a low ceiling. Maybe that's the market inefficiency the Dodgers have been able to really take advantage of, specifically from the scouting to the player development pendulum."

Compared with their quiet scouting successes, the Dodgers' player-development feats were far louder.

# Chapter 8

I N DECEMBER 2019, THE LEGENDARY MANAGER JIM Leyland visited San Diego for the Winter Meetings, baseball's largest annual convention. By then, Leyland had been retired for six years, but he may never retire from what made him most famous: smoking cigarettes and showering love on the men who played for him. One evening, he had just stepped outside the Manchester Grand Hyatt lobby to light up when he saw a contingent of Dodgers player-development staffers. He recognized the man leading the group: Will Rhymes, who once played for him. Leyland rushed over and hugged Rhymes while holding onto the cigarette, engulfing him with smoke and affection. "He might as well have seen Barry Bonds," said one person who witnessed the encounter.

A decade earlier, Rhymes had impressed Leyland during his first major league spring training. He was a five-foot-eight second baseman with little power and no exceptional tools, but Leyland loved his effort. One March morning, Leyland offhandedly mentioned to a group of beat writers that he thought Rhymes would play in the big leagues. One of them quickly

located Rhymes and asked what he thought of Leyland's comments. The remark so surprised him, he overexerted himself the
next few days to impress his biggest fan. No one with anything
approaching Leyland's standing had ever complimented him
before. "I remember the impact it had on me," Rhymes said.
"'Holy shit! Someone's in my corner.'" In time he settled and
made the majors, hitting .266 over parts of three seasons, vali-
dating the manager. Leyland pointed to his development, from
twenty-seventh round pick to dependable depth, as evidence of
an effective farm system.

Months before he ran into his old manager, Rhymes began
running the Dodgers' farm system as their director of player development. "I read him right a long time ago," Leyland said. "I
knew he had a great passion for the game." When Rhymes pre-
pares to speak to his charges these days, Leyland is often on his
mind. "I've always remembered the impact that small things can
have on players," Rhymes said. "I try to do that with our guys,
and it comes from that interaction, how much that can mean to
someone." Leyland's influence has its limits, for so much about
player development changed in the decade between when Leyland first spoke of his pet pupil and Rhymes took over the farm.
"It's so different, I don't even know where to start," Rhymes said.
"I never thought I would want to work in player development. It
just wasn't intellectually stimulating at all. Now it's the opposite:
it's endlessly stimulating."

Under Friedman, the Dodgers have specialized in turning
players with profiles a lot like Rhymes's from organizational
depth into competent players. Because they have achieved consistent success without the benefit of top draft picks, they are the
consensus model farm system within the industry.

Rhymes is the third in a line of former major leaguers Friedman first acquired in Tampa Bay to run the Dodgers farm under
him. The second, Brandon Gomes, Rhymes's teammate on the
2012 team, was another undersized senior sign who maximized
his athletic ability. The first was Gabe Kapler, a muscular man
most recognized for his oft-photographed physique and the sui

generis healthy-living blog he ran in retirement. There, Kapler proposed male athletes tan their testicles to promote testosterone development. He advocated for consuming lean meat and animal carcasses. And he recommended masturbating with coconut oil. He also wrote a baseball blog, where he predicted the future.

"Proprietary information is becoming harder and harder to come by. While there are certainly frontiers of data not yet fully explored, I believe the next real advantage will come not from which team can acquire the most information, but from which team can best put that information into practice. How efficiently and successfully information is shared with managers, coaches and players will equal wins now and going forward," Kapler wrote. "To prepare a major-league club for something truly unorthodox—like switching outfielders on a batter-by-batter basis to minimize the impact of weak arms, poor jumps, or lack of range—the practice should begin at the very lowest levels of the organization. By implementing new ideas in rookie ball, players are less likely to balk when they're asked to do something different in the name of capitalizing on every bit of leverage they can during an MLB game."

Kapler thought like the front office but looked like a player, so Friedman saw him as an ideal conduit to spread the organization's new doctrine to prospects eager to advance to the big leagues. In retrospect, Kapler's arrival in November 2014 announced the beginning of baseball's next analytical wave. If the first wave was sabermetrics' dissemination among hardcore fans, the second its spread within the executive class, and the third when first-moving major leaguers started implementing data's guidance into their games, the fourth was when teams started systematically teaching teenaged prospects how to play the most statistically efficient way. The gap between the early waves spanned a decade. It took a year for the third to transform into the fourth.

Kapler instituted immediate change, telling minor leaguers all about the team's new focus at his first spring training. He arranged higher-quality, mostly organic catering across the team's seven affiliates and banned junk food from the Dodgers complex. "We are the healthiest team in pro sports," Kapler wrote on the whiteboard menu, practically throwing the Red Vines tubs into the trash. Once the minor league season began, he toured the outposts to taste the new food and remind prospects how they would now be evaluated. He moved regrettably fast. "One of the biggest challenges for the way I worked in 2014 was that I had too much certainty," he said seven years later. "I felt like I understood some of the changes that needed to happen without really understanding the entire picture. I feel like I have a better understanding of it now."

On a May 2015 trip to Oklahoma City, Kapler met with a Triple A outfielder named Scott Schebler, who, with a batting average below .200, thought he was struggling. At most stadiums he visited, it was the largest number on the scoreboard when he stepped up to bat. Seeing it made him "madder and madder and madder," he said. Kapler told Schebler that the Dodgers did not care at all about his batting average. He told him he was still hitting balls hard, and over time that was bound to correlate with success. He was not bad, only temporarily unlucky. There was no problem. There would be a problem only if Schebler became so frustrated he altered his approach into something less effective.

Kapler left Schebler a packet of data that showed how he was actually performing. He called the statistics the "real predictors" of success: exit velocity, Weighted Runs Created Plus (wRC+), Weighted On-Base Average (wOBA), strikeout-walk ratio, first-pitch strike percentage, 1–1 count strike percentage, swing percentage on strikes, and chase rate on balls. Only a few of the eight were popular then. But in the seven years since, they have become the language of the game. In the dugout, players often treat a 115-mph line drive as a feat, even if it lands in a glove, and a 66-mph pop-up as a mistake, even if it drops in between the infield and outfield. And if it does fall for a hit, they poke fun at themselves, shaking their hands at first base, as if to say the pitch had so jammed them that it hurt. Many Dodgers now obsess over their barrel percentages and chase rates almost as much as they do their averages.

"Players are going to get bent out of shape about numbers," Kapler said in 2015. "It's inevitable. It's always going to be that way. We just want them to get bent out of shape about the right ones." The rest of the industry has helped them in that mission, as the right numbers are no longer hidden within Kapler's binder but broadcast on televisions nationwide. That year, 2015, marked the transition.

His efforts and forceful style produced adherents and dissidents, galling some coaches tasked with directing the development of future major leaguers while thrilling others. "He's, like, the biggest outside-the-box thinker around," said area scout and instructor Tom Kunis. "That gives you the freedom to expand your mental horizons in player development."

The 2015 minor league managers were all holdovers from the previous regime. They were asked to coexist with new hires who were younger and less experienced. "I think that was really weird for people," Kapler said. "Particularly when those people came into the organization and immediately had a voice, and you had some others in the organization who had been there for many, many years, and had felt like they needed to remain quiet."

After the season, the Dodgers let contracts expire and reconstructed the old schoolhouse with younger coaches, often from the college ranks. They then repioneered what has since become an industry trend, tasking coaches to bounce between the minors and majors. In the 1940s, Branch Rickey and Fresco Thompson first popularized a homogeneous approach, aspiring to teach every Dodger, from Brooklyn to Class D, the same skills. More recently, Kapler blogged about the benefits of uniformity in coaching.

At first, the Dodgers' returns were inconspicuous. In 2016 and 2017, Shawn Wooten worked as the Dodgers' Triple A hitting coach but regularly visited the major league team. When Joc Pederson was mired in a miserable slump with six weeks left in the 2017 season, the Dodgers acquired a last-ditch replacement and demoted Pederson to Triple A. Wooten went with him to Oklahoma City, where they together detected the problem within Pederson's swing, the reason he was so susceptible to strikeouts. It was clear his hips were the hang-up, but locating a solution proved challenging. They tried a number of fixes, none of which stuck. When the Dodgers recalled Pederson two weeks later for September depth's sake, Wooten again traveled with him. It took them all month to figure it out while Pederson hardly played, but before Game 162 on October 1, they finally did. In drills that morning, Wooten had Pederson set his hips just so in a crouch, enabling his head to finally turn as he wanted and track the incoming baseball. With the Dodgers' postseason seed all wrapped up, Pederson batted three times that afternoon, more than he had in weeks. He doubled twice.

The Dodgers coaching staff and front office met the next day to discuss their first-round roster. Wooten unsuccessfully lobbied for Pederson to be included, arguing that his pupil had turned the corner. But when Corey Seager hurt his back in the clinching game and missed the next round, Pederson replaced him. He played here and there in the National League Championship Series, then became the Dodgers' surprise star of the World Series, doubling twice, homering thrice.

Pederson had been an All-Star two years earlier, so his last-second success was not widely attributed to the Dodgers' new approach to player development. Their unorthodox methods became clearer in 2018. The Dodgers hired two former major leaguers, Brant Brown and Luis Ortiz, to rotate between the roles of assistant major league hitting coach and minor league hitting coordinator. When Brown was with the Dodgers, Ortiz was with an affiliate. When Ortiz was with the Dodgers, Brown was with an affiliate.

After the season, Ortiz left for Texas, and the Dodgers hired a thirty-two-year-old named Robert Van Scoyoc to be their hitting coach. Brown became their hitting strategist, a title the Arizona Diamondbacks had created the previous year for Van Scoyoc. Until the Dodgers hired him, that was the closest Van Scoyoc had come to coaching an actual team. After his playing career fizzled as a junior-college reserve, he pivoted to coaching individual players with his mentor, Craig Wallenbrock, out of a business park in his hometown of Santa Clarita. Brown had trained and coached there for years. He even gave a teenaged Van Scoyoc hitting lessons in the mid-aughts.

Wallenbrock has been recruiting clients by word of mouth since the 1980s, when amateur hitters started coming to his San Fernando Valley warehouse to hit. In time, the amateurs turned professional, and the professionals quietly referred him to their peers. J. D. Martinez and Ryan Braun were among the stars to train under Wallenbrock, Brown, and, eventually, Van Scoyoc. In the late 1990s, several UCLA hitters would visit Wallenbrock every Wednesday night. For at least a year, that group included Chase Utley, the future Dodger. Longtime Bruins baseball coach Gary Adams, a contemporary of the late John Wooden, encouraged their treks, both because the training functioned as a workaround to NCAA limits on coaching hours and because he respected Wallenbrock. "He was way before his time, scientifically looking at it," Adams said. "I thought, at the time, it sounded pretty complicated. I always thought he was born to teach hitting like Coach Wooden was born to teach basketball." Adams's professional peers were not as open-minded, for decades discouraging players from visiting Wallenbrock and other outside coaches.

At the time, Wallenbrock worked, too, with a young outfielder named Gabe Kapler, from the summer he was drafted until the year after he broke into the big leagues. A decade in, convinced he had lost what made him successful, Kapler retired to manage a Class A team. A year into that, he resolved to come back and called Wallenbrock, who assured him he was still swinging the same way but that pitchers had adapted to him. He had to adapt again to succeed. When Kapler arrived to see him, Wallenbrock cued a video of two of baseball's best hitters: Vladimir Guerrero and Paul Konerko, telling him to examine their hand positions. Then he showed Kapler video of himself, demonstrating the difference. "He was so much more advanced and in depth than any of the major-league hitting coaches that I'd worked with," Kapler said. The stars' hands moved toward the mound much earlier than Kapler's, enabling them to attack more pitches and better handle the sport's increasing velocity.

Kapler mimicked them, got back into baseball, and, at age thirty-two, produced the best season of his career. That performance earned him a million-dollar deal with Friedman's thrifty Rays, beginning the two men's working relationship. Almost as soon as Friedman hired Kapler with the Dodgers, Kapler suggested Friedman bring aboard Wallenbrock as a consultant. Wallenbrock declined. He had a bad experience in a similar role with the White Sox, he was getting old, and he was happy where he was. A year later, the Dodgers hired Raúl Ibañez to be a special assistant to Friedman. Ibañez was another retired hitter who had worked with Wallenbrock late in his career, to even better success than Kapler. He, too, asked Wallenbrock to join the Dodgers, and this time Wallenbrock accepted on the condition that the Dodgers also hire Van Scoyoc. After Ibañez met Van Scoyoc, then twenty-nine, and learned that the Atlanta Braves were considering hiring him, he cajoled Friedman to bring on both men.

At first, Wallenbrock and Van Scoyoc specialized in winter work. From Thanksgiving until spring training, there were always a few Dodgers prospects hitting at their facility. In need of an artificial hip, Wallenbrock limited his travel, so it was Van Scoyoc who visited all of the organization's affiliates, in a more focused fashion than Kapler's trips. In June 2016, Van Scoyoc visited top draft pick Will Smith in Utah rookie ball. The team believed he had untapped hitting talent, hidden because of a "conservative, handsy swing," as scouting director Billy Gasparino said. Van Scoyoc brought with him a video to show Smith. On it were three hitters: Martinez, Miguel Cabrera, and Smith. Van Scoyoc floated a few ways Smith could change his swing to better resemble the two stars. It was but an updated version of the pitch Wallenbrock had once given Kapler.

When Van Scoyoc visited Smith at the next level the next month, they got to work. Soon the Dodgers promoted Smith again, to the Los Angeles exurb of Rancho Cucamonga, where Van Scoyoc could drive to see him in an hour. They kept practicing his swing. In 2017, it was still conservative, but less so. By the time Smith debuted in 2019, he was among the most powerful catchers in the sport, with the uppercut swing to match. In ninety-one games over his first two seasons, he launched twenty-three home runs. The Dodgers' aggressive development decisions yielded best-in-class results. "There were some scary moments in there," Gasparino said. "Like, 'Is this swing change for the better? Is it gonna work? His strikeout rate got too high; is he sacrificing his hit skill for too much power?'" The answers to these questions, it turned out, were yes, yes, and no. Five years postdraft, Smith had supplied the most value of any first-round pick. He quickly lapped the two more accomplished college catchers who went ahead of him.

Lux, like Smith, welcomed Van Scoyoc on a visit early in his minor league career. Two weeks into his first full season in Midland, Michigan, Lux was hitting .133. He had always felt in control on the field. Now he felt overmatched. "When you've been doing something your whole life and it's worked for you and then all of the sudden it doesn't," he said, "it's super frustrating."

Lux had learned to hit in a much different manner than his new coach was about to teach. His uncle, Augie Schmidt, the former top prospect, taught him to aim for the top of the ball when he swung, to stroke low line drives. It had worked for him, and such an approach, he thought, was the best fit for Lux's scrawny frame. But by 2017, the Dodgers knew that thought was wrong, and now Lux was more muscular and ready to listen. "His talent wasn't showing," Van Scoyoc said, "because the swing wasn't really allowing that." Asking him to be open-minded, Van Scoyoc introduced the concept of maximizing the time his bat spent in the zone to match different pitches' planes. Lux sat out two days of games while they worked on it.

Success did not come at once. Van Scoyoc returned to Michigan multiple times that summer, monitoring his progress. Senior vice president of baseball operations Josh Byrnes also visited for an hour-long statistics session. "How do you think you're doing?" he asked Lux, who was then nineteen. "Shitty," Lux said. Byrnes said he disagreed. He showed Lux his contact rate against pitches traveling 95 mph or higher, another real predictor. He showed him the same statistic for other future stars when they were his age, among them Corey Seager, Carlos Correa, Francisco Lindor, and Gleyber Torres. He was not far off, and that metric better predicts major league success than batting average itself.

In the fall, once the season was over, Van Scoyoc and Wallenbrock redid Lux's swing again. Over the winter, they watched videos he sent to check up on him. That January, he began to feel confident with his new swing. What did it was a drill they called Exit Stage Right, Lux tucking his right foot over his left to start his hitting sequence. It gave him more control over his entire swing, he felt. That year, he starred across the minor leagues. The next year, Lux became the best baseball prospect alive. In 2020, he developed a renewed case of the yips, an unsettling case of COVID-19, and emotional distress after the police shooting of Jacob Blake in his hometown of Kenosha. But Lux spent the off-season working again with Van Scoyoc, and in 2021, he emerged as a key contributor. "Even for someone like Gavin, who was a high pick and semi-famous at times," Gasparino said, "it just never feels like that easy of a path."

The route was often blocked, even in 2021, when Trea Turner took over his position. But from a five-year view, it's clear what happened. The Dodgers drafted an exceptional athlete who, in succeeding despite substandard technique, demonstrated determination and remarkable hand-eye coordination. They bet those traits would take over once his way began to fail him, then meld with their coaching to shape a star. "He didn't want to struggle anymore," Van Scoyoc said. "It's always easier when a guy is failing. He didn't want to go through it again, so he was very forthcoming. I think if I would've approached him before he failed, it probably would have had a lower chance of success."

It was a similar story with Chris Taylor, and Matt Beaty, and Austin Barnes, and hitter after hitter who rose through the Dodgers organization, athletes who found they could not achieve any more with swings so flawed. Once he started working with Van Scoyoc and Wallenbrock, Beaty said, he saw results within weeks. "They turned ground balls to second base into doubles in the gap," he said. "And balls that were usually doubles in the gap had a little more launch angle and went over the fence."

Before the 2019 season, the Dodgers hired Van Scoyoc as their full-time hitting coach and installed Brown as their hitting strategist. Now, Van Scoyoc and Brown helped players get from the minor leagues to the major leagues *and* helped them when they arrived. "We trust them," Smith said. "There's that familiarity with them. You really know that what they're saying is probably gonna help." When Dodgers prospects are promoted for the first time, they typically succeed, notably so in 2019, when Smith, Beaty, and fellow rookie Alex Verdugo hit walk-off home runs in three consecutive games. No team had ever had first-year players do so in back-to-back games. All three players were above-average as rookies, which Van Scoyoc attributed to his experience with them.

"I know where he was drafted, how his career went in the minor leagues, what he's been good at, where he's struggled, his strengths and weaknesses," Van Scoyoc said. "There's a little bit quicker of a learning curve that we have than the average big-league hitting coach, who is reading a scouting report and going off reputation and other people's opinions. We have our own opinions formed on these guys, and I think that makes it a lot easier."

For decades, Wallenbrock and his disciples worked with professional hitters privately, secretly. Teams discouraged, and in some cases forbade, their players from training with him. The Dodgers not only encouraged their hitters to hear his perspective; they mandated it. They created an environment where every new Dodger developed within that school of thought. "You don't want guys to come up here and learn new ways of doing things," Van Scoyoc said. "They should be prepared. To me, that's the whole point of player development."

Wooten left the Dodgers for the Angels after the 2017 season. He's a private coach now, but he still sees his former employer as the industry's pacesetter. Clubs have been trying to catch up. Some come close; others mistakenly believe they are millimeters away. "A lot of teams get really scared to implement mechanics and changes. The Dodgers do not," Wooten said. "Players work with coaches that give them an ability to make in-game adjustments at lower levels. You have to challenge them at lower levels to make those adjustments, because at some point on the major league level, they're gonna have to do it. It's too late to learn by then. Players get so overwhelmed, and it's hard to fix it because they've never done it." Smith's success prompted the Dodgers to attempt more changes during prospects' first summers and autumns. It also convinced prospects they knew what they were doing. In 2018, the Dodgers drafted a college teammate of Smith's, Devin Mann. The first time he met Byrnes, he said he knew Smith's story. "What do you guys see with me?" he asked.

Accidents were also welcome. Months before Friedman arrived, the previous regime used a late draft pick to select an injured high school left-hander named Caleb Ferguson. Scout Marty Lamb had only seen him pitch once, one week before Ferguson tore his elbow. He liked the natural sink on his throws enough to advise the Dodgers to draft him and guide him through Tommy John surgery rehabilitation. After his first year back healthy, Ferguson took two months off to let his body recover. When he started to throw again, his pitches behaved like someone else's. Where his fastball once darted down, it now appeared to jump up. Without trying, he had become a more deceptive spin-rate specialist—throwing the ball with more rotation, and therefore more movement. Hitters were troubled. Both he and the organization were baffled. "The best explanation I can give," Gomes said, "is he came back from his first full season more developed and more mature and it potentially put his arm slot in a slightly different spot."

However it happened, the organization welcomed it. Eighteen months after he appeared anew, Ferguson was in the major leagues, striking out stars with his new fastball. "I still don't know what happened, but I'm not complaining about it," Ferguson said. The team showed him why his new fastball worked, if not how he got it, presenting on Rapsodo software the revolutions-per-minute increase he had been gifted. Ferguson was no Buehler. He was not the type of athlete who had grown up studying how to throw harder. When he tried to throw a ball far in high school, he couldn't even reach the outfield from home plate. But he proved receptive to the insight the Dodgers' technology provided him. After staffers taught him the concept of tunneling, he worked on fitting his curveball into the same visual slot as his fastball, hindering hitters' ability to commit to either pitch.

In 2020, Ferguson became the Dodgers' best reliever until he tore his elbow again. While he recovered from his second Tommy John surgery, Ferguson started to apply what he had learned in baseball to his golf game. He brought his own $500 Rapsodo mobile launch monitor to the driving range and studied his results: drive distance, club speed, ball speed, and launch angle. He is far from the only Dodger to extend his professional learnings to his leisure, even the golf course, long the ballplayer's preferred place to escape. "It probably would not surprise you to learn that if I go to the driving range," Rhymes said, "I'm bringing a tripod, video, and a launch monitor."

For as data driven as the Dodgers are, some of their successes stem from a careful disregard of the data. During one day of fall 2016 instructional-league play, several Dodgers coaches met to discuss the young pitchers they were training. Someone raised a concern about Dustin May, the tall, thin Texas right-hander the team had just drafted. As soon as his left leg landed within his delivery, his knee locked, a concept the analytics community dubbed lead-leg blocking. It could lead to injury, a young coach said that afternoon, mentioning the hard landing of May's heel. That might cause command issues long-term, another coach suggested. Left unsaid was the fear that his frame made him particularly fragile. May's college recruiter said pro scouts consistently remarked, worriedly, that he had no ass.

Up stood Charlie Hough, a sexagenarian veteran of twenty-five major league seasons, the furthest thing from a data nerd in the room. "Walk," he commanded his colleagues. "Stand up and walk." One coach did as asked. Hough asked what part of his foot first hit the ground. The coach looked down to examine the evidence. "My heel," he said. Hough asked if it felt weird. The coach said it did not. "So Dustin's doing something natural," Hough said. "Leave him alone."

The room was silent for a few seconds. "You know how you coach this kid?" Hough eventually said. "You give him the ball, you pat him on the ass, you go back to the dugout, and you enjoy the show." Everybody laughed. Nobody remarked that he still didn't have an ass. And nobody intervened. Not three years later, May was in the majors. "That perspective, combining that with the analytics, is so enormously valuable," said Josh Herzenberg, a coach in the room who now runs research and development for the Korea Baseball Organization's Lotte Giants. Seven years earlier, well before Friedman's arrival, Hough was the coach who counseled failed minor league catcher Kenley Jansen on his conversion to pitching. His strategy then was similar. He let Jansen throw the way that felt natural to him, offering little but encouragement. It turned out that Jansen's natural throwing motion produced unnatural cut that vexed hitters. Jansen became baseball's best closer for the next eight seasons.

One Dodgers advantage is their retention of old-school scouts and coaches, merging their thoughts with data analysis. Yes, an old Dodger Stadium clubhouse became a research and development department. Yes, excerpts of Friedman's public comments can be indistinguishable from quarterly earnings calls. But the organization still values individuality, emphasizing knowledge that cannot be quantified while searching for ways to quantify it.

When the Dodgers hired Rob Hill, the twenty-four-year-old who made his name helping pitchers at Driveline, they paired him with a man who had been coaching professional pitchers longer than Hill had been alive: another sexagenarian named Don Alexander. After the pandemic shutdown, the two pitching coordinators spent eighty-one consecutive days together at the University of Southern California, where top Dodgers prospects trained as alternates, separate from the major league team. "So much of the beginning of the summer was us just getting to know each other," Hill said. "I was also conscious of not wanting to be *that* twenty-four-year-old, that guy that I hear about that creates issues."

In the mornings, Hill and Alexander led young pitchers through drills. In the afternoons, they argued about pitching. In the evenings, they played cards in their Westin Bonaventure hotel rooms and argued some more. By summer's end, they had built a bond. "A lot of it was me helping him put words to things that he had thought, whether that be agreeing or disagreeing," Hill said. "I think that's one of the best things about the organization: We have a bunch of dudes like me, and we have a bunch of dudes like Donnie. We can just marry it in the middle."

The trouble is that determining a direction often requires siding with one side. As in amateur scouting, development staffers are often consulted but rarely directly involved in the decision-making. That remains the domain of Friedman and senior executives. The only way to estimate how much weight a given opinion carries is to compare it to the ultimate choice, and even that is a flawed measure. There's an intentional mystery to it all.

But the union between new and familiar allows the Dodgers to comb more areas in pursuit of growth. And inefficiencies still abound. "In some ways, it's incremental," Rhymes said. "In others, exponential." Take velocity for nonpitchers. "Nobody teaches position players how to throw, or how anything works," Hill once said on a Driveline podcast. His colleague Anthony Brady agreed, terming it the lowest-hanging fruit for teams eager to improve. Hill then told the story of how he plucked some in the summer of 2020.

He showed one curious position-player prospect a video of Padres shortstop Fernando Tatis Jr. throwing a baseball "a million" miles per hour. "I want you to look at his lower half," Hill recounted saying. "See what he does with his front leg?" The player saw immediately. "Oh," he said, "his leg hits the ground and his knee doesn't keep bending. It stiffens up."

"Yeah," Hill said before pulling up a video of this player throwing. "It just, like, keeps going," the player said of his own lead leg. "Yeah," Hill said again. "It's gonna be really hard for you to generate a lot of velocity with your upper body if you aren't stopping your lower half." Soon, Hill said, the player was throwing harder. He declined to say who it was, but claimed that his velocity increased from 76 mph to 85 mph. A 9-mph gain can rocket a pitcher from independent ball to stardom; it's less impactful for a position player. But it's still an improvement, an improvement Hill logged later that day so fellow coaches could understand what triggered it.

Regular logging is essential to what the Dodgers do. They log sleep, weight training, and on-field practice. Coaches are taught to describe both what players think they are doing and, according to the technology, what they are actually doing. The former guides the mental cues they might suggest when the next player needs a change. It makes no sense, but DJ Peters, for years the organization's strongest hitting prospect, entered professional baseball believing he clobbered his home runs by swinging down and getting under the ball. He told Dodgers staffers that childhood coaches taught him that way. They gently showed him he did the opposite of what he thought. After he swung while wearing a $5,500 K-vest, they presented to him in 3D the extent of his uppercut motion and suggested how he might tame it to make more contact while preserving his five-hundred-foot power.

"You have a timestamp on the cues," Herzenberg said. "July 10, we said this, and then the K-vest metrics changed and the tracking metrics changed, and you can actually say what changed and how it worked. So that if he gets promoted on August 10, you have a month of data of a non-arbitrary date with a tangible change."

One league source said he had never heard of this practice during his years working for other major league teams. After working for the Dodgers, he now employs it every day with his new organization. "It sounds so simple, because if you go into the world of science, that's what it is," he said. "You have a hypothesis. You test it. If it maintains itself, you keep testing it. If you prove it to be invalid, then you make an adjustment, a new hypothesis, and you test. That's the process L.A. was really beginning to accelerate and implement during my last couple years there. It's *sooooo* obvious. Why have we never done it that way? But organizations that are near the top or the first people through, you get the yield that they're getting right now."

It's science, but there is an art to the cues. This is the sport in which José Bautista finally broke out, at thirty, after a teammate suggested he swing so early that it felt ridiculous. A successful cue need not work for everyone, just for one player. But if it works for one, it might work for others. Jason Ochart, now the Phillies minor league hitting coordinator, once asked a hitter to be quick to the baseball and then, on his next swing, to get his hands to slot first. As Eno Sarris chronicled at FanGraphs.com, the hitter swung faster on the first cue but kept his bat in the zone longer on the second cue. Yet many teams still do not catalog their cues, do not offer players any sort of structured curriculum.

One ex-Dodgers coach listed six prospects drafted and developed in the seven years since Kapler arrived: May, Lux, Beaty, Smith, Tony Gonsolin, and Edwin Ríos. "All those guys," he said, "were able to speak the tech and the data along with the baseball nuance and the traditional verbiage. They were educated in both of those areas, and whenever they needed to make a small nuanced adjustment to the game, they knew exactly what they had to do."

In 2021, Rhymes said baseball was in its golden age of player development. "Obviously," he said, "people are realizing that and pouring a lot of bandwidth and resources into it." Given the sudden investment, he said, it is fair to maintain concerns about late-coming teams overemphasizing the data at the expense of the people involved. "Any time you see the entire industry moving in one way," Rhymes said, "it's good to maybe consider what they're not doing." For one: no organization is compensating all of its prospects above the federal poverty level. Teams are allocating additional resources to skill development, housing, and nutrition before paychecks, akin to start-ups spending on snacks but not overtime pay for all-hours office work. In 2015, the Dodgers set the pace on nourishment, providing minor leaguers with in-season meals. In 2021, the Astros became the first organization to provide furnished housing for all minor leaguers. Peers copied the former, and, in time, the latter, when MLB made it mandatory for the 2022 season. The two teams are the frequent subjects of mimicry. As one private hitting coach, who requested anonymity to speak freely, said: "Player development isn't just copying what you think the Astros and Dodgers are doing, or poaching their coaches."

Many in the industry expect the pace of progress to continue accelerating, faster than minor league salaries. The question is whether it'll be the right progress. Will teams provide all their prospects sufficient financial support, or continue making incremental improvements while they struggle? Will teams train hitters to be better hitters, or just more powerful ones? Will pitchers reach the majors with controlled pitch mixes that can flummox the best hitters, or just top velocity and something that spins? In every case, fear abounds that the answer will be the latter, that the push for outlandish metrics on the farm will only sentence young men to debt and further fracture the on-field product.

There is little debate that the Dodgers enter the new era ahead. "If you go back and compare orgs over the last several years, you'll see where we stack up. Not to sound like a dick, but it's not coincidental," Rhymes said. "It's gonna take some time, but I think you'll see some narrowing of the knowledge gap as everything becomes more apparent. For now, I think the best coaches have a huge advantage over the average coach, however you term that."

The Dodgers' coaches tend to fit into one of two categories: skill developers or vibe setters.

# Chapter 9

WHEN DON MATTINGLY DEPARTED AS THE Dodgers' manager in October 2015, Gabe Kapler became the favorite to take over. He had played in the major leagues, he had managed in the minor leagues, and now he had worked with the next generation of the organization's talent. His communication skills and eccentricities brought to mind the last manager Andrew Friedman had hired, Joe Maddon, a decade earlier. "Maybe the only guy I can think of like that," Maddon once told *Philadelphia* magazine of Kapler, "is me."

But Kapler's aggressiveness alienated some team members. He recognized later that he made people uncomfortable. "I had the dials up a little too high," Kapler said. He continued in his role while the Dodgers chose an underdog: Dave Roberts, a lifelong connector, who, a decade earlier, had enjoyed a three-year run as the team's center fielder. Roberts was best known for stealing one of the biggest bases in baseball history for the Boston Red Sox. Everyone watching knew what he was trying to do, and he succeeded anyway.

It is probable no job description in baseball has changed as much in recent years as the manager's. At the turn of the century, managers did not consult nightly with executives about lineup formulation. Nor was it immediate nationwide news if they misspoke on any of the 350-plus occasions each year they spoke to reporters. Executives and players must adapt to continually novel information, but managers are tasked with a fundamentally different assignment. It is not a coincidence that only two men on the job in 2021, Tony LaRussa and Terry Francona, predate the *Moneyball* era. As Sam Fuld said when he was hired as the Phillies general manager weeks after becoming a finalist for the Red Sox managerial position, the lines have blurred between the two jobs.

Roberts was an inspired selection, able to navigate through the haze. He had managed only one game in his life, as the interim manager during another interim manager's absence, but he met the demands of the modern role. He is willing to heed the front office's information-based advice in most game situations. He is convincingly optimistic. And he is skilled at staying on message, in his conversations with unhappy players petitioning for more playing time and in twice-daily scrums with inquiring reporters. Most managers are running the same route, but Roberts executes the cuts with consistent precision.

He reliably laughs at the questions intended to inflame. He makes media members feel important with timely taps on the shoulder, unyielding eye contact, and frequent first-name recitations, earning him and his team the benefit of the doubt. He uses similar, pertinent technique on team employees, greeting the team's social-media manager by her Instagram handle, and on players. "He literally says hi to every single guy every single day," Justin Turner said. If Roberts's run of positivity halted periodically, even once a month, players would start to doubt him, according to Turner. "He doesn't do that," Turner said. "It's 100-percent genuine how he is every single day, how he treats everyone. Guys don't think he's full of crap."

Either Roberts is an authentically positive person or one of the great tricksters of his time. But what he presents to players is an act—a well-considered, better-rehearsed one. Baseball is the most individual team sport, particularly at the professional level, where a few additional starts or hits translate to many thousands of dollars. Teamwork is not a necessary part of the game. Every year, Roberts set out to engender anew an environment that inspired an outsized collection of talent to sublimate their desires for the organization's benefit. It was legerdemain. Most in the room knew what he was trying to do, and he succeeded anyway.

His first step was setting the clubhouse's room tone at a sonorous and persistent positivity. Criticism was reserved for private spaces. Juan Castro, a quality assurance coach under Roberts for two seasons, recalled a number of afternoons in which his boss would cheerfully invite him into his office. They'd begin by reviewing some situation from the previous night's game. Roberts would share his opinion, ask Castro for his, and intently listen to his response. Sometimes, Castro would pause mid-answer. "You all right, Dave?" he'd ask. Calmly, forcefully, Roberts would let it all out. For a few minutes, he'd air his grievances, and Castro would aim to make him feel better. By game time, Roberts would appear in the dugout as his standard jovial self. "He gets over the bad stuff quickly," said Gary Adams, his college coach and his managerial inspiration.

In 1968, Waymon Roberts, a Black man from Houston, enlisted in the Marines and met his Japanese wife, Eiko, while stationed in Okinawa. David Ray was born there. The family soon uprooted to California, back to Japan, to North Carolina, Hawaii, and, eventually, California for good. David became a prolific high school quarterback in northern San Diego, running the option, making a snap decision to keep or pitch the ball. When his knee gave out, he reconsidered football. He walked onto the UCLA baseball team and learned to tilt the game toward his strengths. He could not drive the ball, but he could put it into play. So he did, and then he raced to first base, and, often, to second. He had one tool, speed, and another skill, his batting eye, and he forged them and his geniality into a ten-season career.

For as many regular-season games as he won in Los Angeles, for as quick as he was with a smile, Roberts became derided among subsets of the fan base and pilloried by the pundit class for flubbing postseason decisions. Roberts presented himself as inured to the criticism, but his colleagues described it taking a toll on him. His managing strengths were invisible to most outsiders. It's hard to see the defusing of tension when it happens behind closed doors, and harder still to detect it when it's mollified before it emerges.

Roberts and his coaches are in constant search of the moments when players are ready to hear critiques of their play. In exceptional cases, they bring them up in the immediate aftermath. More often, they wait. They have concluded that the ideal moment is an exceedingly rare occasion: when a hitter singles and forces the opposing pitcher out of the game, leaving the first-base coach three uninterrupted minutes to deliver a message. "When they've got a hit, they're in for *anything*," said Roberts, who was the Padres' first-base coach for three seasons. "'Oh man, you're right, you're right, I screwed up.'"

George Lombard, the Dodgers' first-base coach from 2016 through 2020, liked to gently initiate such encounters. "Tell me what you think about that ball last night," he'd say. "Did you have a chance to catch that ball?" To that, the player might admit he should've gotten to it. "Yeah, that's what I saw," Lombard would respond. "I think you could've got a better jump on that ball." The goal, he said, is to "knock them down and build them back up."

Roberts often met a player during batting practice, draped his arm around him, and proffered his guidance. "Most players don't like to be criticized," he said. "It's all about the delivery. There's gotta be trust. When there's trust, then it's an easier conversation to have, and it lands." He built the necessary trust out of towers of public and private praise. When the Dodgers acquired a new major leaguer, Roberts met with him in his office to tell him what he liked about him. Every relationship got off on the right foot.

Roberts even made a habit of commending umpires. Every time he saw "Cowboy Joe" West, the notoriously prickly man who has umpired the most games in the sport's history, Roberts reminded him that West had made him famous. It was West who, with the world watching, correctly called Roberts safe on his 2004 stolen base. That night, Roberts saluted him for getting into the right position to make the call. West moonlights as a country singer-songwriter. During Roberts's first season, the Dodgers once used West's ditties as their walk-up music their first time through the order. "That," Roberts said, "was a little ode to the cowboy." Every year, Roberts earned fewer ejections than his peers.

Roberts set such a palpable vibe that the Dodgers were free to hire assistants of disparate styles. As Rick Honeycutt approached retirement, Mark Prior became the team's pitching coach of the future. Prior had once been the most talented pitcher of his generation. He was tall and strong, his delivery looked impossibly smooth, and he dominated the highest level at twenty-one. Then his shoulder started to hurt and never stopped. He spent six weeks advancing from the minors to the majors and more than seven years endeavoring to make it back, accumulating wisdom from an almost incomparable set of baseball experiences. "The highest of highs," Roberts said. "The lowest of lows."

Years before he called it a career, Prior saw that his superlative talent was gone for good. He sought to survive on work ethic and guile, but he grew frustrated with his supervisors' unwillingness to acknowledge the truth. Across various organizations, coaches coated their words to him in cloying glaze, pretending he could recapture what he had. Only one coach told him the truth every time they spoke.

Ironically, it was the same man most often blamed for Prior's premature retirement: Dusty Baker. Over four years managing him on Chicago's North Side, Baker asked Prior to work deeper into games than any manager would even one decade later. No one knows for sure that his overuse precipitated his injuries, and Prior himself suspects it did not. He sources his downfall to a line drive that fractured his elbow and a fluke collision from which he landed on his shoulder.

With his words, Baker inspired Prior to become a coach, and as a coach Prior was a revelation, attentive and truthful. He told players when they were terrible and when they were great, and they appreciated what amounted to radical honesty in their world. "I found that the more honesty I received, the better," Prior said. "Maybe initially it's more of a gut punch, but in the long run it's better. I've just taken that into my coaching philosophy."

Prior began as the Dodgers' bullpen coach, a role that traditionally constituted little more than babysitting the team's oddballs four hundred feet from the dugout. He did more, though he at first required prompting to divulge his opinions, and he sometimes expressed regret at his bluntness. By the end of his first year, Prior ceased with the apologies. "We joke that he's supposed to be the fluff coach, and he's the exact opposite of a fluff coach," said Chris Gimenez, a fellow former major leaguer who worked on the Dodgers staff for a year.

Prior possesses a dry sense of humor. In the seconds before the Dodgers began to celebrate clinching a division title in 2019, he shouted, "That Champagne better be dairy-free!" He knows how to keep up a bit. During his playing career, his colossal calves were famous. As a coach, he'd roll up to his knee the sweat suit the Dodgers wore on travel days, maintaining a straight face when players remarked on the disproportionate part of his legs. He did this for almost an entire season. "He'll say stuff to me where even I can't tell if he's joking," said Walker Buehler, who considered himself an expert in the deadpan delivery.

When the staff had to confront an underperforming player, Prior's demeanor made for a wicked good cop, bad cop combination with Roberts. He was unafraid to censure a pitcher who strayed from a well-reasoned game plan without explanation. In 2019, he did so several times with embattled closer Kenley Jansen, even in front of his teammates. He would sit with a young pitcher for an hour to unspool the unvarnished story of his career, but when that pitcher, Caleb Ferguson, asked if he could call him Marcus, Prior told him no and vacated the room.

Lost in most remembrances of Prior's short-lived success was his maniacal approach to preparation. Beginning in his sophomore year of high school, he adhered to a precise diet, submitted frequent blood work, and ran regularly. In the late 1990s, none were the norm for professional pitchers, let alone amateurs. On a Team USA trip as a collegian, he asked an assistant coach, Tim Corbin, to accompany him to a tiny hotel gym at sunrise. Corbin became one of the country's most successful college coaches, one of Walker Buehler's mentors. The Prior he knew, he said, would have no patience for anyone who was not obsessed with self-improvement.

Prior started with the Dodgers as an analytics novice. One of his pitchers described him as suffocating in information when he began. But, true to form, he became adept by his second year, and in his third year he took over as pitching coach. He scoured far and wide for tidbits to pass on to players, but he acted sparingly. "I found there were plenty of coaches I interacted with who were very quick to jump to a conclusion: This is the thing. This is what we need to do," said Dr. James Buffi, the Dodgers' R&D biomechanist. "Whereas what I was always impressed with with Mark was his stance of, 'OK, the data is showing this, I get it, but let's take a step back, let's think about the context.' I always thought it was a very measured approach, which I think is really important when you analyze data like this. We're talking about human beings, who are inherently variable. Mark is very measured."

When he was twenty-three, Prior was the world's best pitcher. When the Dodgers' assistant pitching coach, Connor McGuiness, was twenty-three, he was bartending, cutting grass, coaching Little League, and studying for the LSAT. McGuiness had been a crafty lefty at Emory University, nowhere near talented enough to pitch professionally. He hoped to coach but found no inroads. "No one would take my call, man," he said. Law school became an increasingly likely backup. He returned to his alma mater to coach and got in touch with the few club officials he knew.

Because he had not played professionally, they advised him to get a master's degree to make himself more attractive. He did, in management, at Catholic University while working as a graduate assistant for the baseball program. He studied how to develop velocity and implemented a weighted-ball plan for the school's pitchers. He read up on the significance and use of TrackMan.

He reached back out to an old summer ball teammate, Jeremy Zoll, who had by then become the Dodgers' assistant director of player development, Gabe Kapler's deputy. Concerned it might look like he was trying to boost an old friend, Zoll hesitated to recommend McGuiness for months. When an opening came up, he brought him up but undersold their history. He hoped his bosses would see the appeal without his influence, because McGuiness still lacked the traditional track record. They did. McGuiness coached three years in Class A before the Dodgers promoted him to major league assistant pitching coach. He had just turned thirty.

Endearingly earnest, McGuiness made it clear as soon as he met pitchers that he had not reached the professional ranks. He figured they would Google him and learn the truth anyway, so he got ahead of it. "I never say the words, 'Well, this is what I did,'" McGuiness said. "Because I never did it." And he retained a sense of awe about his newfound place in the world. One day in his second season on the job, McGuiness texted his father in what he described as a pinch-me moment. He stood in the Dodger Stadium weight room. Within a few feet of him were three of the biggest baseball stars of his youth: Prior, Clayton Kershaw, and Albert Pujols. "I could never have fathomed this as a possibility," McGuiness said.

Until recently, it was not one. "Connor ended up being at the beginning of a pretty significant shift," said Zoll, now a Minnesota Twins assistant general manager. "There was this weird thing where people were being put in one box or another, just based on their background, not based on their interest or skillset. If you didn't have pro-ball experience, playing or coaching, then pro ball didn't want you. Now we've opened it up enough where people can just do what they want to do based on what they're good at."

Over the winter before the 2019 season, McGuiness helped another man in his mold get hired. Stephanos Stroop had pitched and played the outfield while studying economics at Claremont McKenna. For his senior thesis, he performed a financial analysis of the MLB draft. After a stint flipping houses, he became a college pitching coach and rarely thought of working in professional baseball until McGuiness sent him a text gauging his interest.

Mining the college ranks for coaches is the area where Kapler is most confident the Dodgers changed the sport. "At the time, it was just weird," Kapler said. "We were gonna go hire the Santa Clara hitting coach to a professional job? That's crazy, it was seen as." It turned out that, in college, many coaches' skills were squandered on recruiting responsibilities. When freed to exclusively coach current players, they were often quicker to adapt than professional-baseball lifers.

One spring day early in Friedman's tenure, dozens of minor league coaches, coordinators, and front office staffers gathered inside a Camelback Ranch conference room to provide status updates on many of the organization's hitting prospects. Most of those assembled were returnees, and, after introductions, everyone immediately began to use advanced baseball jargon. Among the many metrics thrown around were projections, weighted measures, and expected and actual statistics from the previous season. "I don't know anything," concluded one coach in the room, who had just been hired away from another major league organization.

That coach now works for another team and requested anonymity because his new employer would not want him publicly discussing these matters. "I knew there were certain things I needed to learn. I didn't know the expansiveness of what that was," he said. "That was a seminal moment in my coaching career, because it really thrust me into the curious state I'm in now and will forever be in. When you start to have those margins exposed to you, you can't look back. It's very much like when you pickle a cucumber. You can't undo it."

With his old team, the coach had rarely been exposed to advanced statistics. With the Dodgers, it took him a year before he felt comfortable tossing around the verbiage and interpreting a handful of data points to reach one conclusion. He felt like it happened fast, because it had to. His peers were all ahead of him, lapping him in an unspoken race. "I really think that's one of the critical components, the secret sauce, of L.A.," he said. "They have a lot of brilliant people over there. There's a lot of brilliant people in a lot of other organizations, but they have been able to leverage that culture to where you're expected to think that way, expected to question the way things have always been done."

Here's one way: Coaches don't pitch. Coaches throw batting practice, hit fungoes, maybe take a few swings for fun. They do not actively train their bodies to keep pitching. Rob Hill does. When the pitching prospects' days are done and no one else is in sight of the bullpen mounds, Hill, the Dodgers' pitching coordinator of technical development, regularly throws on his own. "When all the kids get done with their workouts for the day, the old guys can get out there and chuck the rock," Hill said. "I know I'm not that old, but, yeah."

Hill, born in 1995, refers to "the kids" often. "It's funny because we call people that are older than us kids," said Eric Jagers, Hill's best friend and the Cincinnati Reds assistant pitching coach. Maybe they are the kids. Jagers was also born in 1995. For Hill's birthday one year, Jagers purchased them matching yin-and-yang pendants they continue to wear, Jagers the yin, Hill the yang. The kids met as college pitchers training at Driveline in the summer of 2016. Their bodies broke down, but they proved to be fluent at teaching what they'd learned. Within three years, major league teams employed both.

Now, Jagers and Hill are concurrently pursuing the same goal in their own private race. They both want to throw at least one pitch in their lives that registers 100 mph. "I really enjoy the feeling of doing the thing that I care about the most, even if I'm not one of the best at it," Hill said. "It just matters a lot to me. Some people want to be scratch golfers. Some people like college basketball. I like to throw. I want to throw 100 one day." At last check, he had soared as high as 96.

In 2021, major league coaches and support staff competed in their own velocity contest, for fun, not function. The idea occurred to strength and conditioning coach Eric Yavarone, a brawny former Division I outfielder. It predictably spawned weeks of trash talk. "You have a great body and everything," McGuiness told Yavarone. "But I know I can throw harder than you." McGuiness was right. He beat all comers with one throw at 87 mph. Physical therapist Johnathan Erb, another college outfielder, came in second at 86.

There is edification in Hill's solo pitching pursuit. Before he recommends a tactic to a player, Hill tries it himself first. That goes for throwing, weightlifting, hydrating, anything. "The piece that is probably really attractive to the Dodgers is using yourself as a test subject and being willing to go through it in that regard," said Anthony Brady, his Driveline colleague. "It's really hard to test the efficiency of our program without ever having gone through it, and it's harder to build that athlete's trust that what we're doing is going to work."

There is obsession involved. Hill tends to find obscure goals and train his being on them. He has spent years perfecting his kendama technique and practicing his routines on an arcade video game called *DanceRush Stardom*. "That's how I think of Rob: He's kind of a forged renaissance man," Jagers said. "He'll go through these little phases where he'll pick something up, and then he gets really really good at it, and they are these weird, unique little skills."

And there is meditation. Hill and Jagers approach some throwing days like beachfront showers, rinsing off the sand from a long day in the sun. "It's not that every single session is this mental grind that you're going through with a ton of intense thought," Jagers said. "But the lightbulb may go off, really, at any time. Sometimes you go out there and you're like, 'I'm not going to think about anything.' Then you make one throw, and you're like, 'Oh my gosh, I solved it.' You're subconsciously learning as you go."

They feel lucky to have made their lifelong passion their job. But like many millennials who managed the same, Hill lacks work-life balance. "This is all I do," he said. "People are like, 'Man, I can't wait to go hit the links on Saturday.' And I'm like, 'We've got players to get to the big leagues Saturday.'" He deems the sacrifice worthwhile. "I like helping people actualize their potential," he said, "and I think we have a lot of ways to do that now, which is really freaking cool."

If a pitcher tells Hill he feels like he sinks lower into his body during his best deliveries, Hill will pore through the evidence and offer corroboration. "When you're able to show them how what they are feeling and talking about looks in terms of data, whether it's overlays, videos, biomechanical models, it starts to go really quick," Brady said. "That just builds that rapport and trust factor back and forth. 'This person actually understands what I'm talking about,' as opposed to, 'Here's the data, here's what you're doing wrong, here's what you're doing right.' That's why the Dodgers were so high on Rob."

In his spare moments at ballparks, often many hours before first pitch, minor league manager Mark Kertenian preferred to practice yoga. He took off his shirt and carried his mat into the outfield. If players spotted him, he invited them into his practice or explained its purpose. He summoned others into his cramped office, turned off the lights, draped towels over their eyes, cued ambient music, and led breathing exercises, imploring them to let their breath replenish and relax them. "From the shit he was saying," one player said after his first such session, "I literally felt like I was floating."

Kertenian sent some players personalized Spotify playlists and mixed others special smoothies with organic ingredients he purchased on his meager salary. Another of Kapler's unconventional hires out of the college ranks, he functions more like a guru than a manager. No one cares less about convention than Kertenian. "He just does whatever the hell he wants, quite frankly," said T. S. Reed, who played for him at Cal State Northridge. Kertenian culled that from his father, a man who was once kicked out of his son's college game for smoking a cigar in the stands. Until the Dodgers hired him, like McGuiness and Hill, Kertenian had never played or coached professional baseball. Unlike them, the Dodgers tasked him with managing entire teams. "That's pretty unprecedented, as far as our industry goes," said Shaun Larkin, the Dodgers' field coordinator.

Kertenian regaled his players with his collection of life experiences, wonderful, wild, and awful. After Northridge let him go, his parents divorced, his fiancée had a miscarriage, his fiancée's mother died, and his mother was diagnosed with breast cancer. He battled depression. In sharing his plight, he created an environment where players were comfortable disclosing their own fears and foibles with him.

He told lighter stories, too, like contracting vertigo while driving to Alabama, running out of gas at the base of a mountain pass and bartering for the fuel to reach home, and cooking at an Art Basel pop-up. "I have street cred," Kertenian said. "And I can share with them appropriately, so that they, for a moment, don't feel alone enough where they feel embarrassed. I don't want them to feel embarrassed or like they're letting people down." Struggling players turned to him in ways they had never before turned to coaches. "If I need someone to talk to, it's always Mark," said a onetime prospect, outfielder Brayan Morales. "I would never tell other people what I tell Mark."

At Florida International University, his last collegiate stop, Kertenian coached future Dodgers infielder Edwin Ríos, who predated him at the school. The day he introduced himself to the team, Kertenian pulled aside several players to tell them they could call him if they ever got into trouble—any sort of trouble, anywhere. Ríos laughed because he didn't know what else to do, or what the coach even meant. "You see him for the first time, and it's like: 'Who the hell is this guy?'" he said. "You think maybe it was one of those things where he was trying too hard in his first year. But as the years went by, I realized that's just the way he is."

Elián Herrera, a Kertenian assistant in 2019, reached the big leagues with the Dodgers and Brewers. He played for seventeen professional teams over his thirteen seasons. Never, he said, did he have a coach like Kertenian, a man who both welcomed and risked his own vulnerability. "He is one of a kind who really cares about the players," Herrera said. "Most of the coaches do, but he really shows it. They keep their distance. He doesn't. He tries to make you comfortable. And sometimes, when you show someone you care about him, he can go and play more loose, more relaxed." Players found themselves taking his breathing exercises into games, calming down before they batted or unleashed a key pitch.

Area scout and coach Tom Kunis likened old-school minor league managing to classic football coaching—more chastisement than corrective feedback. They are drastically different sports. By its nature, baseball does enough to sunder players' brains with negativity. This century, the industry has made the long-overdue move toward positivity in messaging. "If you raise red flags every time he fails, you're playing for yesterday every day," Kunis said. "Negativity does nothing. I can still be positive and get a corrective moment in there, and they're gonna listen."

But negativity creeps its way into the conversation. Across the industry, people ask each other, formally and informally, to predict the future. It is the lifeblood of baseball discussion. How long can Corey Seager stick at short? (They've been asking for a decade now.) At what age will Justin Turner have to transition off of third base? Will Dustin May start or relieve? The Dodgers have started emphasizing to their minor league coaches that they are not trained, paid, or asked to be talent evaluators. "I struggled with that for two years," Kertenian said. "And now it's a theme: We are not evaluators. We are developers."

They developed the people. The research and development department developed the models that drove the Dodgers to acquire the people.

# Chapter 10

WHEN DOUG FEARING MOVED INTO HIS OFFICE in the basement of Dodger Stadium, he was surprised to learn it included its own shower. The Dodgers' research and development department took over the ballpark's decrepit visiting clubhouse. As the director of the incipient department, Fearing drew the manager's digs.

Before 2014, the Dodgers carved out a new space for visiting teams to dress, near their dugout. Over the next three seasons, visiting veteran players learned to return to the old clubhouse for the showers with superior water pressure. Then, in series after series in 2017, players opened the doors to find two dozen people typing. "Look at all the computers in here," they'd say to each other. It was a bizarro clubhouse, an on-the-nose inversion of a central qualm of ballplayers this century. With players peering in, the staffers felt like zoo animals. The Dodgers did not make the move for symbolism's sake; it was vacant space in a stadium that had little. But it was impossible to ignore that the times had changed. The nerds had taken over the players' sacred space.

Fearing fell in love with baseball, like millions of other Angelenos, listening to Vin Scully's narration while growing up in the San Fernando Valley. He was watching, alone, at a family friend's home when Kirk Gibson limped into history in 1988. The rest of his family had given up on the game and moved to another room. Eleven and at the peak of his fandom, Fearing stayed put. As he went off to college at Carnegie Mellon, he shed some of his fanaticism. He returned to it a decade later, when he took a year off from work as a software developer to help parent his newborn son. The boy had to sleep sometimes, and, when he did, Fearing found himself following the Dodgers online.

This was 2004, a lively time to catch up to the discourse about the Dodgers. *Moneyball*, recently released, was shaping the conversation about the use of data in baseball, and, on the eve of the season, Frank McCourt had hired book alum Paul DePodesta as the Dodgers general manager. *Los Angeles Times* sports columnists Bill Plaschke and T. J. Simers seized on his ties to tease him in print again and again. They nicknamed him "Google Boy." Meanwhile, the team, largely built by DePodesta's predecessor, Dan Evans, kept winning.

On his nascent *Dodger Thoughts* blog, LA fan Jon Weisman stayed above the fray. Fearing found there an inquisitive community that he appreciated, and that appreciated him. On ESPN .com, Fearing found an outlet for his desire to do the math. He joined six of the site's anonymous fantasy baseball leagues, conducting simple Excel analyses on prospects, sampling innovative roster-construction practices. In several leagues, he devoted a spot on his staff to whichever pitcher was facing the torpid Montreal Expos, who would soon cease to exist. "It was a dominant strategy," he said.

When the Dodgers regressed in 2005, Fearing kept reading and contributing to Weisman's blog. He tracked the organization's farm system and defended some of DePodesta's methods. Halfway through the season, Fearing performed an elementary study of the off-season's best free-agent signings, comparing their salaries with their on-field production. He measured production in terms of value provided over a replacement player, or VORP, a forerunner to WAR that remained unfamiliar to the casual fan. Commenters asked about the intangibles: heart, soul, scrappiness. "Perhaps we should develop formulas for LORP (Leadership Over Replacement Player) and SORP (Scrappiness Over Replacement Player)," Fearing replied. He squeezed in a sick statistics burn: "Even without knowing the formula for LORP or SORP, I'm pretty sure I know how to convert them into wins: Additional Wins = 0 x LORP + 0 x SORP." ("My coefficient," Fearing said in 2021, "would be higher than zero now.")

His sporting interest rekindled and refashioned, Fearing maintained it while pursuing a master's degree in operations research at MIT. Fearing was the only non-MBA student enrolled in NBA executive Daryl Morey's sports management seminar, which featured Bill James as a guest speaker. During that semester, Fearing and a classmate conducted an oft-cited study on putting performance using early analytics from the PGA Tour. After he finished his PhD, in 2010, he interviewed with the Rays. They offered him a full-time job, but at a salary far smaller than he would earn as a professor.

Fearing opted to consult for the team while continuing on the tenure track at Harvard and the University of Texas's business schools. Tampa Bay was advancing from using standard advanced metrics to its own proprietary predictive models, and Fearing advised those models' formulation. At the 2012 Sloan Sports Analytics Conference, he reconnected with an MIT cohort named Timothy Chan, who had become a University of Toronto industrial engineering professor focused on decision making under uncertainty. Fearing researched operational disruption. He especially studied air traffic flow management, quantifying the cost of changes in plans and devising preventative solutions, like de-icing airport runways, to limit the resulting penalties. They reasoned they could solder their specialties, sprinkle in sports, and perform an analysis of roster optimization amid the inevitable yet unpredictable rush of injuries ball clubs faced each year. Ben Zobrist's multiposition success in Tampa Bay influenced them.

They released their paper ahead of the 2013 conference. "Baseball players are like factories producing innings-played at each position," Chan and Fearing wrote, calculating that the most flexible teams held advantages of up to twenty-five runs on the least flexible teams. "We believe our novel identification of the variation in flexibility and resulting value represents an under-explored opportunity for teams to improve their rosters." They suggested teams try players at new positions in spring training to build flexibility.

Future Dodgers general manager Farhan Zaidi sat in the audience for Fearing's presentation, which won top honors. After he introduced the paper's findings, Fearing took questions. One eager attendee asked about the Rays: Given that they employed Zobrist and that their manager, Joe Maddon, was known for his lineup creativity, why did the model rate them so poorly? Fearing tittered. He did not publicize that he consulted for the team. He settled himself and suggested that the Rays had plenty of flexibility in reserve, but none of it was particularly good. "This makes sense with the budget constraints," he said. Zobrist had become an everyday player. The team devoted their payroll to starters, who were so good that the model punished them for it.

Near the 2014 season's end, Fearing approached the Rays with an ultimatum. The current arrangement took up a lot of his free time. He'd have to join the franchise full-time at a salary that could support his family, or he'd have to quit. Suddenly, Friedman left for the Dodgers, and Fearing had his pick between the Rays and the Dodgers. He chose Los Angeles, for Friedman offered him the chance to direct the team's research and development department. The traditional staffing model called for hiring passionate, underpaid undergraduates to learn on the job. Friedman and Fearing reasoned they could not afford to build that way, because they knew exactly how far ahead the industry leaders already were.

Instead, Fearing and holdover baseball-operations staffer Emilee Fragapane recruited candidates who held PhDs in a variety of fields, aiming for an advanced, interdisciplinary approach. Within three years, they hired six such staffers, two with degrees in biomedical engineering, two in statistics, one in quantitative psychology, and one in media arts and sciences. Including Fearing, that meant seven doctors operating out of one old clubhouse. One of them, Dan Cervone, coauthored a 2016 paper building an interface for users to query and examine the new Statcast tracking data, which the league had begun collecting and publishing the previous year. Three months later, the Dodgers hired him.

All told, there have been roughly a major league roster's worth of people performing research and development for the Dodgers in recent years. Organizations do not always make precise counts of such staffs public, but it is thought no team has employed more. *Sports Illustrated* reported that the Dodgers spent more on R&D in 2019 than any major league peer. "We kind of went from zero to 100," Fearing said. "It was only in hindsight that I realized that we ended up building the most robust analytics and R&D capacity in professional sports over four seasons."

That year, Fearing and Chan published an updated, peer-reviewed version of their paper on flexibility. By then, the smarter teams all understood the benefits, although stragglers remained. In April 2021, as he started his fifth season on the job, Diamondbacks manager Torey Lovullo told *The Athletic* that he had just changed his operating philosophy. He explained that he had asked his peers in Oakland and Tampa Bay, Bob Melvin and Kevin Cash, for advice over the off-season. "Their conclusion was that it takes twenty-six players to win a game, and when I heard that a bell went off for me," Lovullo said. "As a result, I have a rotation of players. . . . Different daily lineups and pinch-hitting also plays into our new approach."

Never mind that Lovullo had managed dozens of games against the Dodgers by that point, and the Dodgers consistently carried two or more bench players capable of competently hitting and playing five positions well. An added benefit of that kind of depth: because arbitration compensation is predicated on statistical accumulation, trimming even 10 percent of a player's playing time can meaningfully reduce his next-season salary. Conveniently, elite depth made for unassailable salary suppression. While players rarely complained about the tactics in public, plenty requested regular meetings with Dave Roberts to argue for more playing time. It was here he did his best work, calming players, convincing them their time could come. It didn't hurt, either, that what Dodgers players lost in arbitration earnings, they often made up in supplemental income from annual playoff shares that amounted to hundreds of thousands of dollars apiece. Players on lesser teams mimicking them could not say the same. As the Dodgers' style spread, players suffered financially.

Even the Dodgers' stars regularly rotated positions. In 2018, Cody Bellinger became the fourth major leaguer to appear at least sixty times at both first base and center field, a pair of positions that demand different levels of athleticism and thus do not typically mix. "It's just normal to me now," Bellinger said of playing them both. "People say it's weird. It's normal." In 2019, Max Muncy became the fifth major leaguer to appear at least sixty times at both first base and second base. This flexibility, or optionality, is essential to how the Dodgers operate. It frees them to pursue off-season and midseason improvements at more positions than their peers, because somebody can always slide somewhere to accommodate a newcomer. It liberates Roberts to use the best available pinch-hitter in any game situation and not burn another reserve to defend, because, again, somebody on the field can always slide somewhere. And it insulates the team against the impact of injury. No matter where the hurt player played, the team's best reserve can move from the bench into the lineup, because, of course, somebody—or somebodies—can always slide somewhere.

"Doug did a hell of a job pointing out that one-dimensional players are much more painful than you think, and multi-dimensional players are much more valuable than you think,"

Kyle Boddy said. "And the Dodgers built a position-player system that reflects that." They imported the principles to pitching, too, surely with private research in support; every prominent Dodgers starting-pitching prospect has been eased into the major leagues with shorter stints first. That both shielded them from some injury risk and prepared them for the more flexible roles the postseason demands. "What Doug is really good at is the boring shit," Boddy said. "It's very boring to talk about, like, organizational theory being revolutionary, but I really do believe that it's revolutionary."

Chan, Fearing's coauthor, remained in academia, leading research in the engineering of healthcare and artificial intelligence. He said Fearing could have returned to a university whenever he wished, making his sporting foray a free roll. "His management skills and demeanor make him really well-suited to be working in sport, where you're working in between the people playing and the people analyzing and you need someone to translate between the two," Chan said. "He does that perfectly."

Fearing sculpted the department with a sensibility that veered toward the corny, bookish, and fanatical. A sizable percentage of employees grew up cheering for the Dodgers. One data engineer, Drew Troxell, doubles as a moderator on the public Dodgers subreddit. One ex-analytics coordinator, Ben Zauzmer, published a model to annually predict the Academy Award winners. The systems platform director, John Focht, starred on *Jeopardy!* During his five-show run, another staffer suggested they create a win-probability model for the legendary game show. Focht forwarded links to models that already existed on the internet. "Much like everything else," Focht said the coworker replied, "we need to go beyond what's in the public domain, do research and do it better."

During Walker Buehler's breakout 2018, staffers plastered a Photoshopped *XXL* magazine cover on the door to the clubhouse, or R&D office. Buehler's face replaced that of the rapper Waka Flocka Flame. "Everybody loves Waka!" the headline read. Staffers continue to work out of the clubhouse in the off-season and during road trips, quiet days on Dodger Stadium's field level. They started to spend more time in the wild in 2017, visiting minor league stadiums, migrating east to Arizona in spring training to observe and brainstorm.

One March morning, likely in 2017, Dr. James Buffi lamented to Fearing that there had to be a better way to examine the pitching delivery. In the evening, they retreated to the sparsely furnished condominiums the Dodgers rented for staffers. Camelback Ranch is already quite a drive from Phoenix itself, and their temporary housing sat several miles west of the complex, far from any bars, restaurants, or young people. "There's nothing to do but think about pitching," Buffi said. "Maybe they did that on purpose."

Around midnight, their earlier conversation was still on Buffi's mind. He stood up from the standard-issue desk and began to mime a pitching delivery. A pitcher through high school, Buffi tends to act it out when in search of inspiration. He lives on the top floor of a Culver City apartment complex, and the denizens beneath him bang on their ceiling when he attempts too many late-night deliveries.

As his feet dug into the carpet, he had a realization. What was he doing but applying force to the ground, or collecting energy, and trying to translate it into velocity? What was the body but a collection of hinges and elements that power the hinges? Couldn't he apply everything he had learned in undergrad about designing efficient airplanes to his work with pitchers? "As an engineer at a company, you're trying to waste as little money as possible," he said. "Energy you don't actually use efficiently is essentially money lost. You burn the fuel, create the energy, and then the energy has to make it all the way through the physical machine and out the other end. Any wasted energy is wasted money—and pollution."

In that way, pitchers were just machines trying to efficiently use energy. "Wasting it," Buffi said, "is like wasting money, like wasting injury risk." Buffi likened a pitcher producing energy that did not make it to his arm to bolt cutters creating shear stress on a screw. Everything started to make more sense. "All of the things coaches were saying about here's how you can improve your delivery," he said, "I started connecting those things back to the physics principles, like, *Ohhhh*." Buffi had been analyzing pitching from a statistical prism, according to what had been the biomechanical standard. He, Fearing, and fellow PhD biomechanist Megan Schroeder examined every element within a pitcher's delivery, down to elbow angle at foot plant, and compared it with the same element of a harder-throwing pitcher's delivery, assuming the harder thrower had a better delivery. That produced some successes but more noise.

Examining every movement with efficiency in mind supplied more consistent results. Back at the office the next day, Buffi drew stick figures on his whiteboard and showed them to colleagues, explaining his realization. They laughed at his awful artwork while he ticked through the coaching concepts he had heard over and over since joining the Dodgers, suddenly better understanding why they had endured. Take hip-shoulder separation, a concept pitching coaches cite as a key to velocity. It goes back to the work-energy theorem: any work done on a body, human or not, creates an equal amount of kinetic energy in the body. In pitching, pitchers' lower halves do the work, and their upper halves receive the resulting energy. There are two ways to do more work: use more force or exert the force for a longer distance. A Prius can travel faster than a Model S, if it has way, way more space to accelerate. To further separate your hips and shoulders is to increase the distance over which you exert force. "What that means is even with the same torque, you can do more work on the upper half," Buffi said. "And doing more work adds more energy to the upper half, which can add more energy to the ball, which makes the ball go faster."

Some pitching coaches have intuitively understood this for decades, but relating it to a first principle enabled the Dodgers to study hip-shoulder separation, search for it, and develop it. Before he worked for the Dodgers, Buffi told reporter Jeff Passan, who wrote a book, *The Arm*, about the science of pitching, that he had no intentions of working for a team. He wanted to keep his findings public, and he needed to work with a clinician, "someone in science who can translate the findings into something that can train pitchers." But the allure of the Dodgers proved too strong. And what is an adept coach but a clinician?

Buffi learned that as he lingered in coaches' meeting rooms, especially in the minor leagues. He started to grasp how coaches could identify factors he could not. Once, he and a coach watched a prospect throw an awful, erratic bullpen session. Several pitches in, the coach asked what baseball the pitcher was using. He looked closely and saw it was a major league ball, slicker than what the minor leagues use. The coach handed the pitcher a minor league ball, and the pitcher began to hit his target. "You're telling me the balls are different?" Buffi asked the coach. He had no idea. Nor, when he joined the Dodgers, did he know there was a "whole underground baseball chemistry" industry distributing grippy material that allowed pitchers to increase their spin rate.

Historically, anyone paid to watch a pitcher's bullpen session would know all of that. In hiring outside experts, the Dodgers accepted that they would be plebes in certain spheres. Or, as players put it, they would "lack feel." Undeterred, Buffi began to research the differences in the balls and the effects on various materials on grip. He did not say, but it's likely the Dodgers employed modeling that predicted the effects of sticky concoctions on pitch performance long before MLB began enforcing a rule against them in 2021. Buffi did say he reported back his findings to coaches and players, on sticky stuff and on a variety of topics. "The education thing is a two-way street, and it ends up being a virtuous cycle, informing better research from the analysts and allowing for more conviction from the players," he said. "Also, they can start to connect their feelings and make adjustments more quickly and learn more quickly."

From polling Dodgers pitchers, Buffi learned that most experiments they conducted were trial-and-error in nature. They'd ask several peers for pitch grips and sample them, their decision depending on the imperfect measures of catchers' reviews and their own feelings. Using Rapsodo, Edgertronic, and KinaTrax technology, the Dodgers research and development department offered more specific suggestions and better measures of success. "The way your pitch characteristics look," Buffi said as an example, "we think this slider type will help you a ton, and we have objective information that will help you achieve that slider better."

That starts each year in spring training. In 2020, the Dodgers decided to wait at least a week before proposing new pitches. They wanted to be sure pitchers had settled into their mechanics before suggesting a change. Recent years had revealed the folly in doing otherwise. "I think some guys get infatuated with trying to develop a new pitch," said Connor McGuiness, the Dodgers' assistant pitching coach. "Especially in this new era, people have been chasing certain numbers, pitch characteristics, profiles, X-Y graphs [which illustrate pitch movement] and whatnot. But if your throw's messed up or you're changing your arm angle and everything, you can go down a really dark, slippery slope."

To McGuiness, pitchers slide down because of a fear of missing out. They see the success some of their peers have had with pitch design, and they want in. The Dodgers want to encourage that desire, but they want even more to preserve the skills at which their pitchers already excel. So they limit experimentation to ten or so minutes per spring bullpen session.

Sometimes, that window is enough to enact change. It worked for Ross Stripling in the spring of 2020. McGuiness had him alter his changeup grip by moving his ring finger a few millimeters. Suddenly, he threw the pitch almost 2 mph harder, with more than 100 more revolutions per minute. Edgertronic video showed it was less distinguishable out of hand than the pitch's previous iteration. McGuiness showed the results to Stripling, and Stripling approved. He threw the new changeup all season, even after an August trade to the Blue Jays. Opponents hit .174 and slugged .239 against it, compared with .269 and .385 the previous season. "The less we can do and still accomplish the goal, the better. It's not like you can just go in and rep out reps and keep trying to get a certain feeling. It's a little more sensitive than that," McGuiness said. "If we can accomplish a new pitch without changing arm action, that is the ultimate goal."

The research and development department also aims to provide unbiased reviews of experiments they don't hatch. In the summer of 2018, pitching coach Rick Honeycutt suggested Buehler switch his spike curveball to a conventional curveball. It was a relatively minor change, made because the spike curveball traveled too fast and didn't differentiate itself from the rest of his offerings. Buehler only altered the position of his index finger, draping it over the baseball instead of using the fingertip to grip the ball. He tried it out in one bullpen session and then, to see how it worked, a game. A postgame RPM printout showed a significant increase. "I talked to our nerd guys, and they're like, 'It had 300 more revolutions than your spike does,'" Buehler explained on Stripling's podcast. "It didn't feel great. I didn't love the look of it. But it's a way better pitch." Buehler continued to throw the traditional curveball in 2021. He said the data "gives you confidence to be able to go with something that you might be uncomfortable with."

Buffi, one of those nerd guys, listened to the episode and took note of how Buehler described their exchange for the next player conversation he'd have. He knew Buehler well, but few others, and he craved tips on getting through to pitchers. Buffi is quick with a compliment, quicker with a laugh. Before he met Dodgers players and coaches, he decided to downplay his doctorate and introduce himself as Jimmy. They picked up on his background anyway. "Doctor James," they started addressing him. When he wasn't around, he was a "nerd guy."

In fact, four of the Dodgers' nerds are women, including two of the department's leaders: Schroeder and Fragapane. In October 2016, the Dodgers sponsored Fragapane's trip to the Scouting Development Program, colloquially known as scout school, where, as it sounds, people learned to scout. She was one of two women in a class of several dozen. The other woman, former sportswriter Alexis Brudnicki, wrote in the *Hardball Times* that one would-be scout asked her to put on her proverbial earmuffs before one game while he and several peers graded women in the stands on the scouting scale. Fragapane said the experience gave her a new perspective. "We get stuck in the numbers, and it really helps to go talk to people and watch players more," she once told the *Los Angeles Times*. "It grants us a flip-side view of things that is really helpful." She soon transitioned to a conduit role between the nerds and the team's major league coaches. In 2021, she often watched the Dodgers take batting practice alongside trainers, coaches, and top executives.

On a 2021 panel on the league website, Fragapane alluded to intangible factors like personality—makeup, in baseball speak—that statistical models cannot and do not incorporate. "Trying to 'datafy' the idea of makeup is A, very difficult and B, it's very easy to then build bias into how you're measuring those things and how you're datafying something like makeup," she said. "At the very least, it's something that we are cognizant of and that I really appreciate, especially just even over the last few years, that it's at least on the radar in terms of something that we want to be aware of in how we go about our processes. Even if we don't have a lot of good solutions right now." Fearing, for his part, said humans over-attribute success and failure to makeup.

One curiosity competitors have noticed about the Dodgers' roster construction in recent seasons is its consistent dearth of diversity, especially considering the franchise's history as a trailblazer with Black and Asian players. In 2021, the average opening-day roster included more than seven players born outside the United States, according to the Associated Press. The Houston Astros, the most diverse team, carried fifteen foreigners; the Dodgers had three. The homogeneity is particularly noticeable among position players. The organization has not featured a foreign-born, internationally signed lineup contributor since Cuban outfielder Yasiel Puig, whom they traded in 2018. "I don't think any of that was intentional," Fearing said. "It certainly was not driven by the predictive models." Under Friedman, the

Dodgers have spent plenty to sign international prospects, but they have traded them more than developed them. Seven years in, the best foreign player they had unearthed was Yordan Álvarez. They dealt him to Houston for a reliever before he ever played a game in the organization.

Education is one possible source of the disparity. In the draft, almost all of the Dodgers' selections have attended at least a year of college, and often more. Most international prospects sign with MLB teams at sixteen and agree to terms long before that. As the way the game is taught becomes exponentially more complicated, international signees must confront a language barrier and a formal-education disadvantage. "We had a lot of conversations about: How do we make information and data more accessible to players who might not have an education background?" Fearing said. "That was an intentional focus of the organization's player development." Ehsan Bokhari, the team's quantitative psychology PhD, studied biases in decision making and biases that persist within models.

After the 2018 season, Fearing and Bokhari departed the Dodgers. Two more doctorate holders, Buffi and Cervone, left after 2019. Fearing cofounded Zelus Analytics, a firm that aims to concurrently function like a mini R&D department for several teams in each major sport. Buffi cofounded Reboot Motion, where he analyzes motion-capture data for sports teams, including MLB outfits. Bokhari became the Astros' R&D director. Cervone joined Fearing at Zelus.

New PhDs joined, including Justin Williams, a biostatistics expert who published papers on autism spectrum disorder and influenza's predisposal to secondary infections, and Jacob Coleman, a statistics expert who doubles as a semiprofessional ultimate Frisbee player. Another quantitative analyst, Nick Kapur, concurrently pursued a PhD in statistics. He created an app for the baseball team at his alma mater, North Carolina State, to visualize exit velocity by pitch location or type, count, and other factors.

How did the R&D roster impact the actual roster? NDAs limit the release of details. "The Dodgers are very careful about their employment agreements," one employee said. "You can't talk to the media, now or forever, about the Dodgers." We know a few concrete examples: They advised area scouts on unheralded players to see. Buffi said he and Schroeder spearheaded the emphasis of induced vertical break, also known as apparent rise, which Dodgers pitchers employed to great success. (Fastballs do not actually rise as they reach home plate, but backspin can make them fall less than expected. Players often describe the illusion as a rising fastball.) One analyst said on the *Measurables* podcast he spent much of 2020 working with the team's pro-scouting department to reimagine the way they measured catcher defense.

In time, the department split off into four groups: baseball systems, building and maintaining the computing infrastructure; quantitative analysis, conducting research using open-source programming languages R or Python and SQL; performance science, the home of the most cutting-edge work, exploring body movement; and baseball operations, performing advanced scouting and communicating with coaches. The Dodgers also began hiring in-uniform development coaches for each of their affiliates. Applicants were required to demonstrate programming-language knowledge. Coaches were a bridge between players and the front office. Development coaches buttressed the bridge.

It became clear that change in the minors came faster. Though the Dodgers R&D staffers worked in closer proximity to the Dodgers than most other team employees, those who worked outside of baseball operations rarely interacted with the players. "There's a lot of structure and formalities at the big-league wing of Dodger Stadium, and sometimes it can be a little difficult," Buffi said. "You don't want to mess with people's vibes. Candidly, it was easier to do this kind of thing on the minor-league side of the complex." And easier still to do it on your own.

# Chapter 11

ON MARCH 31, 2017, MAX MUNCY CALLED HIS future wife, Kellie, with some news. The Oakland Athletics had cut him. Three days before opening day, he was unemployed. She said he didn't sound upset. "I'm not," he said. "I'm kind of glad it's over." She flew to Arizona to accompany him on the drive home to Texas, and, along the way, they agreed the news was a relief. He had been depressed for many months. Years of desultory opportunities made him hate the game he had loved as long as he could remember.

Back at home with his parents, Muncy looked into finishing his general studies degree at Baylor, where he and Kellie had met and he had completed three years. The summer semester wouldn't start for two months, so he had some time. He used it to golf. Around his fourteenth day at home, he was watching more and more baseball in the evening, thinking about how he actually missed playing. He told his father, Lee, who suggested they get to work. "When it looked like it might be over," Lee Muncy said, "that's when it really hit him."

Every afternoon for a few weeks, the two Muncys met at Keller High, Max's alma mater, for hitting sessions. Max arrived first, bringing a bucket filled with sixty balls. Lee left early from work as a vice president at TransAtlantic Petroleum. To compensate for his aging arm, Lee set up halfway between the mound and home plate. Max emptied the bucket with five dozen swings before collecting the baseballs and repeating the effort. They worked through three or four buckets each day.

Lee's coaching days had long passed, but he replicated what he remembered. "Where was that pitch at?" he asked after most of his son's swings. "Where did you hit that?" By 2017, Lee had been doing that for decades. He grew up near Cleveland in the 1960s, playing baseball and rooting for the Indians. He played as far as community college before giving it up, transferring to Ohio State and obtaining a master's degree in geology. After his three sons were born and the family relocated to exurban Houston, he coached them all in the sport he loved. Maxwell, the youngest by nine years, displayed the strongest aptitude for the game.

At eighteen months old, his family members insist, Max Muncy could consistently hit a target with a throw from thirty feet. Typically, the target was a tree next to the field where his brothers played. At home, he emulated the swings he saw on television. He stretched his legs, bent his knees, and tried to crouch like only Jeff Bagwell could. He stood up straight, turned his toes inward a few degrees, and swung with Ken Griffey Jr.'s abandon. Lee learned to toss nerf balls to the side of the television so he could watch the game while Max, still in diapers, swung and swung with a souvenir bat. He made their living room his infield, the loveseat his second base.

Max is right-handed. But around the time of his birth, Lee read *The Duke of Flatbush*, Duke Snider's memoir of his Hall of Fame career. The Dodgers star was also right-handed, but his father, Ward Snider, insisted he bat left-handed as soon as he picked up a bat. He reasoned that such a stance would give his son a two-step head start on reaching first base. He examined the average dimensions of major league ballparks in the 1930s, noticed the right-field fence was often shorter, and made his decision, overriding his son's objections. Snider became a star by his twenty-third birthday, and as he aged he realized the gift his father had given him. Stadiums changed, but the distance from home to first stayed the same, and there were always more right-handed pitchers than left.

Lee Muncy resolved to endow his youngest with the same ability. He found it easier than Ward Snider had, for Max was a more agreeable child, and his brothers' superiority forced him to explore any possible edge. From oil and gas conferences, Lee brought home a bunch of branded stress balls printed to look like the earth, with raised continents that could function like seams. For years, Mike and Derek Muncy spun those suckers like hell to their poor little brother. "We could throw it much faster than he could swing," Derek Muncy said. "That's how he developed his eye, by being around the older kids and not being able to swing at the ball that felt like 100 mph. I think he just learned to watch the ball."

When he threw to him, Lee regularly instructed Max to swing at every pitch. It was a counterintuitive approach to instilling patience, but it worked. Because even when they were only hitting in the cage, Lee demanded that Max explain what each swing yielded. They drilled balls low and outside, where he used to pop up. They disputed some outcomes. "If you hit that pitch," Lee would tell him, "you're gonna pop it up."

Max became a versatile Little Leaguer, playing a number of positions, never sticking at one. His predominant skill was always his ability to draw walks. He did that by swinging only at strikes, by refraining from chasing the pitches pitchers wanted him to chase. He did that better than almost anyone. Lee had trained it into him at age six and again at twenty-six. His brothers had reinforced it.

Now, no one is more patient than Max Muncy. Year after year, he sees among the most pitches in the sport, about 4.4 per plate appearance. The league average tends to be about 3.9, though it has risen in recent seasons. The sport's most aggressive hitters, like Muncy's teammate Corey Seager, see about 3.4 pitches per plate appearance. Especially now that starting pitchers rarely last longer than one hundred pitches and relievers not often past thirty, forcing an extra four or five pitches per game can make a difference. With more pitches come more mistakes. These days, a mistake to Muncy often means a home run.

The power emerged out of work Muncy and Triple A hitting coach Shawn Wooten performed after he signed with the Dodgers. With his father, Muncy found fun again. With Wooten, Muncy rediscovered how he drove the ball. They watched clips of swings from his best professional season, 2013, and redid his current version to resemble them. In the intervening years, Muncy had gradually stood farther and farther up, like Griffey. That meant he couldn't keep his bat on the best possible plane to attack approaching pitches.

Wooten had Muncy resume crouching, not quite like Bagwell but closer to it. That sparked immediate improvement. When Muncy started his body lower, his swing caught baseballs while traveling upward, producing more power. "To be honest with you, it was kind of an easy adjustment," Wooten said. "It was just about knowing what the right adjustment is."

Muncy had never made the conscious choice to stand taller. It happened so slowly, over so many professional seasons, that he did not even notice. He knew only that he lost what he once had, not how. At Baylor, he had steadily hit for power while bouncing around the infield. It made sense, then, that Oakland drafted him in 2012. Muncy would have seamlessly fit into the Athletics' draft class of a decade earlier, the one memorialized in *Moneyball*. He got on base, and he looked a little different than the rest. In fact, his first time drafted, by Cleveland, his dad's childhood team, it was as a catcher, where his body type—"girthy," as a teammate put it—fit in fine.

His time in the Oakland organization started wonderfully. In his first full season, Muncy slugged twenty-one homers in ninety-three Class A games and earned the organization's player of the year award. He could not match that power output the next season, but in all of the minor leagues, only four of more than two thousand peers managed to draw more walks than his eighty-seven. Matt Olson, who'd soon supplant Muncy as Oakland's first baseman of the future, led all competitors. Joc Pederson, who'd soon accompany Muncy in the Los Angeles lineup, was second. Aaron Judge was third.

In April 2015, Muncy received his first big-league chance. Ben Zobrist, the man who had revolutionized utility play under Friedman, tore his left meniscus. On his first day, Muncy started at third base, ripping a single into center for his first hit. He waited twelve days until his next start, on getaway day in Minneapolis, where he skied a sacrifice fly to score the game's first run. Five more days lapsed before his third start and five more before his fourth.

That day, Muncy faced White Sox right-hander Jeff Samardzija. As he stood in for a second time, visiting broadcaster Hawk Harrelson introduced him as a career .270 hitter "with a little pop." "I was gonna say, just look at him," said color analyst Aaron Rowand, a retired outfielder. "He's a big boy." Muncy fell behind no balls to two strikes. Samardzija tried to force an end to the at-bat with a low fastball. But he missed up, and Muncy hammered the mistake to straightaway center field. The baseball cleared the fence by inches. Muncy had his first major league home run, and for the next two weeks, he had consistent playing time. Though he performed well, the opportunity vanished when Zobrist returned from injury.

The next season was the same. Muncy enjoyed a two-week stint as Oakland's right fielder, followed by a month-long chance to play second base. The first went OK; the second went terribly. In between, he played everywhere for Triple A Nashville. He continued to get on base but flashed little power. He was not an offensive threat. He was not having a good time. That off-season, the Athletics waived him and no team claimed him. Muncy reported to spring training as a minor leaguer, sensing the end was near.

After it arrived and he retreated to his parents' couch, Muncy heard from no baseball teams, stateside or international, for at least a week. Dodgers general manager Farhan Zaidi was the first team staffer to express interest in signing Muncy. And at first, it was only interest he expressed; the Dodgers did not yet have any space to place Muncy, nor an offer. That came together when Pederson, Muncy's old minor league peer, strained his groin. The timing was just right, as the Seattle Mariners had also reached out with an offer. To replace Pederson, the Dodgers made the aggressive decision to promote top prospect Cody Bellinger, then twenty-one, from Triple A. Muncy replaced Bellinger on the Triple A roster, first as a part-timer, soon an everyday player. He produced his best season yet, with more power and plenty of patience.

Spurred by Bellinger, who became the Rookie of the Year, the Dodgers dominated the league in 2017. One week before September call-ups began, they had won ninety-one games and lost thirty-six, good for an unprecedented .717 winning percentage. From there, it got weird. The Dodgers lost sixteen of their next seventeen games. The best became the worst, made all the more awkward because they had crowded their clubhouse with fourteen September call-ups, one short of the maximum. They'd never again approach that number.

Fourteen call-ups, and no Muncy. He was disappointed to be sent home, but the Dodgers soon offered him another minor league deal, for 2018, and he weighed it for a few weeks. Before the Dodgers made the World Series, he agreed to re-sign. Then he started training at Michael Johnson Performance, a capacious facility on the outskirts of the Dallas–Fort Worth Metroplex owned by the famed former sprinter. Every winter weekday, he worked out for two hours. After a dynamic warm-up, he did medicine-ball throws and footwork practice, agility exercises, sprints, and a full-body weight-training circuit. He reported to spring training 2018 slimmer and stronger than he had ever been. "Max, for him to be a steady player in the big leagues, he needed to take care of his body a little bit," said Chase Anderson, a major league pitcher who trained alongside him. "And he really did."

On April 17, 2018, Muncy received his eighth, and last, big-league call-up. The start to the Dodgers' season was a storm. Two of their key infielders were hurt, and Muncy, finally, was next in line. "I offer a left-handed bat and defensive versatility," he said the day he arrived. "That's what I'm going for right now." That was all the Dodgers were going for, too; he just stuck. He homered in his first start and five times in May.

He became a sensation before the solstice. In 101 June plate appearances, he homered ten times and walked twenty-five times. His on-base percentage was .465; his slugging percentage was .711. The team knew he could not keep this up, but encouraging signs kept appearing. "It's not one of those things where the league can figure him out," Dave Roberts said. "Because he's covering a lot of pitches. And he's not afraid to walk." Roberts did admit he had not been expecting his new infielder's "consistent slug." No one had.

"First, I was just happy he got a call-up," Lee Muncy said one Sunday in New York City, minutes before he saw his son smash his eighth June homer. "Then, he gets to the point where you're happy he's platooning a little bit. Then, he starts hitting lefties a little bit. Now you come to the ballpark and you expect him to be in the lineup. It's surreal."

Max's parents, Lee and Midge, were particularly in tune with their son's career. Whenever they attended his games, they made sure to arrive in time to scout his batting practice. They learned to detect his focus from afar and calibrate their expectations accordingly. While Max was at Baylor, one hundred miles from home, Midge and Lee attended 180 of his 184 college games. During his year in Oklahoma City, two hundred miles from home, they made it to most of the team's home games. And in 2018 and 2019, they attended dozens of Dodgers games. Of course, 2020 halted their streak. But on October 6, 2020, they became two of the first fans in America to attend a Major League Baseball game amid the pandemic.

By chance, the sport staged much of its postseason at Globe Life Field, twenty miles from the Muncy home. For the National League Division Series, only family members were permitted to enter. Those rooting on the Padres and the Dodgers sat on opposite ends of the stadium, at field level. In the Dodgers section were the Muncys; Mookie Betts's parents, in from Tennessee; Cody Bellinger's parents, in from Arizona; and Dustin May's parents, from fifteen miles past Keller.

For Muncy, the 2020 regular season had been a slog. He fractured his left ring finger just before opening day. At first, it seemed fine. He played through it and homered twice on Day 2. But by his thirtieth birthday, on August 25, his batting average was under .200, and it stayed there for most of the year. When Lee Muncy was growing up, even when Max Muncy was growing up, no .192 hitter would ever hit cleanup for an MLB team in October. Even in 2020, most teams wouldn't start such a player in that spot. But as much as peers have copied the Dodgers, most teams still don't think like the Dodgers.

In Muncy as of October 2020, the Dodgers saw a hitter who had not found his form in months, but was still taking pitches, still forcing opponents to work, still walking. His on-base percentage was above average. The Dodgers kept hitting him fourth in their order, surrounded by hitters who were performing far better.

He rewarded their faith. Muncy recaptured some of his lost power and paced the team in on-base percentage through their World Series run. Betts and Bellinger made the big defensive plays. Seager stroked all the line drives. Muncy got on base, as he always had. In fact, he did so about as well as Randy Arozarena, the postseason's breakout star. While Arozarena hit .377 and Muncy hit .250, only four percentage points separated their on-base marks.

There were three key differences between Muncy's attempts to stick in Oakland and his Dodgers tenure. First, and maybe most important, he was a different hitter by 2018, physically and mentally. He crouched into his stance, building a stronger base, and swung with an uppercut, launching the ball into the air with regularity. He did that while maintaining his elite discernment of balls from strikes.

Second, the Dodgers provided him an extended chance and an environment conducive to success. Under Friedman, the organization made a point of eschewing hazing while welcoming new players to the major league roster. Muncy did not have to carry anyone else's backpack or procure much beer or coffee. "He loved that about the Dodgers from Day 1, because they made him feel like he's part of the team," Lee Muncy said. "They didn't keep him in the dark. He likes to be informed and know what's going on. They communicate, moreso than other teams."

And third, he had already failed, already washed out of baseball. In Texas, and then in Los Angeles, he began to approach the game with more aggression and less fear. "The biggest change I made was the mental change, trying not to be depressed about baseball," Muncy said. "Just enjoy it, no matter what happens." He let himself enjoy his home runs, which sparked a few spats. When Giants left-hander Madison Bumgarner confronted him for admiring one lengthy drive he'd hit, Muncy advised him to get the baseball out of the ocean—referring to the San Francisco Bay. That line made its way onto viral T-shirts and gifted him confidence. A month later, Muncy roasted Phillies closer Hector Neris for shouting an expletive at the Dodgers' dugout following a save. "He's blown about eight saves against us over the last two years," Muncy said, "so I guess he was finally excited he got one." That barb made his teammates giggle in the Citizens Bank Park clubhouse.

He didn't speak up much, but when he felt compelled to fight back, his words were snappy. "He's still got that chip on his shoulder, he always will," Roberts said. "I think Max will never forget being at home watching baseball. That feeling never leaves you." The last major event Muncy watched as an outsider was the 2017 World Series.

# Chapter 12

A S THE DODGERS APPROACHED THE 2017 WORLD Series, they heard persistent rumors that the mighty Astros were cheating, were stealing signs in an illicit fashion. Much of the sport heard the rumors. And almost everyone who attended a game at Minute Maid Park in the summer of 2017 heard the trash-can bangs the Astros used to tell interested batters what was coming. Coaches and players steered a television into the clubhouse tunnel, cued a live broadcast, and clanged the can with a spare bat whenever they could tell an off-speed pitch was coming. They did this at least 1,143 times that year, according to an Astros fan who logged every audible bang on SignStealingScandal.com. A front office algorithm helped decipher complicated sets of signs so the bangs could continue in crucial situations.

Few connected the bangs to the rumors and on-field results. With ten days left in the regular season, a White Sox reliever named Danny Farquhar figured it out from the mound, but no reporters asked him about it, he never brought it up publicly, and the specifics remained a secret until *The Athletic* reported them in November 2019. In October 2017, the rumors were no more reliable than the rumors that the Dodgers were doing something, the Yankees were doing something, the Red Sox were doing something.

The Dodgers had confronted similar fears during past post-seasons. In one eighth-inning at-bat during the 2016 National League Championship Series, catcher Yasmani Grandal became convinced the Cubs' Ben Zobrist had decoded their signs and was signaling them from second base. Grandal made the sudden choice to change the Dodgers' sign system; he was pleased to see batter Addison Russell then refrain from swinging at several Joe Blanton sliders. Grandal described himself as "literally paranoid" about protecting the Dodgers' plans. "We know who is getting the signs," Grandal said after that game. "We know what they're doing. We know what they do to get it. In the playoffs, one relayed sign could mean the difference between winning the World Series and not getting there. That's why we have four or five different sets of signs, and we're constantly changing."

He meant when there were base runners who might see what signs he was using. This was traditional baseball gamesmanship, a technique pitchers and catchers strove to prevent but did not consider cheating. Grandal's paranoia had not yet extended to the then-unfamiliar concept of real-time sign stealing without runners on base, aided by technology. He spent hours poring over video before and after games, foraging for tells on his side and the opponent's. Chase Utley did the same, scrutinizing for accidental tips the pitcher provided about what he was throwing. Such research is authorized within the sport's rules, written and unwritten. In fact, many players revere traditional sign stealing and uncovering pitch tipping because of the work required to detect the relevant intelligence and act on it. Because they eliminated the need for that labor, most major leaguers saw the Astros' maneuvers as an obvious overstepping—in a word, cheating.

Some felt differently. As the scandal unfolded, Grandal, by then on the White Sox, indicated to the Chicago sports radio station 670 The Score that he didn't mind the Astros' efforts. "If you're not cheating," he said, "you're not trying." Other involved parties expressed skepticism that the team had even pulled off the procedure in the postseason. Joe Kelly, a member of the Red Sox team the 2017 Astros trounced in the first round, later compared cheating in the playoffs to escaping Alcatraz. "It's virtually impossible," he said.

So it was that most Dodgers deemed it unnecessary to use multiple signs when the bases were empty in the 2017 World Series. It did raise their suspicions when they noticed Astros catcher Brian McCann doing so for his pitchers during Game 1, at Dodger Stadium. Clearly, the Astros suspected their peers were cheating as they were. Dodgers outfielder Andre Ethier recalled to author Jon Weisman times when Houston's players came up to the Dodgers during that series. "They were questioning us, kind of half-joking, 'What are you guys doing? You guys are hitting the crap out of the ball,'" Ethier said. "That should have been the smoke right there. Obviously, they were doing something themselves, and they probably felt we were."

Some rivals remain convinced that the Dodgers staged their own illicit schemes, whether in 2017, 2018, or 2019, after which the league instituted changes that made it far harder. During the 2018 NLCS between the Dodgers and Brewers, anonymous Brewers sources told *The Athletic* the Dodgers were using a camera trained on the catcher's signs to decode their sequences. Informed of the allegations, Major League Baseball investigated but found no violations. In an appearance on the YES Network three years later, former Brewers catcher Erik Kratz referred to who could only be the Dodgers and claimed his team had "caught them doing something *almost* similar" to what the Astros eventually admitted. After he pitched at Dodger Stadium in May 2019, Mets ace Jacob deGrom wandered the grounds to scan for suspicious cameras, Andy Martino chronicled in *Cheated*. He found no evidence. During that series, Mets bench coach Jim Riggleman speculated that the Dodgers operated some sign-decoding system, clarifying that he believed it was within the rules. Others in the industry, unwilling to append their names to the assertion, also voice this. Some go so far as to suggest that the team's R&D department invented technology that allows them to algorithmically detect pitch-tipping from video, or at least narrow down the possibilities, a step up from the Astros' so-called Codebreaker system. Again, no evidence of this has been made public.

Nor is there persuasive evidence of exactly how or how much the Astros cheated in the 2017 World Series. Commissioner Rob Manfred's imprecise report on the scandal mentioned conflicting testimonies about whether the team's system continued unfettered. Sources told Martino it did, throughout the postseason, simply with extra care taken to promptly plug in and unplug the tunnel television before and after each game. To some who were inside Minute Maid Park that month, it seems improbable the trash-can scheme could consistently work in the playoffs. Nearly 20,000 more fans piled into the stadium for every postseason game than the regular-season weekday game when Farquhar caught the Astros. At crucial times in that World Series, it was dozens of decibels too loud for a bang to be reliably detected. It's possible they used a different signal. One theory involves bullpen coach Craig Bjornson, an earpiece, and his positioning in the bullpen. Alternate theories, like a buzzer affixed to players' chests, or a high-pitched whistle that only the Astros knew to listen for, have circulated on the internet, but do not hold up to audit.

It's more likely the Astros did not successfully cheat as often during the playoffs. It's even more likely the Dodgers will never know with precise certainty how and when the Astros cheated. Not because they don't want to know. Series participants have dispersed over the years, affording some former Dodgers the opportunity to ask former Astros, in confidence, what they did. One ex-Astro swore to one inquiring player there was never a buzzer. But the Dodgers will never know for sure if the cheating made the difference in the seven-game defeat, if the twenty-five run Game 5 would have been a little calmer, if Yu Darvish could have avoided wracking his brain to fix his pitch tipping, if Kenley

Jansen's poise would have emerged intact, if Clayton Kershaw's reputation would have rebounded earlier.

That realization deepened some players' frustration as the news emerged. They spent two years digesting one reality, then were forced to ingest another, incomplete version. In February 2018, a reporter asked Kershaw if he had moved on from the pain of the defeat. Kershaw said he was incapable of moving on. "I just kind of absorb it," he said. Asked if that was a healthy approach, he said he wasn't sure. "I'll let you know if I explode at some point." The next years brought their own fresh pain: two more Octobers where the Dodgers were among the few favorites, two more times Kershaw let down his team. And what was Kershaw's melancholic admission after 2019 that "everything people say is true right now about the postseason" but an explosion?

The Dodgers nursed a World Series hangover more than a month into 2018. The last time an Andrew Friedman team had made (and lost) the World Series, it experienced a similar effect the following year. "As bad as it is to say," Rays shortstop Jason Bartlett once told *Sports Illustrated*, "we probably tried to live off '08 in '09."

The Dodgers did the same. They began the 2018 season playing the game by rote. When one of baseball's worst teams swept them over four games in May, Dave Roberts neared nightly outbursts during his postgame press conferences. He always managed to stop short. The peak of his outward panic came on May 10, when he said he expected his players to be as frustrated as he was. "We better be ready to come play tomorrow," he said. Roberts knew the mood he presented would impact players' responses. "Because these guys were all watching me and seeing, 'Is he gonna get pissed? Is he gonna throw over a table? Is he gonna panic?'" he later said. "You won't see me panic."

On the afternoon of May 16, Roberts found comfort in the words of Winston Churchill. "When you're going through hell," he recited to beat reporters, "keep going." That night, the Dodgers lost their sixth straight game, their twenty-sixth in forty-two tries that season. "It's the same story," Roberts said. "We just didn't get it done." That was the worst it got. Justin Turner returned from injury, and Max Muncy emerged as a star. By June, the Dodgers were back in the race. They required an extra game to secure it, but they scuffled all the way back to win the division. In the postseason, they trounced Atlanta and outlasted Milwaukee to earn another World Series bid. There, they were overmatched against the Boston Red Sox.

The Dodgers' only win came courtesy of Muncy, who lifted a walk-off homer to left field in the eighteenth inning of the 440-minute Game 3. Muncy saw forty-six pitches that night, nine more than any other player, twenty-three from Red Sox reliever Nathan Eovaldi alone. (Eovaldi threw six-plus innings.) As usual, Muncy's patience enabled his success. He had seen so many of Eovaldi's pinpoint backdoor cutters that he recognized right away the flaw in his final one: it caught some plate. He met the pitch with the barrel of his bat, and a throng of teammates met Muncy at home plate to yank off his jersey. They profusely thanked him for freeing them to go home.

In Los Angeles, the series is best remembered for the next night's events, for one giant misunderstanding. Rich Hill spun his curveball just so, located his fastball, and dominated through six scoreless, pitch-efficient innings. In the bottom of the sixth, Roberts asked him how he was feeling, as is routine. Hill said he was doing well. But he was the most considerate ballplayer around, and he wanted Roberts to feel comfortable removing him if he deemed it best for the team. He told his manager to keep an eye on him.

Hill walked the first batter of the seventh inning but relocated his release point to strike out the second. At that point, eight outs from a tied series, Roberts decided to jog out to give Hill a boost. But Hill was turned toward the outfield when Roberts emerged, and he didn't see the urgency in his gait. He saw only his manager approaching him, so he did what pitchers are trained to in that instance: he handed him the ball. Roberts did not want the ball, but he believed it would be worse to hand it back. The two men reached a compromise neither wanted:

Roberts went to his beset bullpen, and the Dodgers squandered any chance they had at an upset. Afterward, Roberts revealed what Hill had said to him, insinuating that Hill had asked out of the contest. The next day, Hill felt compelled to clear his name by meeting with Roberts and, later, reporters. He was trying to be a good teammate, he said, not backing down from a challenge. Dodger Stadium fans mercilessly booed Roberts before the series's fifth and final game.

Over and over that off-season, Roberts found himself revisiting the sequence. "For me, it's just disappointing because I pride myself so much on communication," he said. "For me not to communicate to him and him not to know that I was going out there to support him and get him across the finish line, that's what gets my gut." The problem was that Roberts calibrated his communication standard to the typical high-level ballplayer, trained from youth to never show weakness. Hill's unselfishness ruptured his rubric. He didn't need to go out to the mound at all.

All that drama obscured the prevailing issue. All season, and at key times in postseasons past, the Dodgers had been unable to hit when it most mattered. When no one was on base, their offense was by far baseball's best, 18 percent better than any National League peer's in terms of one popular measure, Weighted Runs Created Plus. But with men on base, the Dodgers' wRC+ ranked thirteenth in the sport, roughly average. With runners in scoring position and two men out, they were 25 percent below average, third worst. Their batting average in those situations was the worst.

"You know our average in the World Series?" Roberts asked me that winter. I was unsure if he was speaking in the singular or plural, but he had the answers memorized: .205 in 2017, .180 in 2018. "We didn't get on base, we didn't hit, we didn't do anything," he said. "The bottom line is that we just didn't play well in the last two World Series. To win a championship, you've got to play well in the World Series, and we were outplayed in both. We play two good series and we've won back-to-back championships."

Club executives knew that to be true, even after it became clear that the Astros at least tried to cheat in the 2017 World Series. In Game 7, at Dodger Stadium, trash can bangs weren't to blame for their one hit in thirteen opportunities with runners in scoring position. The cheating influenced the series in innumerable ways, whether or not the World Series games themselves were successfully infiltrated. As one example: the Dodgers designed their preseries scouting reports based on the season's events, but the Astros had juked those stats. Marwin González wasn't near the threat the data made him out to be. But the Dodgers had their chances to hit their way to victory, and they flubbed them.

Baseball's postseason presents almost the opposite challenge of the regular season. The sport's six-month schedule is structured to reward redundancy and longevity. The worst teams have the best weeks; the best teams have the worst weeks. Come the fall, one bad week typically means the end. By following Doug Fearing's template and collecting more competent talent than their competitors, the Dodgers essentially solved the regular season. But the playoffs require excellence, not competence.

Minutes after the 2018 World Series, a reporter asked Kershaw what—who—the team was missing. He appeared to give the question thorough consideration before settling on an answer he knew all along. "We had so much depth at every single position," he said. "It might not be a personnel thing. It might just be a play-better thing."

Within days, Friedman set his sights on making the Dodgers play better, on fixing their postseason offense. Outwardly, he framed it as more of a league-wide predicament than a team plight. "Since I can remember being around advanced processes in the major leagues and player development at the major league level," he said, "the advancements on the run prevention side have dwarfed what's going on on the run scoring side." But internally the Dodgers demanded change, insisted on improvement.

Grandal and Yasiel Puig, the team's streakiest members, did not return in 2019. Friedman and the front office decided to replace Puig with prospect Alex Verdugo, who had the contact ability most of the team lacked. "Having different clubs at your disposal is helpful," Friedman said. They also replaced experienced hitting coach Turner Ward with Robert Van Scoyoc, then thirty-two, the Craig Wallenbrock acolyte who registered one hit his senior season of high school and hardly played in junior college. Brant Brown, he who once coached Van Scoyoc, became the Dodgers' hitting strategist. Brown was fond of saying the two functioned as a "Batman and Batman" combination.

In some industry insiders' estimation, Van Scoyoc was the most unconventional coaching hire the sport had ever seen. But the Dodgers correctly guessed that he would have credibility in their cage because of his high-profile success stories. J. D. Martinez was the bigger nationwide name, but Chris Taylor vouched plenty for Van Scoyoc. He had already recommended him to his closest friends in the sport. Van Scoyoc studied video clips of every Dodger hitter: clips from his career year, clips from his nadir, clips from in between. He arrived at spring training with a plan for each of them that he revealed upon request. "It's a completely different feel than what Turner brought last year," Muncy said that spring. "Turner played for twelve, thirteen years in the big leagues. He's been there. You respect his knowledge, how he goes about the certain picture. Rob's gonna be more of a, 'Hey, here's what the information says. Here's what we need to be doing.'"

Muncy was among those open to the information. He pointed to Trevor Bauer's past project studying frame-by-frame footage of Corey Kluber's two-seam fastball and creating his own pitch in that image. Hitters, he said, could do nothing of the sort. "Trying to find something that can help close the gap is, at this point, a necessity," Muncy said, two years before the league-wide hitting slump that began the 2021 season. "The pitching side is so much more advanced than hitting right now. We're doing our best to keep up with it, but they're getting on a whole other level."

Van Scoyoc understood the uniqueness of his hiring, but he overflowed with conviction in his capabilities. His methods worked on players in part because he projected as much self-assurance as they did. They were not used to witnessing that. "This is a results business," he said. "I don't think I would be in the position that I am if I hadn't proven that I can get results. I'm not afraid of that."

The Dodgers had been obtaining results for years, only not in the postseason. To combat that, one of the coaches' key messages was practicality. "We know we hit homers, we know we're a good offense, we know we're very skilled, we know we're very deep," Brown said. "But what if none of that is going right that night? What can we do to win that game? Basically, the question is: How good can you be when you're going bad?" Brown emphasized the value of two-strike and two-out hitting. "Sometimes, as a staff member, when you announce something or make visible that it's important, then they'll pay more attention to it," Brown said. "So we've been trying to set more value on it."

Part of the plan involved less work. During their season-opening homestand, the Dodgers did not staff the batting cages until five hours before first pitch for night games, an hour later than many players previously hit. The expressed goal was to limit the accumulated workload for the hitters and the hitting coaches. "You gotta put some boundaries around some of these guys," Roberts said. "Because they want to work hard, which is a great thing. But to what end? For some of these guys, there's anxiety involved."

Cody Bellinger noticed the change when he tried to hit before the season's second game. It did not stop him from hitting more homers in the first series than he had in the 2018 season's first month. In the four-game set, the Dodgers notched forty-two runs, a Los Angeles–era record for the franchise in a series of that length. The players did not lodge a protest over the restrictions. "Part of the reason why a lot of us are very good is because we like to get in there and work," Muncy said. "But we're human and the coaches are human, so sometimes you have to put restraints on people to make sure everyone realizes we all need breaks here and there—coaching staff included."

When the Dodgers set off on their first road trip, staffers from a Texas virtual-reality company founded by former Rockies general manager Dan O'Dowd and his son visited Dodger Stadium to install their technology in the team's weight room. By the second trip, players were stepping into imaginary batter's boxes in spare rooms near clubhouses to don Win Reality's portable headset. Bellinger, the sport's hottest hitter, slipped on his batting gloves and grabbed a bat to do so in Milwaukee. A strength and conditioning coach positioned the headset, and Bellinger swung away.

Television camera operators have learned to linger on Bellinger's blank and confused expressions during games. His mien has made him an internet legend. It also captures an essential feature of his personality. Once, he plopped a frozen pizza onto a plastic cutting board and straight into the oven. Another time, he referred to advanced metrics as "the metric system," conflating two unfamiliar subjects. Many times, he used his credit card to withdraw cash from a ballpark ATM, unaware debit cards enabled the same action with far fewer fees. Bellinger's teammates loved to mock him for his ignorance, and Bellinger embraced their teasing.

The son of a bit player from the Yankees' last dynasty, Bellinger possesses a preternatural ability to put failure behind him. His brain lingers on little. It's both a strength and a weakness, because he often lost sight of what made him successful. Or he never knew. "My whole life, I was just swinging," Bellinger once said. "I never had an understanding of what I was really doing. I was just talented enough to keep hitting the ball and have results."

After he became a breakout star in 2017, he played only passably through the first months of 2018. As they pushed for a playoff spot, the Dodgers declined to play him against most left-handed starters. Bellinger reserved his dissent until the following spring, when he argued that he deserved to play every day. "Even when I'm not good," he said, "I'm still really good." He had a point. His skills on the bases and on defense made him valuable—at least playable—even when he was struggling to hit. And he had a higher ceiling, as evidenced by his MVP season in 2019.

On the morning the Dodgers assembled for their first full-squad workout every year, Roberts liked to invite a veteran to address the team after him. In 2019, he asked David Freese, who had supplanted Bellinger against lefties the previous fall. Freese said the Dodgers' upcoming season did not have to be about avenging the 2017 or 2018 World Series. "What's the point?" Freese asked his teammates. "If you keep turning that up," he said, "you're gonna get exhausted." Teammates applauded his message. Even before he spoke, they said, they had learned their lesson. "Playing game 163, you realize that it's not gonna just happen again," said Hill, the team's eldest player.

Since Friedman's first season, the Dodgers had made it a point to carry a veteran or two who functioned as a part-time coach. The first man to fill that role was Utley, a borderline Hall of Famer who approached the game with unsmiling seriousness. He predated Roberts and might have held more influence. In an effort to be like Utley, his younger teammates changed the way they ate, worked out, positioned themselves on defense, and ran to first base on routine grounders. "He's changed everything, man," said one devotee, Kiké Hernández. "If I end up having a pretty successful career, whether he likes it or not, he's gonna have a lot to do with it."

Hernández so worshipped Utley, he wanted to be him. Three weeks after Utley announced his retirement in the summer of 2018, comedian Kevin Hart visited Dodger Stadium to film an episode of a YouTube workout show. A set staffer asked players to sign a consent form. Hernández signed his as Utley, posed for a photo with the paper in hand, and giddily decamped. By the spring of 2019, several players joined Hernández in following Utley's dairy-free diet: Turner, Jansen, Muncy, and Corey Seager. To a man, they swore it slashed bodily inflammation. After he heard all about it in 2020, Mookie Betts experimented even further by going fully vegan.

With Utley on his way out, Friedman acquired Freese for the final month of 2018. In terms of championship win probability added, Freese was the best postseason performer in baseball history. Like Utley, he commanded respect because of his consistency and history. He wielded it, suggesting that reserve players spend the early hours of each game not relaxing but preparing for the likelihood they would be deployed. "He wants to keep the tradition going of the veteran presence," said third-base coach Dino Ebel. "He's not afraid to approach and say, 'Hey, listen, maybe you can do it this way.'"

The Dodgers cruised to a division title in 2019. With their lead at fourteen games in mid-July, Roberts said he was having no trouble keeping the team focused. They governed themselves. "And if not," he said, "they have David Freese to answer to." That season, Freese was joined by catcher Russell Martin, a former All-Star who remained an adequate role player near the end. Martin started to accompany Verdugo wherever he went on road trips, as a chaperone of sorts. When the two visited a St. Petersburg beach on a travel day, it was Martin, thirteen years older, who made sure they departed in time to catch the airport-bound team bus.

He was OK being phased out. The very day the Dodgers anointed Will Smith their primary catcher, Martin provided him a learning experience. In the seventh inning of a tied game in Washington, DC, Martin straddled home plate while he prepared to receive a throw from the outfield. Believing he would be ruled safe because Martin blocked his lane into home plate, Nationals base runner Gerardo Parra did not bother to attempt a slide, and Martin tagged him out. The Nationals challenged the call to no avail. "Honestly," Washington manager Dave Martinez said, "Martin blocked the plate."

Watching from the Dodgers' dugout, Smith agreed with the opponent. "I saw it and I was like, 'Oh, that's definitely not a lane,'" he said. But it was a lane, for Martin had capitalized on a technicality. Parra was out because Martin had left inches of space in front of him that qualified as a path to the plate. After Martin explained it to him, Smith stood slack jawed. "He knows what it takes to win," Smith said. "I'm always trying to pick his brain or learn little bits of wisdom or see what he does."

Those tips helped the Dodgers again advance to the National League Division Series, against the Nationals, where Freese and Martin each hit a cool .500. But the part-timers, the depth, could only do so much. Bellinger again struggled. Roberts again made the confounding decision to entrust Kershaw with outsized responsibility. The Dodgers floundered once more. For the fourth consecutive year, the eventual champions ended their season. It was futile for the Dodgers to keep hoping their competency would win out in October. They needed another position player they could count on for excellence.

Enter Mookie Betts.

# Chapter 13

T HE MORNING OF FEBRUARY 19 BROUGHT THE 2020 Dodgers' first full-squad workout. Dave Roberts planned for Kenley Jansen and Mookie Betts to follow him to the dais, and, for context, he informed them earlier in the day what he planned to say. His theme would center on the idea of a winning player. It wasn't just about the wins, he'd say; it was about how hard they tried each day. He asked Jansen and Betts what they thought about that. Betts only nodded, offering no hints at what he had planned. After Roberts and Jansen spoke, he stood up and unloaded on his new teammates.

Betts had been on the team for nine days, but he had seen enough to make a confident determination: his new teammates lacked intensity in their preparation. This, he thought, was how his Red Sox had trounced them in the 2018 World Series. So he said as much. He added that the Dodgers needed to treat every day like it was Game 7 of the World Series, so that when they arrived at the World Series, there would be no additional pressure.

The criticism confounded some returning team members. Effort had not been the 2019 Dodgers' undoing. They had smarted from the previous year, developing a reputation as some of the sport's hardest chargers. Rival evaluators frequently ranked their effort atop the National League. But Betts demanded a different degree of attention, and he saw the unfurling fallout from the Astros' scandal distracting the Dodgers. Others witnessed the same. "There's a lot of anger being built up inside," Max Muncy said. Players were furious with Rob Manfred for calling the World Series trophy a "piece of metal"; with Astros owner Jim Crane for claiming their cheating "didn't impact the game"; with Astros leader Carlos Correa for insisting they won the championship fair and square and telling Cody Bellinger to "shut the fuck up" for arguing otherwise. Most of all, the Dodgers were outraged that Manfred had granted all the Astros immunity while investigating their wrongdoing.

It was a tense time. Betts meant for his message to come across as a challenge, and he did not care if it came off as a little raw. "He could say it a little bit nicer, some words," Dodgers reliever Joe Kelly said months later on WEEI's *Bradfo Sho* podcast. "It was very well accepted. But if he could've said it a little bit nicer, or articulated it a little bit better, I think it would've came off stronger." As part of his speech, Betts proposed a new rule. Any time a Dodger made a mistake, in a practice or a game, he had to relinquish twenty dollars. Players moved past the Astros and embraced the concept of an error charge. It became a daily topic in the dugout and on the back fields, though no money was actually collected. Most major leaguers valued impressing their peers over a twenty anyway. For whatever little it was worth, the Dodgers dominated Cactus League play.

Two weeks after he spoke, Betts fell ill. He knew what was troubling him, because it comes up once a year: food poisoning. But this was March 2020, so the Dodgers had him examined by team doctors, who confirmed that he had not fallen ill with the novel coronavirus. By the time Betts returned to action, it was March 11, and the world was about to stop. While the Dodgers were playing an exhibition that night, the NBA indefinitely postponed its season. The next day, Major League Baseball postponed its by two weeks. Within a few days, as stay-at-home orders went into place, the postponement became indefinite. Teams closed their complexes and sent their players home.

Like many other Americans with disposable income, Andrew Friedman rode out the shutdown on a Peloton stationary bicycle. His was inside his home office in his palatial Pasadena estate. His players tried to get outside to keep up their game shape, in the hopes there would be some sort of 2020 season. They confronted varying levels of difficulty.

Jansen had custom built a sizable gym in his Palos Verdes mansion, but he lacked a sixty-foot yard, so he threw makeshift bullpen sessions in the middle of his cul-de-sac. Brandon McDaniel, the Dodgers' director of player performance, kneeled onto the cement to catch him. He also fielded the confused questions from Jansen's nonagenarian neighbor. Austin Barnes hopped a fence to play catch with his brother on a Riverside high school football field, absconding when a security guard spotted them. Betts sought out new hobbies to pass the time and hardly practiced baseball. He learned to fish instead, learned catfish were catchable when rain was coming, learned to fillet and fry them at home.

For the latter half of March and most of April, pitching coach Mark Prior functioned as a counselor, acknowledging and comforting disappointed players. Most had stopped or slowed their throwing, and he let them wallow in the disruption of their routine. As May approached and the framework of a potential season emerged, he pivoted into what he called confidence maintenance. He spoke to pitchers at least once per week, generally in the afternoons, after their workouts and after he helped his children learn their California history. He watched their video clips and reminded them of potential go days, when ramp-ups would begin in earnest.

Teams officially began their second spring trainings on July 1, twenty-two days before the rescheduled opening day. A normal year allowed for twice as much time, to accommodate position players, who generally require more time to prepare to face live pitching. That meant many hitters were disadvantaged in the first weeks of the 2020 regular season, but not the Dodgers. Most of theirs had been training, with coaches, for more than a month.

On May 12, Arizona governor Doug Ducey allowed teams to open their in-state stadiums to players. Two of the Dodgers' hitting coaches, Brant Brown and Aaron Bates, lived in Arizona. Another, Robert Van Scoyoc, lived in suburban Southern California. The next week, Brown and Bates started supervising morning workouts at Camelback Ranch. Bellinger, Muncy, Zach McKinstry, Matt Beaty, and Kiké Hernández hit there almost daily, facing a minor leaguer and reliever Pedro Báez. Van Scoyoc soon led more hitters at Dodger Stadium: Corey Seager, Chris Taylor, Justin Turner, and, sometimes, Joc Pederson. On occasion, Jansen pitched to them.

The Dodgers also repurposed the coaches into draft evaluators in their spare time. Ahead of the shortened June 10 and 11 affair, Bates, Van Scoyoc, and Brown watched video of top hitting prospects; Prior and McGuiness studied pitching prospects. It was the updated, pandemic version of the way Friedman once sent special assistants across the country.

Meanwhile, several Dodgers battled COVID-19, and players and owners fought, bitterly and publicly, about the structure of a season. The two sides could not even agree on if they had reached a previous agreement, in March, governing prorated pay. Owners tried the widely ridiculed tack of proposing the same poor offer in different ways. Turner sent out a nineteen-tweet thread quoting a *Baseball Prospectus* article about Cardinals owner Bill DeWitt's deceitful claim that the baseball industry was not profitable. The league eventually imposed a sixty-game season, at full prorated pay, with no fans in the stands, COVID testing every other day, and many specifics still to be sorted out. Plans for an expanded postseason field were announced on opening day. Plans for a postseason bubble were announced in mid-September, about a week before the league required involved parties to quarantine.

As the season neared, Betts struck a pessimistic tone. He criticized the league for its nonresponse to George Floyd's murder and the increasing calls for societal reform. He expressed concern about the laxity in the league's coronavirus protocols. He said he could not be confident the season would be completed. Others with the team were more convinced, but they expected hurdles along the way. "I think there's no question we're going to have a decent number of positive tests, in spring training and the season," Friedman said. In that estimation, he was happily wrong. COVID-19 affected the Dodgers organization, as it did most on earth. Two of the team's international scouts died from the virus. But the Dodgers traversed the entire regular season without a player testing positive for the virus. Several players had COVID-19 in 2020, and others had it in 2021, but no one had it in season. Frequent testing, it was clear, helped reduce the virus's spread.

On opening day, Betts decided to kneel during the national anthem in protest of racial injustice, reversing his earlier stance against kneeling that he described as uninformed. One day earlier, he had signed a $365 million contract with the Dodgers, tying himself to the franchise through 2032. The deal included $65 million dollars referred to as a signing bonus, though he did not receive all of it upon signing. Rather, Betts will receive the money in installments for years to come. Mechanizing it as a signing bonus served two purposes: It made the money eligible to be taxed in Tennessee, where there is no state income tax, rather than California, where there is a sizable one. If the rates remain the same until 2035, the maneuver could divert nearly $8 million from California's coffers to Betts's pockets. And the bonus structure rendered the payouts immune to any work stoppage or cancellation of games. If there was a year-long lockout or the pandemic prevented the playing of future games, the bonus would be unaffected.

The extension emboldened Betts to keep speaking up. The 2020 Dodgers grew to mirror his consistency. Like he had limited his slumps, they halted all their losing streaks at two games. How do you quantify consistency? There is certainly no publicly available measure. But when you witness it, you tend to ponder that question. "That focus, that consistency, I don't know how much better it made other guys in this clubhouse," Clayton Kershaw said. "But I know it did some."

As he watched *The Last Dance* in 2020 and followed the Dodgers from afar, Betts's old first-base coach with the Red Sox, Tom Goodwin, likened Betts to a modern-day Michael Jordan. "I've never seen anybody as committed," Goodwin said. "At first it was just him, but now that he's with the Dodgers, he seems to be calling on his teammates to improve."

The team's role players particularly benefited from Betts's coaching touch. Backup catcher Austin Barnes could've been lifted directly out of a mid-1990s Chicago Bulls bench, scrappy and always ready for action. His uncle, Mike Gallego, wheedled a thirteen-year major league career out of his five-foot-eight, 160-pound frame. Barnes was only marginally larger. On the same WEEI podcast, Kelly named Barnes as one of five lifetime teammates he'd pick to back him up in a brawl. "Austin Barnes, his mentality towards everything in life is just to be a fighter," said Eugene Bleecker, a private hitting coach with whom he previously worked. Barnes, predictably, compared the 2020 season to "street baseball" because of the absence of fans. "Your team versus their team," he said, "whoever wants it more."

His pugilistic sensibility served as a strength. It earned him Kershaw's trust, as he became the pitcher's personal catcher. Kershaw told A. J. Ellis, his friend who once held that role, that Barnes was always willing to wrestle with his stubbornness and force him to be creative. But Barnes's outlook hurt him whenever he started slumping.

Because of his role, he often went days without playing. He spent most of that time thinking about what he had been doing wrong, air swinging in the clubhouse at all hours, repeatedly visiting the batting cage. In Barnes, Betts recognized his own traits reflected back at him. He watched Barnes hit in the cage several times, then offered a few unsolicited suggestions. Neither player has ever revealed the exact content of the message; part of Barnes's fighter mentality involves wordlessly protecting his teammates' secrets. But in an interview with the team's official radio station, Barnes said that Betts supplied him some missing clarity.

"Hitting is hard, but I was making it really hard," he said. "I was probably trying to do a little too much and probably over-swinging a little bit." When Barnes hit his first home run the following week, Kelly suggested that it encouraged Betts to immediately follow with his own home run, his second of the game. An inning later, Betts swatted his third. "Mookie gets pumped on stuff like that," Kelly also said on the station, "when he helps people out and sees success."

Roberts said he had never seen a superstar as engaged as Betts with his teammates. He did not recite all the stars with whom he had shared spaces over his twenty-something years in professional baseball, but they are many: Hall of Famers Jim Thome, Roberto Alomar, Pedro Martínez, Mike Piazza, and Trevor Hoffman; future Hall of Famers Adrián Beltré, David Ortiz, and Kershaw; Hall of Famers on their on-field merits Barry Bonds, Curt Schilling, and Manny Ramirez; and numerous MVPs and Cy Young winners. "I think Mookie has this ability and understanding that to win a championship, you've got to elevate everybody around you," Roberts said. "That's coaches included."

The Dodgers tried to begin the season using Betts in varied lineup spots depending on the pitcher. Once Roberts acceded to his appeals and installed him as the everyday leadoff hitter, Betts and Seager formed a prolific partnership. All year, Seager kept in the kind of form the Dodgers had not seen from him in years. He arrived at spring training healthy and never stopped hitting during the shutdown. He spent most of it in Los Angeles, but also trekked to Minneapolis to visit with Wooten, his trusted hitting coach.

Seager was the lone Dodger who preferred to hit with minimal intervention from the team's coaches. He generally preferred to be alone. "In a perfect world, just let Corey be himself," said Ross Stripling, his former teammate and roommate.

"He's gonna hit with the coach he wants to hit with. He's gonna roll into the field. He's gonna put AirPods in. He's gonna video all of them, evaluate them at his locker, and if you just let him do that, he's gonna hit .310 with twenty-five [homers]. He's just that good."

Seager is the most talented member of an accomplished baseball family. His eldest brother, Kyle, is more than six years older, four inches shorter, significantly stouter, and infinitely balder. He also made the major leagues when Corey was seventeen, supplying his kid brother one more advantage. Corey knew better than most how he projected. Ned Colletti, who drafted him out of high school in 2012, said Seager grasped his gift better than any teen ballplayer he'd ever observed. "He's always had this ability, this presence, at an early age, to understand the dynamics of who he is and what he does," Colletti said.

Kelly was the anti-Seager, the rare major leaguer to whom baseball was a true team sport. Players reach the pinnacle by focusing on themselves. Most don't think they'll thrive or even survive if they stop. After an arduous childhood roiled by his parents' divorce and alcoholism, Kelly's main motivation in adulthood was to back his brethren. Before he joined the Dodgers, he had closed the door on their 2018 team. He sprinted in from Dodger Stadium's visiting bullpen in the final game of the World Series, thinking about all the spirits he was going to crush on behalf of the Boston Red Sox. He threw the Dodgers fastball after fastball, his best pitch.

When Bellinger swung at the sixteenth and missed it, ending the eighth inning, Kelly marched toward his teammates while hollering obscenities, wagging his head back and forth, and banging his fist on his chest. "I saw twenty-five guys getting hyped as if I just crossed somebody over and hit a step-back three," he said. "That moment was the first time in my life where I thought, 'I deserve this shit. I've worked hard for this. My teammates have worked hard for this. I deserve to act like an idiot.' I've never felt that, and I was finally able to enjoy it."

Six weeks later, Kelly signed with the Dodgers for $25 million over three years. They acquired him because of his pitching potential, but for that they overpaid. Kelly remained an inconsistent pitcher throughout his tenure, continuing Friedman's free-agent failures.

Two years into his Dodgers tenure, Friedman famously told reporters that rationality in free agency would never net a team a player. Two teams would always be willing to get silly. "I just may not be good at my job, but I think it's really tough," he later said. He expected it to be his primary weakness when he took the Dodgers job, in part because he brought very little experience pursuing top-tier free agents. The Rays rarely even considered signing such players. "We were protected from ourselves, because of our resources," Friedman said.

In Kelly's case, the Dodgers determined his clubhouse presence would supply a side benefit. They underestimated that. Kelly quickly became the team's resident hype man, their wild card, at times their id. "Joe's just an entertaining person," Kershaw said. He and Bellinger, seven years apart in age, formed a natural friendship, for Kelly was a kid at heart. Many of Kelly's new teammates adopted restrictive, dairy-free diets over the 2018–2019 off-season, and the Dodgers provided strictly nutritious food at their complex. His first weeks with the team, Kelly brought in temptingly greasy bags of Jack in the Box breakfast sandwiches and boxes of warm donuts. He soon invited the team to his house for a Cajun crawfish boil he prepared. In a harbinger of his Dodgers tenure, he hurt his back while minding the pot for five hours.

During the shutdown, Kelly's wife, pregnant with twins, posted a video of her husband breaking a window at the couple's home with an errant pitch. The internet had a grand old time at his expense, admiring a professional pitcher's abject absence of command. Kelly had not been throwing a baseball but a CleanFuego, the puck-like training tool the Dodgers popularized that was much easier to throw away than a baseball. It was designed to fly away when thrown at all improperly. Kelly didn't bother pointing that out, for he was an entertainer at heart. Conveniently, the clip also provided a halfway plausible defense for his exploits on the 2020 season's sixth day.

Roberts called Kelly into the sixth inning of a three-run game at Minute Maid Park, the Dodgers' first there since Game 5 of the 2017 World Series. After quickly retiring José Altuve, Kelly fell behind, three balls to no strikes, on Alex Bregman. Kelly's fourth pitch was a fastball behind Bregman's head. He yawned while Bregman walked to first. After another walk, Kelly spun a first-pitch curveball at Carlos Correa's head. Correa ducked, then glared at Kelly, then toward the Dodgers' dugout. When Correa struck out on a curveball to end the inning, Kelly told him, "Nice swing, bitch," according to Astros manager Dusty Baker. Several Astros started to yell at Kelly. His response made him a Los Angeles legend, the subject of a Sunset Boulevard mural. He tucked his upper lip, extended his lower lip, and made a pouty face toward Correa as he retreated to the dugout. "I guess my expression was what I interpreted in my head what he was saying," Kelly later explained.

Both benches cleared, though only words were exchanged. Kelly denied any intent, citing the viral video. "My accuracy isn't the best," he said. "I broke my window with my newborns coming, two days before they were born." Before the next day's game, MLB suspended him eight games and Roberts one. Such a league response had long been the expected outcome. "Somebody will take it into their own hands, and they'll get suspended more games than any of those guys got for the biggest cheating scandal in 100 years," Dodgers left-hander Alex Wood had said in February. "It'll be pretty ironic when that happens, because I'm sure that's how it'll end up playing out." The only surprise was that a Dodger was responsible, because the pre-pandemic schedule did not call for the teams to meet.

Kelly has never admitted he threw the pitches on purpose. Notably, he doubted that the Astros had actually cheated in the postseason. But he has provided plenty of motive. Five days after the incident, he appeared on Stripling's podcast and accused the Astros players, not the coaching staff, of running their cheating scheme. After serving as the Astros' bench coach in 2017, Alex Cora managed the Red Sox in 2018, and Kelly grew to adore him. Kelly could not stand that Cora and his family were punished for the Houston scandal and the players were not.

The way he grew up, he was always going to do something about it. "If we're wearing the same uniform and someone runs up on you, I'm gonna have your back right away, even if I don't know your character," Kelly once said. "When the pressure gets big, I want to attack it. When the anxiety is up, I want to be the guy to lead."

On the podcast, Kelly referenced Cora's eldest daughter, who was pulled out of her junior high school because of what he described as verbal abuse. "The players get the immunity, and all they have to do is go snitch like a little bitch," Kelly said. "When you taint someone's name to save your own name, that is one of the worst things that you could probably do as a person. It really friggin' bugs me. I think I'll be irritated forever."

Stripling waited to release the episode until MLB heard Kelly's appeal and reduced his suspension from eight to five games. By then, Kelly was injured again. Come September, he had been on the injured list for a month, with only nineteen outs to his name for the year. Players in that position do not often speak up, and that was easier than ever in 2020, with reporters not permitted in the clubhouse. Kelly found a way anyway. Asked on a Zoom about another player's shorter suspension for a similar action, he said he suspected MLB was "just throwing shit out there." He volunteered a prediction about the Dodgers' historic excellence. "Long season, we would've broken all the records," he said. "Short season, we're gonna break all the records." He was right.

The 2020 Dodgers did not have the benefit of 162 games to prove their mettle, but they did have a designated hitter and extra roster spots. Their depth uniquely positioned them to maximize both allotments, as usual.

In 2019, Pederson had smashed thirty-six home runs, or one every 12.5 times he batted, a Ruthian effort. The performance rated 27 percent better than average. In this century's first decade, a hitter like him would have approached, if not surpassed, $50 million on his first free-agent contract. But the Dodgers didn't use Pederson like other teams would. Despite his steady success, he for years remained a part-time player, rarely batting against left-handed pitching. There's sense in it: the Dodgers often had superior options, and the statistics show he's better against right-handed pitchers. But if he played every day, which he steadily petitioned to do, his home run totals would look even better. That would present well in arbitration.

For 2020, his final season subject to arbitration, Pederson's agents and the Dodgers were nowhere close in their discussions concerning his compensation. He opted to file and head to a trial. His agents argued for $9.5 million; the team's lawyers suggested Pederson should be paid $7.75 million because he was a part-time player. They pointed out he had only played fifty-seven complete games all season, because the Dodgers removed him when a left-handed reliever entered to face him. The three-person arbitration panel picked the team's side.

"The teams, understanding how arbitration works, can effectively say: Handle this player this way," said Ed Edmonds, the arbitration authority. "And the Dodgers, because of the roster they have, they're in a different position to treat Pederson that way, then let's say a team like the Orioles or the Pirates, who would've never taken him out of the game." When Pederson arrived at Dodgers camp the week after his lost case, he pledged to play a part in fixing the arbitration process. "I think we all need to kind of come together, and I think we are together, with a group that needs to be better," he said. "Our last collective bargaining was not benefiting the players, I guess you could say. All those things are being addressed, and have been addressed."

Even more than suppressing salaries, the Dodgers' depth insulated them against injuries, the scourge of all high-level sports. They were a frequent problem. The 2017 Dodgers' thirty-eight injured-list trips led a league that averaged fewer than twenty-three. Those figures were artificially inflated, however, because MLB changed its rules before the 2017 season. Out went the fifteen-day mandate an injured player must sit out, replaced by a ten-day minimum. The Dodgers immediately seized on the alteration. Fifteen days is a difficult length of time for a healthy player, particularly a pitcher, to sit out. He must miss at least two starts, an absence that requires him to then build back his arm strength in a minor league outing.

But ten days? Ten days are easy. Start on a Monday, move to the injured list the next day with something nonexistent or minor, and return the following weekend to start again. Throughout that year, the Dodgers shuffled starting pitchers in and out of their rotation and onto the injured list for ten days at a time. Everybody received an occasional break. The best example was when the team sidelined Stripling with what it called "lower body fatigue." When he reported a back injury the next year, he was asked, wink-wink, if this ailment was like his last. "No, no, that one was totally fake," he said. "This one's real."

Roberts summed up the maneuvers as "shortening the season." Effectively, the Dodgers played with an extra roster spot compared with their competition, and they employed similar schemes to shave service time from players' ledgers. When they briefly optioned Walker Buehler to the minors around the 2018 All-Star break, they gained an extra pitcher for a few days and an additional year of his services at a below-market price, because the stint plunged him just under the threshold for a full year. Such service-time manipulation was not unique to the Dodgers, and they did it more gracefully—or secretly—than most. Other clubs waited until late April to promote a star prospect for the first time, making moronic excuses to explain away his absence.

All these moves limited the statistics players could post, and, in time, the accumulation-based arbitration dollars they could earn. They helped the team but hurt the game and its players. In 2019, teams began to copy the Dodgers' injury innovations. The Giants, by then run by ex-Dodgers executive Farhan Zaidi, placed left-hander Derek Holland on the injured list with a bone bruise on his finger. Holland said it was the front office's decision, not his. "I did a fake injury, so I'm not happy about that," he said.

After that season, the league updated its rules again to account for the Dodgers' creativity. The fifteen-day injured list minimum was back—for pitchers. Hitters could still sit out ten days and return. The Dodgers had not yet abused that aspect of the rules. They *had* made liberal use of the seven-day injured list in the minor leagues, as did other organizations. "The phantom," club officials called it. Healthy but struggling prospects received a break from the unrelenting grind and a plane ticket to see Craig Wallenbrock, the club's hitting consultant. "We're taking all the pressure off and just isolating on them for six to seven days without the pressure of having to go into the game," Wallenbrock said. That practice stopped amid the pandemic; the club hoped to resume it in 2022.

After Kelly wreaked his havoc, the Dodgers' season was devoid of drama. The Padres played them tough, but the Dodgers outlasted them and everyone else. On the night they clinched, they followed league edict and refrained from a customarily wild celebration. Seager still showed up for his postgame Zoom wearing a visibly soaked commemorative shirt. "I didn't realize it was wet," he said. "It's probably sweat."

The Dodgers toasted to their accomplishment with individual flutes of Champagne. Perhaps a few were flung into the air. Roberts spoke up about the distinct challenge awaiting them. The next night, players and coaches entered a week-long quarantine at the Langham Huntington, a Pasadena resort built during the Gilded Age. Coaches' family members quarantined separately. If the team survived that stage, including a crapshoot best-of-three series against a feeble opponent, they would reunite with their families and fly to Texas for another isolation of unknown length. They did. On October 2, the Dodgers set off for Dallas–Fort Worth International Airport.

# Chapter 14

THE DODGERS PACKED FOR A MAXIMUM OF twenty-six nights at the Four Seasons Resort and Club Dallas at Las Colinas. They were there for twenty-five. The first ten days were all fun and games, literally. They spent four nights settling in before sweeping San Diego in three relatively smooth games. Joe Kelly stepped up in the series's tightest moment. Then four more free nights awaited the Dodgers, followed by a best-of-seven National League Championship Series with no scheduled days off, unlike anything any of them had ever experienced.

The monotony set in during that second break. The players had agreed to the confinement called for in the bubble, and they were used to it; many of them had long subjected themselves to a similar sort of voluntary confinement on road trips. Within the Dodgers' 2019 traveling party, players regularly toted their own high-definition monitors to play video games in style inside their hotel rooms. But road trips never lasted longer than ten days.

Especially for the childless players, the experience had the feeling of a high-tech, high-class summer camp. Hotel staffers provided prepackaged breakfast, lunch, and dinner daily at designated times. Snacks were always available on every floor. Players could swim, play ping-pong, play video games, play cornhole. They could not golf, but some veterans stayed in villas overlooking the resort's pristine course, adjacent to the eighteenth green. A group of Dodgers convened on one balcony, chipped balls toward the hole, and asked a young player to scamper out undetected and recover them.

The Dodgers were not accustomed to seeing so much of each other, and no one else, for such a lengthy stretch. Players tend to scatter across the Los Angeles sprawl. During a typical season, some will reside in the Beach Cities, others West Hollywood, the San Fernando Valley, Glendale and Pasadena, and some even in the Inland Empire. At the wrong time, traversing the traffic on such a circuit could take eight or ten hours. During homestands, players don't see much of each other away from the stadium. At the Four Seasons, they were seconds away from a teammate's room. They'd wake up and greet someone standing on the next balcony.

It all started to feel like a lot after a while. "It's kind of like having kids," Mark Prior said. "Like those first couple months where you're not sleeping and you just do not remember them." There were also approximately thirty Dodgers-affiliated children on the premises. For them, the experience was a delight. After months of coronavirus restrictions limiting social interactions, they had an entire roster's worth of playmates. "Our kids are never gonna have a better vacation than that," assistant hitting coach Aaron Bates said.

Most baseball men like to follow a routine. The bubble both facilitated and challenged those desires. On the road, Prior generally likes to walk to a third-wave coffee shop near the team hotel and sample their wares. He refuses to support Starbucks, preferring locally owned establishments that roast and brew to precise specifications. Prior planned ahead; he and the few coffee connoisseur coaches simply brought several pounds of their favorite beans to Texas and fashioned the Four Seasons into their own coffee shop, specializing in Chemex cups, and the stadium a drip specialist. There was one problem: they ran out of beans during the World Series. They ordered more from a local roaster so they'd arrive quickly.

Few are more routine oriented than third-base coach Dino Ebel, who prefers to run four miles on a treadmill every morning, then devour several servings of oatmeal. While the hotel took care of the oatmeal, the gym on premises was reserved for the umpiring crew. There was a track, but Ebel could not stand it. "It was like running in circles: boring," he said. "I'd rather run on my treadmill looking at my garage door. That's not boring to me." There was a solution. The Dodgers coaches bused to the stadium two hours before the players. Ebel learned to eat first and then run his miles there. The coaches all worked out together. "It went from not being able to see each other," Bates said, "to seeing each other every moment of the day."

Milestones were reached inside that Four Seasons. Joc Pederson's daughter, Poppy, celebrated her second birthday. Director of player performance Brandon McDaniel's youngest child, not quite eleven months old, started walking. Gavin Lux listened to fifty episodes of *The Joe Rogan Experience*. Families put on a makeshift Halloween event for the children, who trick-or-treated from room to room across the resort.

Back at the ballpark, the Braves proved a formidable NLCS opponent. Several longtime Dodgers have remarked that, throughout their run of eight division titles, only the 2018 Red Sox presented a stiffer postseason challenge. Atlanta's first baseman, Freddie Freeman, hit better in 2020 than anyone alive. Outfielder Ronald Acuña Jr. wasn't far behind. The young Braves starters were pitching well. Their bullpen was as bottomless as the Dodgers', and it featured a more consistent closer.

In the tied ninth inning of Game 1, the Braves pounced on Blake Treinen and Jake McGee, two of Dave Roberts's most reliable regular-season relievers. In the middle innings of Game 2, Atlanta attacked rookie right-hander Tony Gonsolin, who made his first postseason start on short notice because Kershaw's back flared up again. After a ninth-inning rally finished ninety feet short, the Dodgers were down two games to none. They halved that deficit in Game 3, stockpiling eleven runs in the first inning and gliding to an emphatic victory.

The next afternoon, veteran left-hander Alex Wood argued that the series's first two games had finally awoken him and his teammates. "It really felt like that was the first game of the year that we put it all together, in all aspects," Wood said. The Dodgers were then 49–19, historically successful, and yet Wood's assertion rang true. As good as the Dodgers had been, they had the talent to be better. Wood spoke of the inevitable stagnant feelings that sustained success produced. Told what his player said, Roberts spun the stagnancy as a reward for the organization's success. "That's something to be proud of," he said. "I expect our guys, regardless of circumstance, opponent, to play a certain brand of baseball. I expect the intensity to be the same every night. That's obviously maybe unrealistic at times. But, in the postseason, certainly not a big ask."

In Game 4, Roberts's ask was still too much. The Dodgers submitted a lifeless performance. An Atlanta rookie right-hander ran roughshod over them, Kershaw was mediocre, and two relievers flailed behind him. The game did not finish until nearly 11 p.m. local time. It was past midnight by the time the Dodgers returned to their rooms, their season officially on the brink. The coaches tucked their kids into bed and reported to the conference room to prepare for the next night.

It was going to be a doozy. Both teams planned bullpen games. Dodgers hitters had to be prepared for a half dozen pitchers, probably more. Seven Dodgers would pitch. But four games into the series, a sense of stillness came over some of the exhausted staffers. "Ironically, it was probably the calmest and most relaxed I'd been the entire season," Prior said. "Mostly just because, at that point, your hands are tied. We just gotta win. There's nothing else to do."

For players, there was nothing to do but rest and text on the group chat. Kershaw started the conversation. Justin Turner wrote in early. Venezuelan reliever Brusdar Graterol sent a hefty, boisterous paragraph that included a preemptive apology for his English, although teammates said his grammar was perfect. Memes and GIFs pinged players' phones. The Dodgers had group texts before 2020, but the pandemic accelerated the move to virtual communication. Motivational talk once confined to the clubhouse was now almost exclusively conducted on a GroupMe thread, befitting a millennial-laden team more comfortable expressing themselves through their phones.

The conversation amounted to a collective affirmation exercise. Walker Buehler likened reading the messages to repeatedly hearing, as a child, that America contained fifty states. "A lot of times, you know things, but when you hear it again, you feel like you know it more, even if you already knew the fact," Buehler said. "It's that reassurance, the continual positive reinforcement from people that you respect. Also, the situation is not fun for anyone, and they're still happy, excited." Over the off-season, Wood scrolled back through the thread and screenshotted his favorite messages. "It was just so raw and real, the true belief that a lot of guys had in theirselves," he said.

To play their best, the Dodgers needed to be faced with the worst outcome. Until then, they coasted, because they could. "The thing that stood out to me that was a lot different than the two other World Series teams we had is that we were just fuckin' better than everybody," Wood said. "That intensity, that teamwork, we didn't really have to go to that next level at any point during the season. We just out-talented everybody. We just showed up and won every day. But to win a World Series, you have to come together on a deeper level than just a group of guys that are better than everybody. We never really knew if we had that in us, or we hadn't seen it. Then you get your teeth kicked in, and it's like, 'Who are we?'"

Mookie Betts answered the question. When Game 5 began, the Dodgers quickly fell behind by a run in the first and two in the second. In the third, the margin was about to widen when Betts sprinted in to save them. Kelly was on the mound, teetering. With one out, the Braves had runners on second and third. Dansby Swanson knocked a soft liner to right field that looked like it might fall in for a single, but Betts came charging in to snare it. On third base, Marcell Ozuna saw Betts coming. He was so afraid of his speed and throwing arm that he left too early to legally tag up.

After a replay review, umpires called Ozuna out on the violation. The Dodgers' dugout ignited. "If you're talking about momentum shifts," Roberts later said, "that's the play of the year, for me." He cited a number of factors: the sheer difficulty of the catch; the score of the game; the suspense built by the Dodgers' replay request; and the fact that he might have had to call in his highest-leverage reliever, Treinen, if Betts did not make the play. Its significance to the Dodgers' championship hopes was assumed.

If Betts had let the baseball pass him, the Braves would have scored twice. If he had trapped it off the outfield grass, the Braves would have scored once and had runners at the corners with one out. If he had even left his feet to catch it, Ozuna likely would have scored on a sacrifice fly. As it was, Betts corralled the ball inches from the grass and, on the run, released his throw home. His transfer and throw were imperfect, but the threat was enough. Betts argued that his actions were instinctual. He hones his instincts with work.

The sequence was Betts's best postseason play since Game 4 of the 2018 American League Championship Series, when he threw out the Astros' Tony Kemp trying for second base on a liner into the corner. Betts sprinted to it and gloved it, then turned and delivered a no-look throw on target to second. On that, too, he made a nearly impossible play look so smooth that Kemp was blamed more than Betts was praised. But three times a week from that February into October, Betts and Red Sox outfield coach Tom Goodwin had worked on that particular play, pivoting to throw out runners on balls hit down the line. Throughout the summer of 2020, Betts and Dodgers outfield coach George Lombard practiced the catch-and-release throw.

Four minutes after Betts's heroics, the Dodgers scored their first run on a Corey Seager home run. Two innings later, Betts reached on an infield single and stole second, averting a likely inning-ending double-play ball off of Turner's bat. There were two men out and two men on when the Dodgers' Will Smith bested the Braves' Will Smith with a three-run home run. There would be a Game 6, and Buehler would start it. When Wood, poking the bear, asked if he was nervous or scared, Buehler scoffed at him.

The next night, Buehler scattered seven singles across six scoreless innings, his longest outing all season because of recurring blisters and his decision to rest his arm during the shutdown. Behind him, the Dodgers bullpen held the line. Seager and Turner began the game with back-to-back home runs, and Cody Bellinger singled in an additional run. There would be a Game 7.

If not for the back injury that delayed his initial outing, the start would have been Kershaw's. Instead, the Dodgers pieced together another bullpen game. Dustin May opened and gave way to Gonsolin. Neither was sharp, but the next three relievers faced eighteen batters and recorded eighteen outs. Julio Urías, the pitching prodigy, was responsible for nine alone.

Soon after Urías signed with the organization in the summer of 2012, the week he turned sixteen, the Dodgers assigned special assistant Juan Castro, a retired infielder, to mentor him, for the two hailed from cities two hundred kilometers apart in the Mexican state of Sinaloa. It took Castro until he was twenty-eight to establish himself as a major leaguer, but he stuck around for a decade. In terms of talent, Urías stood untold tiers above him. Some within the Dodgers organization believed he could've handled the majors before he turned eighteen, in 2014. More became convinced the next year.

He debuted in May 2016, three months from twenty, in New York City. He pitched to a 3.50 ERA over his first sixteen games, fourteen of them starts. But when they returned to New York to meet the Yankees in September, the Dodgers demoted Urías to the bullpen to preserve his innings for the postseason.

Urías disagreed with the decision. By then, Castro had become a quality control coach on Roberts's staff, and he met with his fuming mentee at Yankee Stadium. "This is for your own good," he said several times.

The next year, Urías tore the anterior capsule in his throwing shoulder. He missed thirteen months, but made it back to the major league team just in time to throw three September games and crack the 2018 NLCS roster. From there, Roberts turned to him in relief in seven of twelve games. Urías's slow upbringing forestalled his arrival as a dominant starter, but it almost unwittingly prepared him for his star turn in the 2020 postseason.

Urías enabled the Dodgers to reach the World Series. Bellinger propelled them. The former MVP regressed in 2020, registering his worst statistical season yet. But his underlying numbers were better than the obvious ones. Bellinger had been walking and avoiding strikeouts. In the postseason, he demonstrated newfound restraint, spurning or spoiling the primitive pitches he once chased. In the seventh inning of Game 7, he battled Braves reliever Chris Martin to an eight-pitch at-bat. Martin finally missed over the plate with a fastball. Bellinger sent it out to right field for the go-ahead home run. Thirty-four minutes later, he caught an Austin Riley fly to finish the NLCS. The Dodgers would get a third crack at the World Series.

By the time it began, they had played a dozen games at Globe Life Field. The Rays, their opponents, had played none. The Dodgers' confinement created some advantages. The stadium's foul-line fences produced unusual ricochets, and the Dodgers outfielders had long since learned to play the caroms. It was all new to Tampa Bay. Because their two previous playoff rounds had been in San Diego, the Rays also brought fewer family members to the Four Seasons. The Dodgers' contingent swarmed the resort.

Crudely, the Rays were the discount Dodgers. They lacked the offensive potency of the Padres or Braves, but they compensated with depth. Tampa Bay was the only major league team with a comparable collection of competent position players to the Dodgers'. Their pitching stash was likely superior. As Rays manager Kevin Cash phrased it in September 2020: "I have a whole damn stable of pitchers that throw ninety-eight miles per hour." His horses were tiring. The Rays had hurdled thirteen games in fourteen days to advance to the World Series. While they had one more day than the Dodgers to rest before it began, it was a travel day.

The series's first three games developed about as expected. They featured twenty-one, twenty-two, and twenty-three strike-outs apiece. The team that struck first won each evening, and the Dodgers brought a one-game edge into a far wilder Game 4. They took an early lead on two solo shots before the Rays halved it with one of their own. The Dodgers remained in front when, with a two-run sixth-inning lead and two men on, Roberts summoned right-hander Pedro Báez from the bullpen. For years the fans' bête noire because of his deliberate pacing and high-profile failures, Báez had rehabilitated his image. On that night, he reminded them of the bad old days.

Báez garnered two strikes on Brandon Lowe with his changeup. In a two-and-two count, catcher Will Smith called for one more change. Báez shook him off in favor of a fastball, then aimed high but missed over the middle. Lowe slammed the mistake for a three-run home run. In the dugout, Roberts shook his head. After the inning, Roberts told Báez he was done for the day, but he reconsidered when Pederson vaulted the Dodgers ahead with a two-run single in the top of the seventh. He asked Báez if that was all right, as if Báez could answer in anything but the affirmative. He trudged back to the mound and surrendered the tying home run. Roberts later expressed regret that he had instructed his reliever to relax. He had made another crucial communication error in another Game 4 of the World Series.

It got worse. The Dodgers leapt ahead again, and Roberts called in Kenley Jansen, his erstwhile closer, to handle the ninth. Jansen let on two Rays but secured two outs and two strikes on Brett Phillips, a reserve outfielder who was batting for the first time in seventeen days. Smith called for a high cutter to end it.

Jansen left the pitch over the plate, and Phillips shot it into center field for what appeared to be a game-tying single. Playing center for the first time in six weeks, Chris Taylor bobbled the ball. That tempted Randy Arozarena, who had been sprinting from first to third, to try to score. Taylor picked up the ball and hit the cutoff man, Max Muncy, who turned and fired an offline relay throw. Smith rushed to catch it and apply a tag, unaware that Arozarena had tripped two thirds of the way home. The throw eluded Smith's glove. Wallowing in his misfortune, Jansen neglected to back up home plate. Arozarena recovered and scurried the final few steps home, ending the comedy of errors by scoring the game-winning run. The series was tied.

While Phillips rejoiced in the outfield, Roberts jumped down a step, ripped off his cap, and spat in disgust. He had managed nearly eight hundred games, and he had never reacted with such repugnance. "His first expression was like what Vin Scully said: 'I don't believe what I just saw,'" said Gary Adams, Roberts's college coach. "But his expression changed. It went from that, in an instant, to a face that said, 'We'll get them tomorrow.' It was that determined look, and then he turned around and hustled down the tunnel."

The Dodgers promised to bounce back, and they did. Game 5 exhibited the value of Roberts's buoyant optimism and Kershaw's newly tolerant attitude. Up one run, Kershaw issued back-to-back walks to begin the fourth inning. After the lead runner, Manuel Margot, stole third, Kershaw accepted that Margot would score, that the game would be tied. He aimed only to preserve that tie, giving himself wiggle room. Then he made pitches, tempting Joey Wendle with inside fastballs, spinning sliders past Willy Adames. Soon there were two outs and Kershaw was on the verge of escape. Seeing his chance to score slipping away, Margot attempted to steal home. Kershaw stepped off the mound and threw home, as calmly as he might have tossed an intentional ball. Austin Barnes tagged out Margot. Kershaw had done even better than he hoped.

One of Kershaw's signature strengths is his ability to improve when opponents reach base. Year after year, he is even better with runners on than without. Whether it is stubbornness, a product of the strikeout era, some combination of the two, or something else entirely, no one has ever more effectively curtailed rallies. Of the 676 major leaguers who have completed 1,500 innings since 1900, Kershaw's 79.4 percent strand rate through 2020 stood alone atop the list. Trailing him are Hall of Famers Whitey Ford and Sandy Koufax.

The skill had failed Kershaw in October. His postseason strand rate was a below-average 67.8 percent, reflecting how he had been hurt by his teammates, his managers, and himself. Inherited runners often scored. Too many times, he faced two batters too many. He placed untold pressure on himself. But 2020 had ushered in a new, better perspective.

The Dodgers stood one win away, and they had an ace in the hole. If the Rays rendered Game 7 necessary, Buehler would be ready to start it. For Game 6, the Dodgers deployed one last bullpen game. The Rays sent out left-hander Blake Snell, a former Cy Young winner. A seventh game was a smart bet, especially after Snell started pitching. He had his best stuff, a pinpoint fastball and corresponding changeup, plus two breaking balls.

Betts began the game with a strikeout, worrying himself. Much like in the 2018 World Series against the Dodgers, he was not hitting his best. Coaches acquired the distinct sense that he was overdoing it. "Just hunt results," hitting coach Robert Van Scoyoc began telling him, tongue halfway in cheek. "Don't worry about swing aesthetics. We're trying to win a World Series." Betts laughed it off, as he had laughed off Kelly's attempt to snap him out of his 2018 slump. "We all know you're holding the record for the biggest 0-fer streak in World Series history," Kelly told him then, when he was hitless in eleven at-bats. "You already have the record. What else worse could happen?"

After Snell struck him out again in the third inning, Betts approached Bates in the Dodgers' dugout. "He's about to throw a [complete game]," Betts said. "No," Bates told him. "He's about to go two times through the order, and you're about to absolutely rake as soon as he comes out of the game." Bates was being flippant, but the Dodgers had reason to believe Snell would not sniff the ninth. It had been fifteen months since he finished six innings. Not once in his major league career had he completed eight.

Sure enough, the moment Barnes singled with one out in the sixth, Cash came forth to remove Snell. The Rays had long since determined that Snell was ineffective the third time through an order, especially one as talented as the Dodgers'. Their diagnosis is increasingly common in the major leagues; after two looks at what a pitcher offers on a given night, hitters tend to identify adjustments that enable breakthroughs. This happens just as the pitcher is tiring and losing precision. The data reflects this, as hitters tend to perform 10 to 15 percent better when facing a pitcher a third time. (Because of selection bias, that probably understates the advantage.)

The Rays' problem was that Snell's replacement, Nick Anderson, was wilting with fatigue after a robust regular season. Betts laced his third pitch down the left-field line for a double. Anderson soon fired a wild pitch, allowing Barnes to score and Betts to take third. On Seager's subsequent grounder, Betts used his impeccable instincts to notch the fateful run.

The Dodgers turned to Graterol to begin the seventh inning. The team's most excitable player, he could not control his emotions in that moment. His first three pitches were wild sinkers. Luckily, Adames chased the third and tapped into an easy out. After Muncy stepped on first to secure it, Prior called down to the bullpen, requesting Urías warm his arm. Just then, Andrew Friedman's iPhone rang. Commissioner Rob Manfred was calling with the news that Justin Turner had tested positive, twice, for COVID-19.

Friedman left his box behind home plate and entered the Dodgers' clubhouse. He stayed on the phone and tried to follow from a delayed broadcast as Urías entered and finished the frame. When the stadium rose for the seventh-inning stretch, Friedman walked toward the dugout. The first person he saw was athletic trainer Yosuke "Possum" Nakajima, who became the messenger, bringing him Roberts and Turner. Turner went to the clubhouse with Friedman while Roberts returned to the dugout, reached his arm around hitting coach Brant Brown, and explained the situation. Ron Porterfield, the Dodgers' director of player health and COVID-19 compliance officer, walked down the right-field line to where families were watching and retrieved Kourtney Turner, the player's wife. She joined her husband in an equipment room.

The news trickled throughout the Dodgers' dugout and bullpen, especially after Edwin Ríos took Turner's place at third base to begin the eighth. But there was no official notice. Some players figured he had been injured. Some assumed it was a false positive, since no one else had been removed from the game. The game continued as if he had suffered some standard muscle strain.

Betts added a home run and Urías kept pitching, the left-hander's precision and aggressiveness stunning the Rays into submission. Their final two batters struck out looking, their last on three pitches. Urías crouched and pumped his fist so fast his entire body vibrated with elation. Barnes, his catcher, triumphantly raised his arms, then bounded into Urías.

During the last inning, Kershaw was so anxious he wandered onto the bullpen mound. When it ended, he smiled like a child as he barreled toward his teammates. Many who knew Kershaw were themselves overwhelmed with emotion as they watched, even on television. "All the weight, all the expectation, all the pressure, all the commentary, you could see it all just falling off of him," said A. J. Ellis, his best friend. "And then he got to where he wanted to be: jumping around with teammates and celebrating with those guys." Dozens of Dodgers pulled Kershaw in for hugs. Kiké Hernández gripped his back as if his survival depended on it. Muncy cried as he clutched him. Roberts kept repeating how happy he was for him. "As a man that does not get very sentimental, it was one of the few moments in my life I've ever actually gotten chills," said Ross Stripling. "It's almost like I felt the burden come off his shoulders right in front of me."

Kershaw felt it, too, though he had not acknowledged its entire weight until that moment. "I think you don't really realize what you're carrying while you're carrying it, you know?" he later said. He had blinded himself to the impact his pursuit had on his friends and family, particularly his wife. "Everybody who's ever spent any time around him has seen what he's been in pursuit of, what he's been chasing after," Ellis said. "To see him running towards it and finally catch it is really special."

Lee Muncy watched the celebration from behind the backstop. Only family members who had been inside the bubble were permitted onto the field. So Lee and Midge just watched, contentedly. The most momentous days of Lee's life flashed back in his brain. He thought about graduating from high school. He thought about getting out of the Army. He thought about witnessing the birth of his three boys. And he thought about what he saw in front of him. "It's the World Series, the Los Angeles Dodgers," Lee Muncy said. "Your son's playing for them. He's batting cleanup on the team that wins the World Series. It's like, 'Wait a minute now. Do they know this is my son? He's just an everyday guy. How does this happen?' It's just amazing, it is. It's hard to believe sometimes, but we believe it. Yeah, we do."

For the first part of the Dodgers' celebration, Turner remained in isolation. He sent out a tweet that read, in part: "Can't believe I couldn't be out there to celebrate with my guys!" After some of those guys entered the room to coax him out, he decided he could. Wearing surgical masks, he and Kourtney emerged on the field. Witnesses said league officials asked him to leave on multiple occasions. He declined, and soon shed the mask to pose for a team photo with the trophy. He hugged a number of teammates. Roberts was too thrilled to demand that Turner leave. Friedman claimed he lacked the jurisdiction. "Him being a free agent," he said, "I don't think anyone was going to stop him from going out."

Turner later apologized for his reckless decisions, but the league and the team should never have afforded him the chance or choice to come back on the field. The league's protocols called for immediate isolation. Manfred admitted that someone should have been assigned to monitor Turner there and transport him to the resort sooner than they did.

Some of them unnerved as details emerged, the Dodgers returned to the Four Seasons for one last night. Many players celebrated in an outdoor area set up for them. The childless crowd stayed out until the sun rose. Alcohol was available, unlike at the stadium. Kershaw downed Michelob Ultra and stuck out his tongue for teammates' photos. Because they had been exposed to Turner for more time, hitting coaches and position players took three rapid tests before boarding the team plane bound for Los Angeles the next afternoon. Pitchers and pitching coaches took two tests.

The champions landed back at Los Angeles International Airport near sunset on October 28, to a crowd of airport employees who assembled to take photos. Betts carried the trophy down the airstairs. The Dodgers loaded into three buses for the trip back to Dodger Stadium, where they had parked their cars. Members of the traveling party were ordered to self-quarantine for two weeks. Because many of them no longer had the keys to their in-season housing in Los Angeles, they were asked to drive, not fly, to their off-season homes. That was not always possible. It was a nervous time. Some Dodgers were in contact with Los Angeles health officials, asking when they could be certain they were not infected so they could safely visit at-risk family members. Even fourteen days, they were told, were not guaranteed to be enough.

Two days after bullpen catcher Steve Cilladi arrived at his Arizona home, his wife and daughter showed symptoms of illness. "Son of a gun," he thought, "I'm asymptomatic." Turner had sat directly in front of him for the celebratory team photo. Cilladi and his family underwent repeated tests. His wife and daughter's symptoms stayed mild, he never had any, and no one tested positive. Their scare was brief. Turner's case did not become an outbreak, though several members of the organization tested positive following the World Series. Sources indicated those cases came from outside the league's Four Seasons playoff bubble. Though the bubble proved penetrable, it was riskier to attend the series outside it than inside it.

Ahead of the World Series, the Dodgers conducted a ticket lottery for interested team employees. Some around the team were uncomfortable attending. Friedman's brothers attended several games, but their father, J. Kent Friedman, opted against it for safety's sake. He later told the Houston Jewish History Archive that his sons reported back that he had made the right choice, as much as it had pained him not to go. "Although everyone had to wear a mask to get into the stadium, once inside and once people began drinking, masks went away, spacing went away," he said. "It was a very uncomfortable situation for them."

Two seconds after he caught the baseball that won the World Series, Barnes seamlessly slipped it into his back pocket before flinging his glove and mask into the night. He had scripted the maneuver in advance. He had not gotten as far as considering what he would do with the baseball thereafter. After the game, a league official affixed to it an authentication sticker. Barnes stuck the keepsake in his backpack and brought it to his Riverside home, where he stored it for several restless weeks.

Barnes was more comfortable catching the ball than protecting it. Everyone, it seemed, saw his slick move. Every fan he encountered, every radio host he spoke with, every friend he saw, had the same question: Where was the ball now? Because he did not want to advertise its location, Barnes never knew how to answer. "It was a lot to be responsible for, leaving my house and wondering, 'Damn, is that ball gonna be OK?'" he said. Thankfully, Lon Rosen, the team's executive vice president and chief marketing officer, eventually came calling for it. Barnes brought the baseball to Dodger Stadium himself. His work was done.

"It's weird, because it's just a baseball," Barnes said. "But what it's done, what it's been through, what it symbolizes, is a lot more than that. That was the ball that brought a lot of joy to the city of L.A. to Dodger fans. It's an important baseball. It's seen some stuff."

# Chapter 15

BEFORE AUSTIN BARNES SURRENDERED THE baseball, Andrew Friedman started sending texts about winning another World Series. "Let's be pigs," he wrote to team staffers. "To a fault," Friedman said, "all of us are probably a little too focused on 2021 without relishing in 2020." He was prescient. The Dodgers' gluttony culminated in the February 5 signing of reigning Cy Young winner Trevor Bauer, a known online harasser.

For years, Bauer had wielded his Twitter platform to bully, troll, and inflame. He tweeted more than a dozen times at a young woman who had mentioned him as her least favorite person in sports, digging into her posting history to find evidence that she consumed alcohol before turning twenty-one. He once invited another Twitter user to commit suicide. "We won't miss you," he wrote. He told a fan asking about the Cleveland Indians' logo, the red-faced Chief Wahoo, to shut up, that he had never met someone who thought it was racist. (Cleveland has since retired the logo and renamed the team the Guardians, because it deemed the old branding offensive.) The Dodgers weighed his history against the pitcher he had become and decided it was worth it. They boosted his platform.

Boiled down to the bitter, concentrated truth, baseball's plight is simple. Too many teams care more about profits than winning. The league's revenue-sharing system enables even consistent losers to turn a continual profit, or at least break even while their valuations steadily increase. A select few teams, the Dodgers included, care so much about winning they are willing to accept almost anything if it gives them a better chance at a championship. From their warped perspective, a player's misconduct can even be an advantage, lowering the acquisition cost, transforming him into a distressed asset. This strategy, too, makes adhering teams plenty of money. That cash, the thrill of the chase, and the persistent absence of any accountability requirement blinds them to the consequences of their actions.

In recent years, both the Yankees and Astros traded for discounted closers after they were involved in domestic-violence incidents. Neither Aroldis Chapman nor Roberto Osuna was convicted of a crime, but both accepted MLB suspensions without exercising their right to an appeal. Their new employers accepted the public would castigate them—for a time. "Sooner or later," Yankees owner Hal Steinbrenner told *USA Today*, "we forget, right?" Steinbrenner said this not five hundred days after Chapman fired eight gunshots into his garage during a domestic dispute with his girlfriend. In that span, the Yankees had twice acquired Chapman.

In the case of Justin Turner's knowingly COVID-positive celebration, many guilty parties were lucky their shared lapse in judgment did not yield a superspreader event. When the Dodgers decided to pay Bauer more money annually than any baseball player ever, they quickly faced worse repercussions than they imagined.

During Bauer's introductory press conference, Friedman referenced investigating the pitcher's online history while pursuing him. "From our standpoint, it was important to have that conversation," he said. "We came away from it feeling good about it. Now, obviously, time will tell. But I feel like he is going to be a tremendous add, not just on the field, but in the clubhouse, in the community. That's obviously why we're sitting here."

Friedman noted that the Dodgers obtained as much information as they could about Bauer. He argued that his front office deserved trust because its vetting process had succeeded over his six-plus years in Los Angeles. "The most important thing is every teammate we talked to, all the feedback we got from every organization he was with, was not only incredibly positive in terms of the type of teammate he is, but also in terms of the impact he makes on each organization," he said.

This was a damning indictment of the scope of their research. The *Washington Post* later reported that an Ohio woman, alleging that he choked and punched her during sex without her consent, had received a temporary restraining order against Bauer in 2020. "I don't feel like spending time in jail for killing someone," read a text message to her delivered from a phone number registered to him, according to the *Post*. "And that's what would happen if I saw you again." (In an email to team employees two days after the *Post*'s report, Dodgers president Stan Kasten said the club had been unaware of the Cuyahoga County case. It's worth noting that the Dodgers had agreed to trade for Chapman in December 2015, also unaware of the domestic dispute until Yahoo! Sports reported the contents of an October police report. Other teams were aware. For example, the *Boston Globe* reported that the Red Sox had uncovered the incident while exploring a Chapman trade and halted their pursuit.)

The Dodgers became Bauer's fourth organization. His first, the Arizona Diamondbacks, traded him after seventeen months because he "had a really tough year with his teammates," the team president told *USA Today*. *Sports Illustrated* quoted multiple members of his second, Cleveland, calling the clubhouse of twenty-five men "twenty-four plus Trevor." In a contravention of clubhouse code, Bauer criticized the performance of the team's closer. "I could've fixed Cody Allen's curveball in two days last year," he said, "but I couldn't tell him anything because he's a veteran and he doesn't want to listen." No members of the Cincinnati Reds, Bauer's third team, publicly grumbled about him, but the team made little effort to retain him after the best season of his career.

On the field, Friedman said, Bauer's talent was obvious. He so valued his durability. "But I actually think from a cultural standpoint, from a continuing to strive to get better in everything we do, I actually think he's gonna be a tremendous asset in that," Friedman said. "It's not for me to speak for Trevor, but in our conversations he's alluded to past mistakes he's made. You know what? We're all gonna make mistakes. What's important for me is how people, including myself when I make mistakes, how we internalize it, what our thoughts are about it going forward."

Friedman had a point, but not the one he wanted to make. When he spoke that day, Bauer evinced no understanding of how he had inflicted harm on people who lacked his platform. This was precisely the problem. He spent more time complaining about a fan who followed him to, but not inside, a hotel elevator in pursuit of an autograph. When asked about his behavior on social media, he referred to "mistakes" but extended no apologies or promises to stop. He called it "a very nuanced issue," without chronicling any nuances. He offered only platitudes about being "a positive member of the community."

(Warning: The following four paragraphs contain graphic details of alleged sexual assault.)

Then, on June 29, the Los Angeles Superior Court granted a young woman a temporary restraining order against Bauer. Their encounter began in a strikingly similar way to his past public transgressions. She teased him on social media, and he responded. She had tagged him in her Instagram story. The woman later recounted in court Bauer showing her how he scrolls through every tweet sent to him, reading every one. She recounted it as "how he gets his high." The woman and Bauer had met twice, once in April and once in May, both times at his home, for what both parties agreed was initially consensual rough sex that she alleged devolved far beyond what she consented to. In her application, she alleged under penalty of perjury that, over the two meetings, Bauer had anal sex with her without her consent, choked her to the point that she lost consciousness, and punched the left side of her jaw, the left side of her head, and both cheekbones, among other body parts.

"I remember this vividly and it was extremely startling and painful," she wrote of the second encounter. "I was absolutely frozen and terrified. I could not speak or move. After punching me several times, he then flipped me back onto my stomach, and began choking me with hair. I lost consciousness again. I re-gained consciousness even more disoriented. I had a terrible pain behind both of my ears. I tasted blood in my mouth and felt that my lip was split open. My whole body hurt and I could not even tell if he was having sex with me."

The next day, she checked herself into an emergency room near her San Diego home. A doctor diagnosed her with an acute head injury and assault by manual strangulation. According to her affidavit, Pasadena police officers soon encouraged her to phone Bauer while they recorded the call. She testified that Bauer admitted on the call to punching her in the butt while she was unconscious. The tape was never played or admitted as evidence in the proceeding. In one of his written communications with her after the second incident, Bauer used the passive voice when she told him the doctors' prognosis. "I feel so bad that this happened," he wrote. In a June 29 statement to reporters, Bauer's co-agent, Jon Fetterolf, disputed the woman's desires, not the details she alleged. "Mr. Bauer had a brief and wholly consensual sexual relationship initiated by [the woman] beginning in April 2021," Fetterolf wrote. "We have messages that show [her] repeatedly asking for 'rough' sexual encounters involving requests to be 'choked out' and slapped in the face. In both of their encounters, [the woman] drove from San Diego to Mr. Bauer's residence in Pasadena, Calif. where she went on to dictate what she wanted from him sexually and he did what was asked." Bauer's representatives sent to reporters what they claimed were the mentioned messages.

The next day, *The Athletic* reported the contents of the woman's exhibit within the restraining order, including photos of her bruised face, and the Dodgers traveled to Washington, DC, for a series against the Nationals and the customary champions trip to the White House. Bauer accompanied them on the flight, but not the following morning to the Oval Office, where the party was limited to members of the 2020 roster. When he addressed the team, President Biden called the Dodgers "a pillar of American culture and American progress." At the time, Bauer remained on schedule to start in two days.

Five months after he predicted great things, Friedman was not commenting on his prized acquisition. When the woman alleged assault and presented proof of her injuries, the Dodgers abdicated the responsibility they welcomed when they signed Bauer.

As of the White House visit, the only club official who had spoken on the matter publicly had argued that the decision to start Bauer was out of his hands. "I'm in the position of following the lead of Major League Baseball," Dave Roberts said. "Their recommendation was to—he was our scheduled Sunday starter, and to have him move forward and start that game on Sunday. And so for me to try to read into it any more outside of just following what they had advised me and us to do, I just choose to kind of follow their lead."

It was exactly that: a choice. If the Dodgers did not want to start Bauer, they did not have to start him. If they wanted to release him, they could release him. Such actions might result in Bauer or his agents filing a grievance, and the Dodgers could be forced to pay out the rest of his contract. But all that was within the bounds of the law, and the Dodgers chose not to do it. They skirted the issue, because MLB placed Bauer on administrative leave shortly after the team left the White House. While the league and the Pasadena Police investigated his actions for weeks, Bauer continued to earn millions of dollars from the Dodgers.

For four days in mid-August, Bauer sat before the Los Angeles Superior Court on the fourth floor of the Stanley Mosk Courthouse, two miles from Dodger Stadium. Seeking a five-year restraining order, his accuser testified for twelve hours, laying bare her history of alcoholism and intimate details of their encounters. She said she felt like a rag doll when he choked her on the second occasion. Bauer uttered only three words: "Yes, your honor," when judge Dianna Gould-Saltman asked if he intended to plead the fifth to every question the woman's attorneys wanted to pose.

His attorney, Shawn Holley, a veteran of O. J. Simpson's dream team, spoke for him. As Fetterolf had hinted was the legal team's strategy, Holley aimed not to dispute the violence the woman alleged, but to prove that she had requested it. "Did you not think that it was of critical importance," she asked in her closing argument, "to tell the judge that you asked for it?" Holley succeeded. Gould-Saltman ruled that the woman had given affirmative consent with her texts, and further determined Bauer did not pose an active threat to her, rebuking the woman's overstated claims in her initial declaration that Bauer had been calling and texting her nonstop.

On her way to obtaining that ruling, Holley admitted that Bauer had choked the woman to unconsciousness but insisted her claim that Bauer was sodomizing her when she regained consciousness "strained credulity." Holley alternated between positing specifics, such as that the woman had mounted Bauer first during sex, and questioning them, asking if lubrication was involved in the anal sex. With what she said were her apologies, Holley reported that contrary to the woman's stated hopes, there had been no emotional connection between the two. And didn't she tell Bauer, Holley asked, about how she used pain as her escape and high once she became sober in January 2020? The woman denied saying that.

Despite the courtroom win, Bauer faced an uncertain legal future and an even more tenuous professional outlook. The police continued to investigate. As Gould-Saltman said in her decision, the photos of the woman's injuries were "terrible." The forensic nurse examiner who saw the woman about twenty-four hours after her last encounter with Bauer said her vaginal bruising was the worst she had seen in three years of caring for sexual-assault victims. The Dodgers began distancing themselves from Bauer before he appeared in court, canceling his upcoming bobblehead night, removing his merchandise from their stores and website, and giving his Dodger Stadium locker to his high-profile replacement, Max Scherzer. No matter the outcome of any future proceedings, some within the sport suspected he would never again pitch in Major League Baseball.

It was not necessarily a matter of what fate the justice system had in store for him. What Bauer admitted to in Fetterolf's initial statement already made him unwelcome by the code of many clubhouses, including that of the Dodgers. What Holley ascribed to him during the hearing, as a league official observed in the courtroom, exposed him to potential league punishment. While the Dodgers accepted Julio Urías's presence in their room after his arrest for alleged domestic battery, the facts of that case were far different. Witnesses reported seeing Urías shove a woman in a mall parking lot. She denied that it happened and declined to press charges. He accepted a twenty-game suspension for what he called "inappropriate conduct." After the allegations against Bauer emerged, he denied culpability, instead positioning himself as the victim of attempted extortion.

Even if his career is over, Bauer's influence on the sport will continue in absentia. He arguably impacted the modern game more than any other active player. A statistic that gained relevance in 2021 is literally called a Bauer Unit, for the research he conducted connecting a pitcher's spin to his velocity. The ratio between the two, he determined alongside Driveline staffers, cannot be altered without the aid of sticky substances. In other words, there are only two known ways to increase the spin on a fastball: throw it harder, or throw it with something sticky on your hand.

Such foreign substances have long been against the rules. But the game's history with grip aids is just as lengthy. Problems arose when modern players found stickier and stickier stuff, both homespun concoctions and goos and gunks meant for a variety of other activities. High-speed cameras made it easy to detect and quantify the apparent rise the additional spin imparted on pitches. After Bauer's college teammate and personal nemesis Gerrit Cole appeared to benefit from them in the first starts that followed his 2018 trade to the Astros, Bauer started mentioning the substances on social media and in interviews. "If only there was just a really quick way to increase spin rate," Bauer tweeted. "Like what if you could trade for a player knowing that you could bump his spin rate a couple hundred rpm overnight . . . imagine the steals you could get on the trade market! If only that existed . . ." He challenged the league to enforce the rule book ban.

In 2019, Bauer revealed to *Sports Illustrated* that he experimented with Pelican Grip Dip during one 2018 inning, when his spin rate shot up more than 300 revolutions per minute, a statistically significant jump. He said then he'd be the best pitcher in the big leagues if he used Pelican, but that his morals prevented him from doing so. Starting in September 2019, he recorded the best spin statistics of his career and continued to until the league began to enforce the substance ban in June 2021. That stretch was the best of his career. At the hearing, the woman who accused him of sexual assault testified that he told her he used Spider Tack, the stickiest of all substances, a tacky goop designed to help World's Strongest Man weightlifters hoist huge boulders. When the league announced plans to enforce the substance ban, Bauer raised a ruckus. He had asked for just that, of course, but he moved the goalposts when the league finally said it would do what he asked, protesting the policy's rigidity and the decision to enforce it midseason. Because of the variance in his spin statistics, scouts for rival teams questioned how good of a pitcher he really was. (They wondered this about other pitchers, too, including Cole, whose performance regressed after June 2021.)

Bauer was used to getting what he wanted. He refused to adapt to professional baseball's traditions, insisting that professional baseball adapt to him. It usually did. Former Cleveland catcher Eric Haase told FanGraphs that the team still had old-school sensibilities when he joined in 2011. "When Trevor Bauer got over there (in December 2012), it really started that revolution of tech," he said. When the Diamondbacks drafted Bauer third overall in 2011, many of the league's pitching coaches prohibited pitchers from playing catch beyond 120 feet to warm up, believing it harmed their arms. Since high school, Bauer had been long-tossing from distances greater than 120 *yards*. "If you watch him long toss, it's like Mark McGwire in BP," said Alan Jaeger, a loss-toss advocate for more than three decades. "You don't forget it."

The act is now common, as is much of how Bauer chose to train as a teenage pitcher, including strengthening the rotator cuff with J-Bands, Jaeger's creation. "He has so radically changed the way that the entire baseball world looks at training and development," Jaeger said. "He has been the torchbearer. Trevor has played a profound role in changing the culture of baseball forever. It's like Curt Flood." That is hyperbolic. Flood helped create the opportunity for Bauer to choose his employer and make millions by challenging baseball's reserve clause and propelling the push for free agency. The league blackballed him for filing a lawsuit. Bauer argued that his efforts grew the game, but his iconoclasm mostly just made him more money, as he peddled his own merchandise and expanded his social-media following. Few players attempted to mimic his online presence. He carried greater authority on pitching.

In December 2013, eight starts into his major league career, Bauer posted a video to YouTube in which he demonstrated why and how he threw each of his pitches. Calling it "pitch design," he included three camera angles of each throw, slowed down to individual frames. At the time, the video attracted little attention. His YouTube channel had only a few hundred subscribers, not the 400,000 it would reach in 2021. (One of the first was Robert Van Scoyoc, the future Dodgers hitting coach, who grew up in the same town as Bauer. He commented on the pitch-design video with a critique.) The clip became a treasured guidepost to people pursuing pitch design professionally. "I remember watching it and not having any idea what he was talking about," said Eric Jagers, who graduated from high school in 2013 and is now the Cincinnati Reds assistant pitching coach and Driveline's assistant director of pitching. He felt like he was in elementary school and Bauer was teaching a graduate course. "Very, very ahead of his time," Jagers said. "Now we have better tools and systems to kind of do that on a mass scale, but it's an absolute fact that Trevor is kind of the godfather of that all. He and his dad, Warren."

In Driveline's early years, Bauer was the model their experts followed, the first big leaguer to whom they had access. He spent one off-season developing a two-seam fastball with his trusty high-speed camera, the next a new slider, the next a changeup. Employees then tried to replicate his processes with everyone else they saw. "Really what we did at Driveline was take what Trevor does, and kind of put that on a mass scale so that we could not just get some of the best in the world better but distribute that out to college kids, [junior college] kids, high-school kids," Jagers said. "There was some pretty compelling evidence that doing a lot of these things and learning from the past was going to help teams win. That's what we were after, just sort of trying to exploit a competitive advantage and scale that out to as many players as we possibly could."

They so successfully scaled that, in time, pitchers as accomplished as Clayton Kershaw trekked to Seattle to see what they could do. His trip there, and any improvement he derived from it, is directly connected to Bauer. He is only an obvious example. Hundreds of pitchers now embark on pitch-design projects each off-season. More than a dozen current or former Driveline employees now work for major league teams, spreading Bauer's influence across the sport. Long before the temporary restraining order, his ideas on pitching were more palatable than his personality.

In 2021, only four prominent players remained free agents into February. Bauer and Turner were two of them. Turner anticipated that his decision to celebrate while harboring a murderous virus could affect his free-agent market. "It was definitely a big question mark and a big unknown how people were going to perceive that and how people were going to pursue me," he said. "But once I got into conversations not only with the Dodgers but other teams, and cleared the air on that stuff, it all just kind of started moving forward and building momentum."

His apology aided his cause. The Toronto Blue Jays and Milwaukee Brewers both chased him, but the Dodgers re-signed Turner to a two-year contract just as players filed into spring-training camps. Together with Bauer's, the deal sent the Dodgers skyrocketing over the luxury-tax threshold. The reunion was delayed because Turner first sought a four-year pact, and because the Dodgers did not begin negotiating until the New Year. Nor did they with Bauer.

All off-season, Friedman repeatedly told agents who represented rival clients that he was not in the market for Bauer. Many knew better than to take that as fact. After the 2018 season, the Dodgers had also come in late with a short-term offer at a record-setting average annual value for Bryce Harper. He picked the Phillies because they offered more overall money, and because he had tired of having to comment on his next destination.

Bauer sought the attention and additional earning potential that came with another possible trip through free agency. He did not sign until February because his market did not materialize as he hoped. Some teams thought better of courting him. Others were unwilling to spend. In the end, only two clubs submitted competitive offers: the Dodgers and the Mets, who, under new owner Steve Cohen, were desperate to make a splash. The night before Bauer announced his decision, Friedman said, he went to sleep believing the Dodgers were out of the running. Things changed the next morning. The sides agreed on a three-year, $102 million contract. Bauer got the record average annual value he wanted; Friedman secured a short-term commitment for a distressed asset.

Mets president Sandy Alderson had publicly pitched Bauer as a good fit for New York City. "Look, professional wrestling was built around villains," Alderson said on SNY. "Entertainment has always been about good versus evil." He rejected the perception that Bauer could cause problems within the New York fan base or clubhouse. "Generally speaking, if a player is performing," he said, "they can probably get away with almost anything in the clubhouse, in terms of their teammates."

Alderson's wrestling argument was a typical one. Many inside the industry welcomed the development of villains, and no one disputed that Bauer was a natural fit. Before the assault allegations, Oakland Athletics outfielder Mark Canha called Bauer's star turn the best thing that happened to his sport in years.

"That brand of baseball is baseball's future," Canha said in May 2021. "That's what baseball needs to become. This is extreme, and I'm getting worked up talking about it, but throw out the unwritten rule book, throw out everything you knew about baseball. Watch Trevor Bauer. That's what baseball needs to become. That's exciting. That's not hits; it's strikeouts. It's pageantry. It's wrestling. It's entertainment. Stop acting like this game is something that it's not. It's entertainment. When you're talking about the business side of it, what is it to these owners? It's entertainment. That's what the bottom line comes down to: the money."

Bauer clearly understood Canha's point. "Storylines sell," he once told an ESPN panel who asked what he would change if he were commissioner. "If you look at WWE, I think that's a great example. If you look at what the Paul brothers have done, the Kardashians have done, just showing people their lives, creating a storyline with their lives and people are so tuned into it, the more we can do that with baseball, the more people are gonna tune in. Not because they want to see the game as much, they want to see what their favorite personality is gonna do next. I think that's the age we're in. The more we can embrace that, the more we can lean into that and produce content like that, produce storylines like that in baseball, the more compelling it's gonna be."

His methods worked. In a sport starved of public figures, Bauer's brand was among the strongest. He constantly centered himself for the sake of brand development, and his YouTube vlogs attracted an adoring audience. But Bauer presented there a reality-show take on baseball, manufacturing drama wherever possible. Teammates learned to steer clear of him whenever he was holding his camera rig. He was the star of every episode, and he was often alone. Was this really baseball's best hope for sustained or increased relevance? It turned some on to the game, but it turned others off.

In private, some close to him said in the spring of 2021, Bauer was willing to listen to what they had to say, even occasionally complimentary. To the public, he acted as if he was on an island, solely responsible for his success. When, two months into that season, home runs were his primary undoing, he spoke as if he were about to launch his own inquiry into the source. "I'm gonna look at some distributions of pitches and pitch types and locations and try to figure out if there's something I can adjust," Bauer said. Of course, Dodgers coaches and R&D staffers had already been doing that exact work, with more resources than any individual could possibly have.

Bauer claimed to spend an hour each day logging data about his body performance and collecting forty to fifty metrics. He employed at least three quantitative analysts to study the results and synthesize them into a color that captured his readiness on his start day: red, yellow, or green. In the hours before he took the mound, he said, he presented Roberts that color. "We've gotten to the point where we're pretty good at predicting what's actually going to happen out on the field, just based on my mea-surements that day and a couple of days leading up to it," Bauer said on his YouTube channel. Roberts said he was "very dismissive" of the color. "I really don't take much heed," he said.

Before the allegations emerged, Roberts was more willing to contradict Bauer's assertions than any other Dodger he had managed. The night Bauer conceded his eighteenth and nineteenth home runs of 2021 in his seventeenth start, the pitcher said it was "definitely bad luck" to blame. "I don't think that luck had anything to do with those two homers tonight," Roberts said.

Friedman had previously acquired players with a history of misdeeds, among them Josh Lueke, who pled guilty to felony false imprisonment with violence after he was charged with rape. During his tenure in Los Angeles, the Dodgers did not tell the police or the league that a seventeen-year-old girl alleged one of their prospects, James Baldwin, had sexually assaulted her, and another, Alex Verdugo, had been present, as *Sports Illustrated* reported. When a maid at the team hotel accused another prospect, Luis Rodriguez, of sexual assault, the club sent him home but again did not report it to authorities.

Friedman had also employed players who avowed racist views like Bauer's claim that Barack Obama was not born in the United States. In fact, nine years earlier, Friedman had signed another free agent, Luke Scott, who loudly shared the same notion. Far-right perspectives were neither unique nor extreme within Major League Baseball or the Dodgers. For months in 2021, reliever Blake Treinen's Instagram profile included a link to the personal website of Mike Lindell, the purveyor of pillows and baseless claims that Donald Trump won the 2020 election. In July, Treinen declined to visit the White House and posted a link to a trailer promoting Operation Underground Railroad (OUR), the QAnon-connected nonprofit that claims to assist government agencies in rescuing the victims of human and sex trafficking. It was under criminal investigation, *Vice* reported, for a host of alleged violations, including OUR operators engaging in sexual acts with the victims, creating demand for the victims, and laundering money to for-profit businesses. "This is the real Pandemic," Treinen wrote of OUR. "Save the Kids!!!"

The Dodgers accepted this behavior from good players. But Bauer's alleged assault was high-profile enough, gruesome enough, that it became untenable for the team to continue providing him a uniform. The police investigation and legal battle would determine his off-the-field fate and whether he would continue earning the sport's heftiest salary.

# Chapter 16

O N APRIL 9, 2021, THE DODGERS COLLECTED THEIR World Series rings before their home opener. Fans filed into Dodger Stadium for the first time in eighteen months, since Game 5 of the 2019 NLDS. To commemorate the occasion, team staffers assembled an unusual presentation. Every Dodger received a congratulatory video from a childhood idol. The clips ran on the big screen as introductions before each player jogged out from the dugout to collect his ring box.

The look on Clayton Kershaw's face as he opened his rivaled his smile running in from the bullpen to celebrate the championship. Joe Kelly's playfully pouty face replicated the face he had made to the Astros. Jogging to fetch his, Justin Turner tried to make up for lost time. "This would've sucked if you weren't here," the team's television station caught Andrew Friedman telling Turner when he handed him his ring. "How long you been waiting for this?" team president Stan Kasten asked. "My whole life, man," Turner said. Turner said he didn't care if it was considered selfish, he was motivated to capture another championship so he could celebrate it in earnest, dogpiling and embracing his teammates as the rest of them had before he returned to the field.

COVID-19 was still top of mind. The Washington Nationals, most of them, were back in town. Several of their players were in quarantine because of a virus outbreak. The Dodgers had not yet crossed the 85 percent vaccination threshold that would grant them additional freedoms at the ballpark and on road trips. Across the country, vaccinations were increasing. Postpandemic hope was on the horizon.

The Dodgers were busy confronting the challenge of repeating. Dave Roberts had framed it in animalistic terms during his annual spring address. "When we were chasing a championship, there was an intent, a hunger, a fire," he said. "We were the hunter, as opposed to being the hunted. We haven't done anything in '21." When speaking to reporters in February, Roberts asserted that there was a reason why no team had repeated as World Series champions since the 1999 and 2000 Yankees, the longest-ever stretch among the four largest American professional sports leagues. And then he clarified: he was sure there was a reason, but he did not know what it was.

The 2000 Yankees were not an especially good team. Winners of only eighty-seven games, they snuck into the postseason because of a weak division, then seized on a charitable slate of October opponents. In total, they outscored their opponents by fifty-seven runs. The 2021 Dodgers surpassed that mark for good in May, but they did not have the benefit of a weak division. The Dodgers' direct competitors, the San Diego Padres and San Francisco Giants, have pruned what was once a substantial edge.

The two rivals present different challenges. The Giants are run and managed by ex-Dodger executives, Farhan Zaidi and Gabe Kapler. They are coached by multiple ex-Dodger coaches. They have the financial wherewithal to consistently compete with the Dodgers' payroll. The Padres are also run by an ex-Dodger staffer, but he left ages ago. A. J. Preller has since become the sport's most aggressive executive, not its most frequent dealer but its most decisive. Their ability to sustainably spend is an open question.

The season shaped up to be a three-team race before the Padres faded. The Dodgers remained the most talented of the three, but by a smaller margin than in 2020. Knowing they were likely to face each other come October, and appreciating the advantage of a division title, the teams competed for the same midseason reinforcements. The Dodgers won that contest. One month after the assault allegations against Bauer emerged, Friedman replaced him by consummating a trade with the Nationals for right-hander Max Scherzer. He also acquired their shortstop, Trea Turner. The two All-Stars were probably the two best players dealt at a frenzied deadline. The Giants might have acquired the next best: the Cubs' Kris Bryant. To get his new duo, Friedman ceded his top two prospects: right-hander Josiah Gray, purloined from the Reds, and catcher Keibert Ruiz, superfluous in the Dodgers' catching-rich organization. By acting a day early, Friedman paid a lesser price than contenders who waited. On deadline day, the Toronto Blue Jays surrendered a similar package for one top talent: right-hander José Berríos.

Scherzer was the bigger name, Turner the bigger addition. When the trade was made, he had been baseball's second-best position player since the start of the 2020 season, about a full year's worth of games. In that span, he clubbed thirty homers and amassed a .924 OPS. Both Baseball-Reference and FanGraphs measured his play as worth 6.9 Wins Above Replacement. When the Dodgers acquired Mookie Betts, his last season featured twenty-nine homers and a .915 OPS. By an average of Baseball-Reference and FanGraphs measures, he had been worth 7.0 WAR. Turner was that good. Betts was the superior defender, Turner the better base stealer and the sport's fastest player. He supplied short-term defensive flexibility and a medium-term replacement in the likely event Corey Seager departed as a free agent.

The Dodgers front office knew Turner well. In their final months with the Padres, executives Josh Byrnes and Billy

Gasparino had drafted him thirteenth overall in 2014. Byrnes had also drafted Scherzer, eleventh overall, in 2006. He deserved less credit for that, for he traded him three years later. There were more organizational ties. Scherzer and Kershaw had long been friends, and Walker Buehler and Scherzer had developed a relationship in recent years. Before they met, Byrnes said the two right-handers shared a fixated mindset. Scherzer liked to run outside for his exercise, often near stadiums in the hours before games. In Washington, he'd take to the streets of the Navy Yard district. During road trips to Dodger Stadium, he could be spotted jogging around the vast lot's perimeter, beyond all 16,000 parking spaces. During his first homestand, a surprised stadium security guard spotted him sprinting through nearby Elysian Park.

On the days none of them started, Buehler, Kershaw, and Scherzer walked off the field together following pregame workouts. During his three months with the team, Bauer, the pitcher Scherzer replaced, typically walked off alone.

Scherzer made his Dodgers debut against the Astros, at Dodger Stadium, the eager fans pausing their boos to hail him. When the Dodgers had visited Houston in May, Kershaw completed there what he could not in 2017. He coaxed whiff after whiff out of the Astros and bequeathed the bullpen a sizable lead in a comfortable win. When Kelly relieved him, the standing ovation was so loud that Kershaw gleaned who was replacing him strictly from the sound. Kershaw grinned when Roberts came to the mound to pull him. He never smiled upon removal in years past.

It is not that Kershaw is calmer now that he has won it all. "I don't think any past result, even a World Series championship, will mellow him out," Roberts said in spring training, and early-season action attested to his accuracy. Kershaw still became enraged at the Padres' Jurickson Profar for swinging late and perhaps purposely into a catcher's glove so as to elicit a catcher's interference call. Kershaw still decried the Angels' Taylor Ward for bunting in a game the Dodgers led by thirteen runs.

It is that he has been learning to, sometimes, redirect his energy to more productive places. During 2020 postseason games, the Globe Life Field video board displayed live readings of each pitcher's spin rate, induced vertical break, and horizontal break. While he watched from the dugout near the Dodgers' starting pitchers, assistant pitching coach Connor McGuiness often found himself rhapsodizing about the opposition's metrics. He saw breadcrumbs everywhere that hinted at what pitchers intended to accomplish. More than once, McGuiness said, Kershaw leaned over to him, nodded toward the scoreboard, and asked how a statistic applied to him. "The brilliance of him is the curiosity," McGuiness said in 2021. "It's never died. He's always curious how to evolve with the game. All of a sudden, there are a lot more questions this year than there were last year."

During the Dodgers' May trip to Houston, Kershaw bested Zack Greinke, his old teammate. Greinke marveled afterward at Kershaw's ability to recover from ailments that felled others. "Maybe it's more common than I realize, but it's like, he's had some injuries where you think that's gonna hurt him, and somehow he bounces back," he said. "I wouldn't say he's as good as ever, but it's pretty impressive how good he's done the last couple years. He'll have a bad game and you'll think that that might be the starting of it. But then he always comes back." By "it," Greinke meant the end. There was no end in sight for Kershaw, only another run at free agency at season's end.

When he said at his Dodgers introduction that winning begat clubhouse chemistry, Friedman was right. But he realized in Los Angeles that model veterans helped culture it in high-stakes environments. For the first six weeks of 2021, the Dodgers lacked the part-time veteran presence once provided by the likes of Chase Utley, David Freese, and Russell Martin. Albert Pujols, plucked off the Angels' discard pile in his forties, filled that role. He filmed Will Smith's ring-ceremony video, then hit next to him in the Dodgers lineup. "He told me that he grew up watching me play," Pujols said of Smith. "I'm like, 'Please don't. You're gonna make me older.'"

More cheerful than he had been in years, Pujols hit better than he had in years and became a clubhouse favorite. By his third day with the team, Pujols was taking swing tips from Betts and hitting coach Robert Van Scoyoc during early batting practice. Pujols needed no help with one skill, the lone area of his game that improved with age: situational hitting. He was consistently above average at advancing runners, and despite the hitting coaches' efforts, the Dodgers had been below average at the assignment before his arrival. "When you have a big spot and you need to move the ball forward, he's got a nose for that better than any player that I can remember seeing over the last fifteen, twenty years," Friedman said. "His ability to move the ball forward, drive in key runs, is real."

In the minors, situational hitting remained a distant dream. Coaches concentrated on encouraging any contact. In their season opener, the Dodgers' Low-A affiliate, in Rancho Cucamonga, met the Angels' and set a new league record with thirty-five strikeouts. The next night, the teams matched it. The circumstances conspired against the hitters; because 2020 minor league play was canceled, they were playing their first professional games in twenty months. "I think we've had growing pains, and the strikeouts are the symptom of those growing pains," Craig Wallenbrock said. "But it's going to correct itself, or we're going to be able to correct it, as they relax the COVID restrictions."

If he were distributing credit, or blame, for the 2021 state of play in the minor leagues, Wallenbrock said, the plurality of it would go to the advancements in pitching instruction. Pitchers were ahead of hitters. Then, tied for the next most impactful, he ranked the shift; the absence of umpire accountability; and the overemphasis on the lower body in the swing at the expense of the hands. He put COVID-related restrictions on coaching time in fifth place. Hoping to counter the latter two factors, Wallenbrock ordered a set of Chinese meditation balls, or Baoding balls, from Amazon and left them for Low-A players to incorporate into their daily life. He prayed they might improve motor skills.

Kyle Boddy, the Driveline founder, placed the onus on short-sighted management. "Only caring about the major leagues and not caring about the quality of the product that really grows it," he said, "is exactly the problem we have in baseball." Pitiful minor league salaries validated his claim. Boddy spoke nine games into the season. The Nationals' Low-A affiliate in Fredericksburg, Virginia, had lost each of the nine by a cumulative margin of seventy runs. "I didn't know that it would be this bad," Boddy said, "but I did know it was gonna be bad."

It got better. The FredNats won some games. Strikeout totals started decreasing. But the need for change remained. "I think hitters are now going to train to put more balls in play," said Kapler, the Giants' manager. "If you ask me what my level of certainty on that is, I'd say it's not very high. But it's my bet." Kapler spoke while watching his team take batting practice inside the Dodger Stadium visiting batting cage, against a breaking-ball machine firing dimpled foam balls to approximate spin. Indeed, one transformation is already afoot. From the minors to the majors, teams are taking more batting practice against machines and less against humans. Among the reasons: Newer machines are getting better at replicating breaking balls, and they can produce more velocity than any coach who throws batting practice. Also, down on the farm, more and more new coaches can't throw consistent batting practice.

Many stakeholders see contact rate as the game's central dilemma. "We talk so much about keeping traditions and not changing, but in reality, as hitters, we have to evolve," one league source said. "We have to change. If we don't do that, you're gonna continue to see the strikeouts go up, people are gonna continue to call our game boring, and we're gonna continue to Homer Simpson back into the bushes."

The forces that so swiftly altered baseball in the twenty-first century are not fleeing. The data will only increase in complexity, as kinematic data literally adds a dimension to the calculus. The statistical models will grow more complicated. The resulting insights will be far more individualized than what players have seen to date. Executives will continue to rummage everywhere for any eensy edge and continue to present the resulting havoc as mere unintended consequences.

Some of it is unintended, sure. But for the Dodgers, and for their most aggressive adversaries, a lot has worked exactly as envisioned: treating problematic players as distressed assets, gaming arbitration, manipulating service time, faking injuries, "shortening the season." More than a decade ago, Friedman understood that defensive shifts were bad for entertainment but good for winning. He stuck with them, the sport followed, and every 2021 ballgame featured fewer balls in play as a result. Especially for the first-moving teams, the methods work. The Giants snapped their streak of division titles at eight in 2021, but the Dodgers' on-field prosperity is undeniable. They consistently win more than 60 percent of their games. They won the (least-watched) World Series. For the foreseeable future, they will annually have a shot to win another. It is easier to envision their success than the sport's.

The distrust between players and owners, or the league office, won't abate and may broaden. In June 2021, prominent Mets first baseman Pete Alonso revealed what he described as a rampant belief among players: The league annually fiddled with baseballs to reduce the earning potential of the forthcoming free-agent class. When it was dominated by pitchers, he said, the league juiced the ball. When it was dominated by hitters, as the 2021–2022 class was, the league made it harder to hit. He submitted no evidence to support his theory. The same week, the league announced plans to begin enforcing its long-ignored rules against pitchers using foreign substances on the mound, and hitters pronounced the subject "the next steroids of baseball ordeal."

On Day 1, umpires checked seventy-five pitchers and found no sticky stuff. On Day 2, they checked more and found the same. The only object they denuded was, nearly, Scherzer, still a National. He was checked three times because Phillies manager Joe Girardi requested an additional examination after Scherzer ran his hands through his hair several times. Repeatedly exclaiming he had nothing on his person, Scherzer started to disrobe to prove his point. Umpire Alfonso Márquez asked him to stop. Scherzer's thinning hair was confirmed to be clean, and the game continued. Scherzer's GM, Mike Rizzo, called Girardi a "con artist." Backing his friend, Kershaw suggested that managers like Girardi be levied some sort of penalty if their accusations were not substantiated.

All the haranguing over substances pitted members of the players association against each other during critical CBA negotiations. If that was the league's plan all along, maybe its leaders are cannier than they seem. But it at least appeared to be a welcome consequence. Lost in the 2021 season's myriad controversies was splendid play from so many stars. The league has long enjoyed the ability to draw attention away from its athletes.

Those athletes are more athletic than ever. The best available training is more effective. When the rules permit and the stars align, the best ballplayers furnish maximally entertaining action. There are just more hindrances standing in their way. Men like Betts are the way forward, but he is an anomaly, the superstar who looks and behaves like a role player.

Buehler argued that Betts became a star because of those bona fides. "People undervalue size and how that affects how you learn to play this game," he said. "Mookie obviously wasn't the six-foot kid in Little League. For him to be successful in Little League, he had to try to hit the ball the other way sooner than the giant kid." Buehler spoke from the experience of a similar upbringing, grasping how to pitch with his small frame before he learned to throw exceptionally hard. "He learned all the little things he could do to be successful before it turned into, 'Oh, you're athletic enough and we can tap into that elite movement,'" Buehler said. "He probably had a closer swing to what his swing is right now than a lot of major leaguers. He just does it stronger now, more so than the guy who was strong enough to hit home runs and then learned how to change his swing."

To Buehler, fundamentally sound players share an oft-overlooked trait. To master a fundamental inherently meant to learn to do it differently than whatever way came naturally. So those skilled in fundamentals were also skilled at learning to implement tiny tweaks to their game. From the Dodgers' dugout, Buehler angled his head in Turner's direction.

"If J. T. doesn't learn how to inside-out the ball for the majority of his life, is he then able to, hand-eye-coordination-wise, alter his swing completely?" Buehler asked. "We always want to get one percent better and all this hoo-rah shit, but you can get better at learning. Guys that learn get better at learning and can make smaller changes. What happens in our game is not that people have a problem adjusting, but that people adjust too far all the time: 'I was early on the changeup, so now I'm gonna wait, and now I'm late on the fastball.' When you learn a lot, you learn how to make a lot of really, really small adjustments really often."

Collecting players capable of this, then, might be pivotal to the Dodgers' success. It is also one of the persistent problems facing the broader sport: there aren't nearly enough of those players to go around. The amateur showcase circuit has been churning out opposite talents, all brute force and little precision. Another, even greater obstacle: it's not clear the league sees any of it as an issue.

"Let's not get it twisted: The league has created the product that's on the field right now—with the likes of Andrew Friedman and Farhan Zaidi," said pitcher Alex Wood, naming his most recent bosses. "The league wants to make as much money as possible. How do you do that? Let's hire an MIT grad, a Harvard grad. [Zaidi went to MIT. Friedman went to Tulane.] Let's use numbers and analytics that give us something concrete for how we evaluate, how we judge, how we play against other teams, how we position, how we put our lineups out there, all of that. And that turns into where we're at right now. Players are having to adapt to what the game has turned into."

The union's 1,200 members are not in agreement about what the game has become or what kind of game they want.

There are still active players unhappy that the league outlawed body-slamming catchers and cleating second basemen. Players are nearer agreement on what they see as necessary changes to compensation structure in the CBA negotiations. They are determined to procure more pay for their younger members, whether by raising the minimum salary, speeding up the onset of arbitration eligibility, or shortening it. Most players are convinced owners are elated with the pace at which their investments are accumulating wealth. They believe they can get what they want.

During the 2021 season, it was not clear if they would be willing to stomach a strike to secure it. Agents are relatively impartial observers of the league's labor relations, and some of them worried that MLBPA executive director Tony Clark felt pressured because he so soundly lost the last CBA negotiations. "You just hope that he doesn't go in there trying to win at all costs," one agent said, "and that being the antagonistic approach that leads this thing down a difficult path." It wasn't especially antagonistic early. The two sides avoided leaks for months after beginning negotiations in April. Beyond better early-career compensation, players were committed to ensuring that more teams try to win. It's not clear if expanded playoffs would incentivize or disincentivize competition, but owners desperately wanted them for the additional millions they'd reap, so the territory was ripe for players to recover something in return.

Finding a compromise that improves the on-field product will be a stiffer challenge. Inefficiencies made baseball entertaining, whether in laughing at its absurdity or in witnessing the real-time pursuit of an edge. The clandestine exploitation of every minuscule margin bores many of us. Part of the problem is that those doing the exploiting don't see it the same way. "There was some level of inconsistency that existed in the game, just because there wasn't the data to show otherwise," said Doug Fearing, the former Dodgers R&D director. "It's unlikely we're going back to that. But that also provides an opportunity, because now we know that teams are trying to optimize their decision-making around the rules. You can adjust the rules and teams will respond."

How big of an opportunity, really? Would any rule changes amount to more than a momentary fix until the highest-powered teams processed a new way to exploit them? Maybe there is some secret blend that will tame the lions for at least a few seasons. Say, some defensive shift restrictions, to produce more singles; wider bases, to entice more steals; fewer roster spots for pitchers and a reasonably grippy baseball, to force and reward restrained pitching; more distant fences, to hinder homers; and maybe a slightly smaller strike zone, or an inching back of the mound, for good measure.

It's possible that cocktail, any cocktail, could produce unforeseen consequences. Ideally, the changes would come quickly and alongside some embracing of responsibility. At the 2021 All-Star Game, Manfred voiced a desire to ban the defensive shift before the 2022 season. He presented it not as a rule change but a restoration to the way the game was played a half century ago. Of course, he vocalized the same interest on his first day on the job seventy-eight months earlier, but did nothing about it.

For years, Roberts favored the defensive shift, the gambit his boss propagated. In June 2021, he revealed he had recently changed his mind. He began advocating for rules that required two players on each side of second base or, if three players were on one side, all three to stay on the dirt pre-pitch. "I just think that sometimes we end up kind of talking out of both sides of our mouths as far as trying to promote offense, but allowing for other things that kind of suppress it," Roberts said. "So, I guess if I had my druthers, I would do away with it."

While he was at it, Roberts proposed that teams start paying their flexible contributors sums more commensurate to their worth. "In some things, I think we're just too slow-moving," he said. "When you're talking about Gold Gloves or All-Star selections, the industry itself has valued versatility. But for now, players aren't getting compensated for versatility on the defensive side, and they're not getting recognized by the league. We just gotta make adjustments."

Roberts is a manager, not a GM, and he must live within our existing society as much as the rest of us. But there are few richer ironies than the man who supervises the sport's most shifts, and perhaps its most interchangeable roster, calling out his industry for duplicity on those matters. He spoke as the winningest regular-season manager since 1950, the manager of the reigning World Series champions. If he does not have his druthers, who in this world does?

# Epilogue

AFTER THE FIRST INNING OF THE LAST GAME the Dodgers played in 2021, Clayton Kershaw was the first person to greet Walker Buehler in Truist Park's visiting dugout. Kershaw's elbow was hurt for the first time in his life. Buehler was pitching without the standard starter's rest for the second time in his life.

Thirty hours earlier, Buehler had agreed to do so when Max Scherzer told the Dodgers his arm felt dead. Since he pitched an inning in relief to vanquish the San Francisco Giants from the National League Division Series, he had not been recovering at his normal pace. That forced the Dodgers to start a diminished Buehler in Game 6 of the next round and hope that Scherzer's arm would rebound enough for him to tackle Game 7.

There was no Game 7. The Atlanta Braves smothered Buehler, who could only bend down and grip his knees as the Dodgers' season slipped from his grasp. After Eddie Rosario's decisive three-run home run. unincorporated Cobb County was home to the two worst postseason outings of Buehler's career. The first time, in 2018, he was a young hotshot who temporarily lost his command. The second time, he was a blooming ace stepping up to pitch at less than his best because two future Hall of Famers' arms prevented them.

With the Dodgers' blessing, those pitchers had pushed themselves beyond what their aging bodies allowed. Kershaw told The Athletic that he "really came back too early" from a July elbow injury. On the eve of the postseason, the elbow started aching enough that his year was over. Scherzer, Dave Roberts said, lobbied for days to pitch in relief against the Giants. (Scherzer denied doing so.) He was then unable to pitch as planned in Game 1 against the Braves. Soreness lingered during his Game 2 start. He resumed his running routine the next afternoon, but he could not complete his between-starts throwing.

Neither of those developments should have surprised the Dodgers. Kershaw had been forging his own injury timetables for a decade. In justifying the Scherzer decision, Roberts spoke of an unspecified "cost." He also noted that Scherzer had pitched in relief two years earlier—against the Dodgers—and bounced back to start well three days later. He did not mention that, later that postseason, Scherzer had to be scratched from a World Series start because he could not lift his pitching arm.

The warning signs had sounded for weeks. Peerless upon his Los Angeles arrival, Scherzer faded toward September's end. In the sudden-death Wild Card Game, his pitches lacked their typical movement. The Dodgers pulled him before he could complete five innings, his playoff low over the last decade. Because of their bench, they won anyway. Chris Taylor entered in a double switch and later launched the winning homer.

In the next round, the Dodgers met Farhan Zaidi's Giants, who possessed superior depth. This was rare. It had been at least three years, arguably longer, since any team could rival the rear of the Dodgers' October roster. But Zaidi had procured many of the men who supplied that depth, and he was doing the same for San Francisco's squad. Gabe Kapler, the Giants manager, brought with him updated versions of the ideas he spread through the

Dodgers' farm system. Kapler smarted from two sloppy seasons in Philadelphia to become an improved, inspirational leader. Where at his previous stops his trenchant methods landed better with younger players, in San Francisco he won over even Buster Posey, a three-time champion in his final season.

The Giants relied on rejuvenated veterans and platoons populated by waiver claims and small-scale free-agent signings. The Dodgers depended on stars. If they were to win, it would be on the strength of those stars. They won, but barely. San Francisco shut them out twice in the series' first three games. When the Dodgers evened the series at two, Roberts performed a pump fake.

The teams thought so similarly, he said, that they already knew each other's playbooks front to back. For the decisive game, he promised Vince Lombardi's power sweep. The next night, he revealed the Air Coryell in a text to Kapler. The Dodgers would not start their announced Game 5 starter, left-hander Julio Urías, but an opener: right-handed reliever Corey Knebel. This forced the Giants to guess when Urías would enter and reshape their platoon-laden lineup accordingly.

The ploy was designed to budge the odds on likely late-game matchups in the Dodgers' favor. At that, it succeeded, probably forcing one more right-handed hitter to bat against a right-handed pitcher and one more lefty to face a lefty. If it were the last game of the World Series, it would have been a brilliant gambit.

It failed because of what came next. Roberts pulled Urías after four innings and called in his last trusted reliever, Kenley Jansen, for the eighth inning. When Jansen's spot in the batting order came up during the Dodgers' rally in the top of the ninth, Roberts pinch-hit for him and summoned Scherzer to close.

The idea had been to leave Scherzer in the bullpen unless an emergency arose. A buzzed Scherzer revealed postgame that the Dodgers' script called for Urías to last five innings and Jansen to throw two. Instead, Scherzer covered the chasm, aided by a generous check-swing call. A half-hour later, soaked in alcohol and sandal-clad, he celebrated by running the Oracle Park bases alongside his toddler daughters. He declared that the Dodgers' decision to use an opener had worked, despite the outside doubt. He promised to party that night and sort out his status the next day.

Roberts uttered a sober version of the same answer. In a testament to their rivals' roster, the Dodgers' decision-makers felt they had to exhaust every option to advance. And they had great options, at least in the short term. "Knowing you have an ace in the hole," Roberts said, "is a good feeling." It's also fleeting. After the Dodgers landed in Atlanta, Scherzer told staffers he wouldn't be able to start Game 1 of the NLCS. The Dodgers deployed a bullpen game in defeat, then a still-sagging Scherzer in Game 2. To buttress the beset bullpen when Scherzer started, the Dodgers asked Urías to prepare for an inning of relief. This sent more dominoes falling, for Urías let in the tying runs and the Dodgers lost.

After they staved off a 3-0 deficit with a late Cody Bellinger home run, Urías produced perhaps his worst start of the year in Game 4. He said his usage had not provoked his failings, and there is no way to definitively know. Either way, it was a worst-case outcome for the Dodgers, who lost by seven runs and lost Justin Turner to injury. Again, they needed to beat the Braves three times or head home without a World Series bid. In 2020, that situation spurred them (and their group text) into action. While they again exchanged texts in 2021, the circumstances were less motivating, more tempting them into concession. Before Bellinger's homer, Roberts said, the Dodgers were "dead in the water."

The atmosphere ahead of Game 5 was not lifeless, just awkward. Four hours from first pitch, Mookie Betts spoke as if he had accepted the inevitable. "Obviously, going into this series we had to throw Scherzer and whatnot," he said. "So we were kind of behind the eight ball at the start." Three hours later, controlling owner Mark Walter tried to walk down a staircase toward the Dodgers' clubhouse. Blocking the way, a security guard asked for identification. Walter said he did not have any. The guard said he could not pass. Walter gestured to the logo over his chest and took on a tart tone. "I'm the owner of this team," he said. The guard let him through.

Their pitching staff still reeling from the earlier decisions, the Dodgers started Joe Kelly, who struggled and hurt his arm in the first inning. It looked like they were done until a suddenly resuscitated offense rallied for eleven runs. In the morning, they met at Dodger Stadium before boarding a cross-country flight. Lined up to pitch in thirty hours, Scherzer couldn't throw without pain. Throwing at the same time and slated for Game 7, Buehler reported feeling fine, so the Dodgers swapped their Games 6 and 7 starters. Buehler perished before the series went further.

The Braves won only eighty-eight regular-season games, a stunning disparity from the Dodgers' 106. Statistically, Atlanta's victory represented the third-biggest upset in postseason history, but that distorts the two teams' similarities and overstates the talent gap between them at the time they met. At the trade deadline, Atlanta architect Alex Anthopoulos had improved his team in Andrew Friedmanesque fashion. He would know; he worked for Friedman in 2016 and 2017, a stint he often referenced as his graduate school. During the 2021 season, the underachieving Braves lost superstar Ronald Acuña Jr. to injury and No. 3 hitter Marcell Ozuna to administrative leave after he was charged with domestic violence. To replace them, Anthopoulos acquired four undervalued outfielders ahead of the trade deadline. Men with decades of experience could not recall an executive shoring up one position with so much quantity at once. But Anthopoulos understood the power of depth, and all four additions abetted the Braves' efforts to come back in the National League East and eliminate the Dodgers.

When it was over, the Dodgers assured each other that the best team doesn't always win. They told reporters they believed they were the best team. "It's crazy," Jansen said. "All these years that I've been here, and everybody just wants to beat the Dodgers." Maybe the collective target on their backs they cited was real. Maybe they made it real in their minds and ceded an edge to teams that played sans self-imposed pressure. Or maybe peers had been emulating the Dodgers long enough to locate their own success. In 2021, as in 2020, Friedman or someone he had hired ran the winningest regular-season team and all four semifinalists. MLB owners wanted to hire men he had molded, whether he had hired them as interns or midway through their careers. This both challenged and reinforced his supremacy.

On his way home for the winter, Betts echoed Roberts' words of eight months earlier. "There's a reason why it's been so long since there's been a back-to-back," he said. Like Roberts, he did not present a reason. Perhaps the reason is that championship teams are so desperate for a dynasty that their intemperance systematically undoes them. The Dodgers had been self-admitted gluttons. Their bingeing brought them only a pricey contract with a problematic pitcher they paid not to pitch, and a departure from the depth they made their hallmark throughout the first six seasons of Friedman's tenure.

Friedman thought his July trade for Trea Turner made the Dodgers' lineup the best he had assembled. "But," he noted, "it didn't quite play like that over those two months." The problem was not just the underperforming lineup but the bench. It turned out that several young players still lagged behind their expected development schedules after the 2020 shutdown. Max Muncy's October absence due to a dislocated elbow exacerbated the deficiencies. Where in seasons past competent players Kiké Hernández and Joc Pederson surfaced in key pinch-hit situations, in 2021 the Dodgers turned to Steven Souza Jr. He had accumulated nine hits over the previous three seasons, but Roberts batted him nine times in October alone. A perennial edge became a disadvantage, or, at best, a wash. Meanwhile, Hernández and Pederson starred on palatable salaries for their new teams. In free agency, they had not fled for riches but opportunities.

Pederson, one of the Braves' midseason saviors, wrote in the Players' Tribune that multiple Dodgers asked him after Game

6 to please beat the Astros. A week later, he did, as the Braves won the World Series in six games. For the fifth time in six years, the champion had eliminated the Dodgers from the postseason. The exception was their own 2020 win. Anthopoulos missed his team's celebration because he contracted a breakthrough case of COVID-19 during the World Series. Exactly as in Justin Turner's case, the news was first reported in the minutes after Game 6 while the rest of the roster partied on a Texas ballfield. "I had flashbacks to last year," Friedman said of learning the news. One difference: Anthopoulos stayed home after learning of his test result.

The Dodgers had not retreated to being the hunted instead of the hunters, as Roberts warned against in February. They had just hunted too hard, exposing themselves to the ravages of injury, misfortune, and exhaustion. Friedman had broken one of his few omnipresent rules: Don't be desperate. Ironically, he had done so not to alleviate a decades-long championship drought but to pursue the first 21st-century dynasty. Fortunately for them, he had not acted so aggressively that he ruined the team's chances at 2022 or 2023 titles. Rivals still expected the club to contend in coming Octobers.

Awaiting the Dodgers first was free agency. Kershaw, Scherzer, Jansen, Taylor, and Corey Seager all earned the right to depart. The consensus called for Kershaw to return but at least one, and probably both, of the cornerstone position players to depart. Buehler termed it a crossroads. "We're gonna have to build from within like we always do," he said. This was truer than he realized. Before the World Series was over, the Dodgers had already lost three valued minor-league coaches to bigger jobs with new teams. More interviews were afoot.

For the league, too, a crossroads approached. The CBA expired not six weeks after the Dodgers flew home for the winter. To some, that offered hope. The winning manager, baseball lifer Brian Snitker, said he looked forward to any new agreement extending the the designated hitter into the National League. "It'll be a better game to watch," he said. But players braced for a rancorous, protracted offseason. When pressed, most in the industry predicted a lockout.

Before Game 1 of the World Series, Rob Manfred and Tony Clark met on the field at Minute Maid Park. Speaking separately to reporters, they equivocated about the negotiations. Manfred then defended the Braves' team-sanctioned tomahawk chop, offensive to many Native Americans, on the strangest of grounds: One regional tribe had recently started a partnership with the team, and, as reported by ESPN, stopped criticizing the team. He described that as unwavering local support. "We don't market our game on a nationwide basis," Manfred said, in a singular self-own. Immediately, many tribal organizations spoke up about their disdain for the racist gesture and the team's dehumanizing name. No one needed to critique his marketing claim. It was somehow wildly inaccurate, given that he spoke at the incongruously named World Series, and exactly accurate. As Manfred uttered those words, the game of baseball continued to vanish from the national consciousness while the league's controversies commanded the conversation. The players were better than ever. The business of it was worse.

# Acknowledgments

Thank you to all the scouts, coaches, executives, agents, ballplayers, former ballplayers, mothers, fathers, siblings, and cousins who lent me their time.

Thank you to Ben Adams and Clive Priddle at PublicAffairs for believing in this project. Thanks to Ben, my editor, for repeatedly and thoroughly improving it. Thank you to my agent, David Patterson, at Stuart Krichevsky Literary Agency, for making it happen. Thank you to Aemilia Phillips, Kaitlin Carruthers-Busser, and Mike McConnell for your help along the way. Any remaining errors are mine.

Thank you to the beat writers whom I relied on reading, before and while I worked on this book. Among those whose work was most relevant and impactful here: Ken Gurnick at MLB.com; Bill Shaikin, Dylan Hernández, Andy McCullough, and Jorge Castillo at the *Los Angeles Times*; Alex Speier at the *Boston Globe*; Jen McCaffrey at MassLive.com and *The Athletic*; Evan Drellich at several shops, including the *Houston Chronicle* and *The Athletic*; Sam Miller at the *Orange County Register*, everywhere else he's been, and wherever he goes next; and Marc Topkin at the *St. Petersburg Times* and *Tampa Bay Times*.

Sheryl Ring's Beyond The Box Score coverage of the Trevor Bauer hearing helped me understand the legal intricacies involved. Ed Edmonds's Collection on Sports Law at Notre Dame's Kresge Law Library helped me understand the history of salary arbitration. Jeff Passan's *The Arm*, Ben Lindbergh and Travis Sawchik's *The MVP Machine*, Jared Diamond's *Swing Kings*, John Dewan's *The Fielding Bible*, Andy Martino's *Cheated*, and, of course, John Helyar's *Lords of the Realm* were valuable resources for various parts of the book. Daniel Okrent's *Nine Innings*, Michael Lewis's *Moneyball*, and, later, Barry Svrluga's *The Grind* influenced how I learned the sport. Vin Scully, on television, taught me baseball and taught me to love it.

At my several sportswriting stops, so many accomplished colleagues have ventured far out of their way to endorse, enrich, and mentor a Brazilian kid who wanted to write about baseball. Thanks especially to Kevin Arnovitz, for teaching me to watch the games in critical ways; Gary Klein, for setting an admirable example of elite beat work every day for decades; and Jesse Sánchez, for convincing me that Latinos could make it in ballwriting. Thank you also to Jim Barrero, Tim Brown, Jerry Crasnick, Mike DiGiovanna, Steve Dilbeck, Beto Durán, the late Pedro Gomez, Ken Gurnick, Rich Hammond, Todd Harmonson, Dylan Hernández, Tony Jackson, Joe Lago, Eric Neel, Claire Noland, Eric Nusbaum, Hideki Okuda, Bill Plaschke, Bill Plunkett, Ken Rosenthal, Mark Saxon, Chuck Scott, Glenn Stout, Rachel Ullrich, and Jon Weisman. At my current job, thank you to Amy Brachmann, Kevin Jackson, and Ben Osborne for your positivity and flexibility.

Thank you to the teachers, Jim Klipfel and Vilo Del Rio, who showed me the value of research. Thank you to my friends Stephanie Apstein, Alex Convery, Rustin Dodd, Chris Kirkham, Dennis Lin, Andy McCullough, Aaron Mendelson, Ryan Menezes, Javier Panzar, Nick Piecoro, Mike Piellucci, Sara Randazzo, and Davy Rothbart for reporting or writing (or both) so well you motivate me to try to come close. Thank you to all my friends not near this business who encouraged and guided me with questions from outsiders' perspectives. I know I'm lucky there are too many of you to list here.

Thank you to Susan and Greg Kay for my first tickets to Dodger Stadium and so much else. Thank you to my godmother, Carolyn Taylor, for buying me my first baseball book, *The Southpaw*, when I was a couple years too young for it. Thank you to my grandmother, Carminha, and my aunt and uncle, Beth and Hugo, for your unwavering support. Thank you to my mom, Solange, for your unsurpassed commitment to motherhood, for reading to me in your second language, for learning baseball because I expressed an early interest, for everything. And thank you to my partner, Chloe Stepney, for your patience, devotion, and consistency.

**Pedro Moura** is a national baseball writer for FOX Sports. Previously he has been a senior writer at *The Athletic*, where he covered the Dodgers, as well as a reporter at the *Los Angeles Times*, the *Orange County Register*, and ESPN.com. His work has been cited in *The Best American Sports Writing*. He lives in Los Angeles.

PublicAffairs is a publishing house founded in 1997. It is a tribute to the standards, values, and flair of three persons who have served as mentors to countless reporters, writers, editors, and book people of all kinds, including me.

I. F. STONE, proprietor of *I. F. Stone's Weekly*, combined a commitment to the First Amendment with entrepreneurial zeal and reporting skill and became one of the great independent journalists in American history. At the age of eighty, Izzy published *The Trial of Socrates*, which was a national bestseller. He wrote the book after he taught himself ancient Greek.

BENJAMIN C. BRADLEE was for nearly thirty years the charismatic editorial leader of *The Washington Post*. It was Ben who gave the *Post* the range and courage to pursue such historic issues as Watergate. He supported his reporters with a tenacity that made them fearless and it is no accident that so many became authors of influential, best-selling books.

ROBERT L. BERNSTEIN, the chief executive of Random House for more than a quarter century, guided one of the nation's premier publishing houses. Bob was personally responsible for many books of political dissent and argument that challenged tyranny around the globe. He is also the founder and longtime chair of Human Rights Watch, one of the most respected human rights organizations in the world.

·     ·     ·

For fifty years, the banner of Public Affairs Press was carried by its owner Morris B. Schnapper, who published Gandhi, Nasser, Toynbee, Truman, and about 1,500 other authors. In 1983, Schnapper was described by *The Washington Post* as "a redoubtable gadfly." His legacy will endure in the books to come.

Peter Osnos, *Founder*